"I'VE WORKED HARD—FOR WHAT?"
"WHERE HAVE ALL THE YEARS GONE?"
"IS THIS ALL THERE IS?"

At mid-life a vast number of American men have an intimate encounter with desperation and inner turmoil. They feel they have gone as far as they can along the path they have taken by choice or chance. They feel they must find a new direction or resign themselves to a dead end.

This remarkable book offers a brilliant new perspective of life-cycles that explains this lust for change. It tells every man (and every woman concerned with him) what signs to look for, and what dangers and decisions must be faced at a crossroads where self-knowledge and understanding of options can make all the difference. You will learn about:

- Exploring your uncharted self
- The risks and rewards of starting over
- Revitalizing your marriage, or changing partners
- Finding new veins of energy for renewal and creative change
- Coming of age—from boy/man to man
- And more

"Reflects understanding and holds out hope . . . highly recommended!"

—*The Levinson Letter*

"A serious, sensible treatment of a widespread problem."

—*The Free Lance-Star*

THE MALE
MID–LIFE CRISIS

Fresh Start After Forty

Nancy Mayer

A SIGNET BOOK

NEW AMERICAN LIBRARY

SIGNET TRADEMARK REG. U.S. PAT. OFF. AND FOREIGN COUNTRIES
REGISTERED TRADEMARK—MARCA REGISTRADA
HECHO EN CHICAGO, U.S.A.

SIGNET, SIGNET CLASSIC, MENTOR, PLUME, MERIDIAN AND NAL BOOKS are published by New American Library, 1633 Broadway, New York, New York 10019

First Signet Printing, February, 1979

10   11   12   13   14   15   16   17

PRINTED IN THE UNITED STATES OF AMERICA

*This book is dedicated to Carl and Daniel,
whom I not only love but also respect
and admire.*

Contents

Preface

This book is about new beginnings. It is about beginning again in the middle of your life. It is about starting fresh at a time when society says you should be settled down. More specifically, this book is about American men in transition—men in their thirties and forties and fifties who are changing their lives in remarkable, and sometimes radical, ways.

Why should a woman write this story? This question was posed many times in the course of my interviewing, sometimes politely and at other times as an attack. Men implied that I must be a castrating female. Women accused me of betraying my sisters.

The facts of the matter are both simpler and more complex. What is simple is the journalistic route that led me to my subject. After having been a writer/editor in the mental health field, I began my career as a free-lance writer in the late sixties by publishing, first in *New York* and then in such other popular magazines as *Cosmopolitan*, *Travel & Leisure*, and *Pageant*. While I was researching an article on middle-aged men and young girls, a friend used the phrase "male menopause" to describe a syndrome that seemed to be afflicting many of his contemporaries who were having trouble aging. This phrase, which I had never heard before, both amused and intrigued me. In the course of writing articles on a wide variety of subjects—everything from the advertising business to middle-class pot-smokers to suburban politics—I had met scores of men who seemed, somewhere along in their forties, to be going through something strange, something disconcerting. "Male menopause" seemed a handy label with which to pull together the problems they were having with their wives, their girlfriends, their jobs, and themselves.

As a writer, I viewed this topic as being new and newsworthy. Not much had been written on this subject in 1971, when it first began to interest me. In fact, with the prominence of the women's liberation movement, not much was being written about issues related to men at all. Since most of the people I had been interviewing for magazine articles were male, I did not think it odd to consider writing a book that would deal primarily with men. Moreover, I had already learned that when it came to a man's revealing his true feelings, my being a female interviewer was, if anything, an advantage. In the presence of a woman there was less need for a man to sustain a strong front, more permission to express his emotions openly.

In the course of my preliminary research my approach shifted—in focus and in depth. What began as a somewhat bemused, lighthearted exploration of the male menopause turned into a more far-reaching look at the larger subject of the mid-life crisis. I had discovered the work on adult development being done by social scientists, and was immediately fascinated. Inspired primarily by the work Daniel J. Levinson and his colleagues at Yale University were doing on the male mid-life decade, I realized that the boundaries of my project had expanded. Partly in the interest of simplicity, but predominantly in the interest of my own sanity, I decided to retain my original focus on men, rather than try to include women as well, as I explored the multiple dimensions of the mid-life crisis.

More complex than the journalistic explanation are the personal reasons why I chose to write about men. When I first began this project I was a divorcee in my mid-thirties, living and working in Manhattan while raising two children. Having been married to a college professor for ten years and having lived in the relatively sheltered atmosphere of academia, I was rather naïve when I first moved into the big city. Predictably, while playing the mating game I had my heart broken not once but several times. And so it gradually began to dawn on me that there were certain mysteries about men in their middle years that I had not yet solved. Many of my male friends were going through major upheavals and monumental changes—at work and at play, with wives and ex-wives, with lovers and friends, and most strikingly in relationship to themselves. Just as the men I was interviewing in my professional life, the men in my personal life seemed to be going through something peculiar. Something I was having trouble comprehending and coping with. Something I wanted to know more about, for my own self-preservation!

My interest in men's lives has another component, which is more difficult to describe. It is related, I think, to the feminine mystique, to the silent code so prominent in the 1950s that decreed that women should serve men and be subservient to them; that women should marry an achiever, rather than achieve themselves. In short, that women should satisfy their desire for power and success not directly but indirectly—*through* a man. What, then, was I to do with the part of me that craved adventure, the part of me that was ambitious and bright? Growing up, I had no female models or mentors—none, at least, who interested me or earned my respect. The women I knew were engaged in wifely, "womanly" pursuits—boring and limited pursuits, for the most part. Thus it was that I often turned to males for stimulation and support, not just because I admired them but also because I *identified* with them. From adolescence on I was interested in men not as other but as self. Their lives had a special significance for me—a special magic—because they seemed to be living out a part of me that I, being female, was forbidden to act upon. Except in fantasy.

Given this symbiotic entanglement with men, it is not surprising that I learned, early on, to be a superb listener—attentive, responsive, discriminating. That talent, combined with my predisposition to identify with the male, has been as important as my journalistic skills in the creation of this book.

Above all, this book is about growth and change. It is about growth as an organic process that continues throughout a person's entire life. Not surprisingly, a similar process affected this book itself at every stage of its existence—from conception to completion. At times, in fact, it became a project whose mushrooming proportions seemed overwhelming. Like the dinosaur, its bulk and mass appeared upon occasion to prophesy extinction. But despite startling disappointments and oppressive setbacks—such as editors departing and collaborators clashing—the project was revitalized repeatedly. Time and time again, what seemed like a permanent demise turned out to be just another death-and-rebirth. Another metamorphosis.

Thus, during a six-year period that was marked by stops and starts, the book changed form continually, evolving, growing, transforming itself. It took on a life of its own, and in the course of three complete rewrites its central theme changed from male menopause to the mid-life crisis; and then, finally, to the concept of second acts after forty—new directions and fresh starts.

Needless to say, I grew along with my book. The exploration of this mid-life period as a crossroads, a time of transition and transformation, had an enormous impact on my own life. Six years ago I was thirty-seven, and now I am forty-three. But I am not just older. I am wiser and warmer, stronger and softer, brighter and bolder. More open and more honest. Almost everything in my life is different now from what it was then.

My hair is short and curly instead of long and straight. I walk and talk and dress differently. I have even changed the contours of my body. Thanks to a regime of daily exercises, I am stronger and more supple now than I was six years ago. Also more energetic. I have been meditating regularly for several years, and recently not only gave up caffeine but also conquered a three-pack-a-day cigarette habit.

I have moved to a new home, and gotten rid of many old possessions that no longer suit the self I have become. I have severed some relationships that were debilitating and formed new ones that are more nourishing. There have been generational shifts, too. My role as a mother has changed dramatically. I have survived, and sometimes even enjoyed, my two sons' adolescence. This year, my elder son, Carl, left home to enter college; and my younger son, Daniel, is becoming more independent every day. Moreover, as so often happens at mid-life, the balance of power between me and my parents has shifted, too. Like it or not, I have had to assume some responsibility for my father as he has become sick and incapacitated, to take charge of a man who, throughout his life, always needed to control others.

And so I have been growing—growing up.

I did not make these many changes completely on my own or all at once. They have occurred slowly, sometimes painfully, and with lots of support. Three years ago, I embarked on psychoanalysis, and have found it to be an invaluable tool for change. I have also benefited greatly from Ira Progoff's "intensive journal" method of exploring the deep levels of the psyche, a method that is Jungian in its approach. In addition, the Esalen Institute, in Big Sur, California, has had a tremendous influence on my personal development and will be a continuing part of my life for many years. There I have been learning to get more in touch with my own feelings and fantasies and to become more connected to my body. I have participated in workshops that use Gestalt therapy, Feldenkrais and Alexander movements, bioenergetics, tai chi, sensory awareness, hatha yoga, massage, guided fantasy, and deep-breathing exercises. But Esalen is more than techniques, more than brilliant teachers. It is a humanistic community dedicated to conscious and responsible living; and it is for me personally, as well as for many other people, the most important educational institution in this country today.

As part of my personal journey, I am also changing my career. No longer satisfied with the distance and detachment that writing imposes, I want to participate more closely, and more caringly, in the process of how people grow and change. Thus I am now completing my educational and training requirements to become a psychotherapist.

Like the men in this book, I, too, am starting fresh in the middle of my life, making many joyful and exciting discoveries along the way. Which is not to say that it has been easy. On the darker side of every metamorphosis, my own included, are moments—or even months—of anxiety and confusion and despair. This, too, is a part of change. There is loss and there is loneliness. It was helpful to me, as I imagine it will be helpful to those who read this book, to know that some of the pain is related to a particular stage of life. Knowing what to expect, what to anticipate, makes the mid-life crisis more manageable.

To gather material for this book, I spent a full year at the outset first reading widely, and then interviewing all sorts of people. I talked to physicians, surgeons, psychiatrists, psychologists, social scientists, business executives, personnel managers, and industrial consultants. To obtain case histories, I followed numerous leads to find men, and some women, who were willing to contribute their own stories. All together I interviewed more than two hundred persons. In a few case histories, real names are used. But in most, where anonymity was preferred, the person's name and place of residence, and sometimes other identifying material, have been changed. All the men who contributed their personal experiences were most generous with their time. In turn, they appeared to derive some comfort, and some catharsis, from sharing their story. (With some notable exceptions, the majority of men in this book are white middle- and upper-middle-class.)

Although this book contains many firsthand accounts, it is

not so much about the particulars of life in the middle years, as about the possibilities. Looking at the American male from a life-cycle perspective, I have been less interested in proving what is than in exploring what might be. For this reason I have deliberately *not* sought out "typical" or average men. Nor have I attempted to cover all classes, professions, social, religious, or ethnic groups, or economic categories. To the contrary, I have sought out men who are in some way special— men who have lived deeply and daringly. As examples of *optimal*, as opposed to typical, aging patterns, they serve as models for what other men can become—if they are willing to revise their expectations about life's possibilities and their own post-forty potential. It is my hope that this book will contribute to such a revision.

Thanks are due to many people who helped in the birthing of this book. First, I want to express my appreciation to each and every one of the men, and women, who shared with me their own personal experiences and who cannot be acknowledged by name. I am grateful for their candor and courage.

Knox and Kitty Burger, my agents, have won a special place in my heart by being who they are. Going way beyond the call of duty, they stuck by me through these many trying years as friends and fans, counselors and confidants. I am enormously grateful for their love and loyalty.

June Adler, my dearest friend, lived through the agonies of creation with me more closely than anyone. She gave me much comfort, support, and love throughout. There is no way to express thanks for such a gift other than to say that her presence was essential to my surmounting the bad times, and celebrating the good. Albert Goldman, another loving friend and mentor, provided constant encouragement and constructive criticism throughout. I am deeply appreciative of his unfailing faith in me. My long-time friend Dr. Meyer Friedman also gave me his blessings, as well as the benefit of his critical intelligence, just as he has done for the past twenty-six years. His help has been invaluable.

Deep-felt thanks also go to Richard Kluger for his aid and encouragement at the beginning; to Ken McCormick for his editorial guidance; to Roberta Ashley and Jim Hoffman for reading the manuscript at various stages and helping me improve it; to Leah Wallach for her vital editorial contributions; and to Resa Cronin and Joanne Henkelmann for their good will and enthusiasm applied to the task of typing.

I am enormously indebted to Dr. Alfred Jones for helping me to open so many doors in my head and heart, and in the world as well. His belief in me has been the catalyst for my own mid-life metamorphosis. And finally, I am profoundly appreciative of Carl and Daniel Mayer, my two sons, who suffered most during this book's long labor and who, despite their resentments, never failed to shower me with love and laughter.

Nancy Mayer
New York City
December 1977

Section I THE PROBLEM THAT HAS MANY NAMES

Chapter 1 A Portrait of Harry at Forty-three

There comes a time in the life of every American man, somewhere during his forties, when his penis acts less playful than it should, when his body is plagued by niggling little breakdowns, and when each heart palpitation alarms.

It is a critical time and a painful time.

Suddenly a man feels shocked by how quickly time has flown, angered by an awareness that his youth has slipped away, and terrified by the recognition of his own mortality. It seems like only yesterday, he thinks to himself with chilling surprise, that I celebrated my twenty-first birthday.

What's happened to my life? he wonders. What's it all about, anyway?

Depression descends on him, gnawing his gut, and disturbing questions intrude into his daily life. Driving home at night or sitting glumly in a bar or lying awake at 4 A.M., he begins to ask himself:

- What am I breaking my ass for?
- Is this really all there is?
- What have I accomplished, anyway?
- Why isn't it making me happier?
- And what the hell *would* make me happy?

Christ, he mutters, here I am turning gray, and I still don't know what I really want to be when I grow up!

Not feeling grown-up yet at a time when you suddenly discover you are growing old is profoundly unsettling.

Equally unsettling is the conviction, certain and stabbing, that there are no easy answers to the agonizing questions that now arise. Nor do any simple solutions seem to be at hand.

How come nobody ever told me it was going to be like this? a man on the brink of middle age is likely to wonder. How come nobody ever warned me?

The sad truth is that we Americans are still more concerned about how to make a good living than about how to live. And despite our current struggle to mature, we have not yet begun to confront the complex problems that all adults encounter as they go through the different stages of their life. Instead we remain incurably fascinated and obsessed by youth—the appearance of youth, the style of youth, the sound of youth, the touch of youth.

The magic of youth.

No one wants to grow old in America today. Why should they? We all know that in our society the elderly are dismissed, or discarded. We all know that in our society growing older means giving up the magic and getting nothing else in return. No rewards. No recognition.

So it is hardly surprising if a man shudders, and recoils in horror, when he begins to sniff the first faint scent of his own aging flesh.

There goes the magic, he laments.

He feels just like the embittered fellow in a *New Yorker* cartoon who commented: "It's a real American tragedy— *Wunderkind* at twenty, *Ubermensch* at thirty, *kaputt* at forty."

Usually too his misery is compounded by the feeling that he is totally alone. His depression and self-doubt strike him as being a personal curse—something he must suffer through silently, something he cannot share.

If asked to talk about himself at this stage of life, his thoughts and feelings, his hopes and fears, a man is likely to sound confused. Resentful, too. And he is likely to complain about almost every area of his existence. To hear what he might say, let's listen to Harry, an imaginary man whose words and thoughts and gestures are based on many different real men. His problems and his predicament are not unique.

Harry is every American male somewhere during his forties.

When the alarm clock goes off at 6 A.M., Harry lunges for it and groans.

Christ, what a horrible dream, he thinks. I was in this

haunted house . . . dark . . . menacing . . . eyes glaring at me . . . arms grabbing at me . . . hippie kids hooting and hollering . . . waving shotguns around . . . I was scared shitless . . . wanted desperately to get the fuck out of there . . . but every door I tried was locked . . . every window, bolted.

His heart pounding, he shudders.

Trying to blot out the nightmare images, Harry reaches for a cigarette and glances for reassurance at his wife, Sue, burrowed under the blankets and still fast asleep.

Swinging his legs onto the floor, the joints creaking, he sits on the side of the bed for a few minutes, head in hands, body sagging, attempting to clear his brain before standing up. A regular morning habit.

Finally Harry lopes toward the bathroom, pees, and then reaches gratefully for the shower faucet. Stepping under the hot water, he begins to soap himself automatically. Arms first, back of the neck, around to his chest, and then the belly.

I'm too damned fat, he thinks, pinching the handles of flab around his middle. Gotta get back in shape. Like when I played football. I was hard then, solid. Now everything's getting soft. Disgusting.

Twisting the faucet, Harry turns his mind to the day ahead. It's going to be a bitch, he thinks, the cold water streaming down his face as he contemplates the problems awaiting him.

After toweling himself vigorously, he suddenly becomes conscious of a terrible throbbing in his temple. Peering at himself in the mirror he sees blood shot eyes, darkly circled, deep furrows across his brow, and a scruffy salt-and-pepper stubble.

"Whatta sight," he mumbles. You're getting to be an old fart, fellow. Can't drink the way you used to, either. Christ, it feels like a goddamned jackhammer's ripping through my skull this morning.

Harry opens the medicine cabinet, gulps down three Excedrin before picking up his razor, and then returns his gaze to the mirror.

Strong jaw, though, he thinks, and most of the hair's still there. So what if it's turning gray? Some of those guys at the class reunion were as bald as a baby. Anyway, Brenda says the gray makes me look "distinguished." And she sure was right about getting my hair styled. Gotta admit, Brenda has some good ideas sometimes. Mmmmmmmm, she sure can turn me on, that kid. Gets me horny just thinking about her . . . those gorgeous big boobs . . . the way she moans and wiggles when she sucks my cock. Not like Sue. Hell, Sue still thinks that's dirty . . .

Harry lights a cigarette, inhales deeply, and then balances it with practiced skill on the edge of the sink. As he begins shaving, his thoughts return to the day ahead of him.

Delivery problems again, he thinks. Why is that god-damned factory always screwing up? Nobody does anything right anymore. And Joe, the guy's just not performing. I gotta fire him, been dreading it for weeks, but I can't put it off much longer. And the boss gets back from vacation this afternoon. That means trouble for sure. The old SOB, I can see him now, marching around like a five-star general, look-ing to pounce on everybody. . . .

Suddenly Harry remembers he has a lunch date to be inter-viewed, a date he's already postponed twice and isn't looking forward to. Why did I agree to do that anyway, talk about myself and my life? he wonders, frowning irritably. Guess I had no choice after Ben told that writer dame to call me. "Do it," he said. "You might learn something." Never did ask him what he meant. Oh well, might as well get it over with. . . .

Christ, what time is it? Gotta hurry and get the hell out of here before the thruway really jams up.

After dressing rapidly in the dark and bolting down a glass of orange juice, Harry charges out of the house before any-one in the family awakens. By 7 A.M. he's on the road, with roughly an hour and a half's drive before him.

Traffic's not bad this morning, he observes, turning on the radio to get the news and stubbing out a cigarette in an ashtray overflowing with butts and candy wrappers. Shit, he grimaces in disgust, this car's a goddamned mess again. Why can't Sue get it cleaned out when I ask her to? She never lis-tens anymore, never does what I want.

Harry sighs deeply and settles back for the long drive, his shoulders hunched together tightly. Along the thruway the trees are turning red and yellow, bright reminders of a new fall season. But Harry doesn't notice. Scenery bores him, always has. Besides, he's got too many things to worry about.

By eight-forty, his car safely garaged, Harry is striding briskly into the office building where he works as general sales manager for Consolidated Gadgets. Hurrying off the elevator at the ninth floor, he's anxious to attack the papers on his desk before the phones start ringing. Damn phones, they drive him crazy. That's why he comes in early, tries to get some work done while it's still quiet, while he can still think.

Marching resolutely toward his office, with the weight of his heavy briefcase beginning to numb his right arm, Harry sees that his usual coffee and Danish are on his desk. But Linda, his secretary, is nowhere to be found.

I'd better start without her, he thinks, settling into his chair. Scowling, Harry puts on his bifocals. Acquired three months ago, they pinch and still feel strange. He resents them fiercely, maybe because he remembers all too vividly the day his father got his.

Wow, he's really an old man now, Harry had thought.

That realization had scared him. And now, with the ritual being repeated, he felt like an old man too.

Ignoring his pinched nostrils, Harry sorted a mass of papers into different piles, and then began making notes on a large yellow pad as he studied the latest sales figures. Last month's reports looked bad. He'd have to whip those guys into line, really lay into them, or else his own head would be on the carpet soon.

Half an hour had passed when Harry suddenly heard Linda ask disapprovingly, "Mr. Wilson, how come you have one cigarette in your mouth and another burning in the ashtray?"

Stabbing out both cigarettes simultaneously, Harry squirmed. Damn, he thought to himself, I've been doing that a lot lately. I'm going to fucking set myself on fire if I don't watch it. What the hell's wrong with me, anyway?"

Aloud he said, "Thanks, honey. You saved my life! Now get your pad like a good girl and let's go to it. There's a lot to cover this morning, and it's almost nine-thirty."

The muscles in his right shoulder were aching, and he could still feel a dull throb in his temple. Harry hated dictating, didn't have the knack for it. Linda wasn't much help either, always stopping to ask him how to spell words. But she was a good kid; reliable, too. So Harry tried to be tolerant, sipping his coffee and joking a little as they struggled through this daily chore together.

When it was finally over the rest of the morning seemed to fly. There were never enough hours to do everything he had to, although, God knows, Harry scheduled himself tightly, didn't waste time bullshitting around, either.

Mornings were especially hectic. Salespeople streamed in and out of his office, and the phones rang constantly. By eleven-thirty Harry had juggled more than a dozen long-distance calls, most of them troublesome. Aggravated by one delivery foul-up after another, he was at the end of his rope when the plant manager from Georgia started stalling too. Harry tried listening sympathetically, then he tried pleading and cajoling. Nothing worked.

"I'm sick and tired of your phony excuses," he finally screamed, cutting the fellow short. "Get that stuff here Thursday or it's your goddamned ass!"

Harry slammed the phone down in a fury, still cursing loudly to himself.

"You seem upset, Mr. Wilson," Linda said, poking her head in from the outer office. "Can I get you anything?"

"A glass of water would be great, honey," Harry replied. "On the double." He could feel his stomach tensing, sour juices flowing. Maybe some Alka-Seltzer would help.

During the next hour he met with some junior salesmen from Chicago. His stomach was subdued, but he still felt agitated. Working on a short fuse today, he thought, as he found himself becoming impatient and sarcastic. Then he'd really gone too far with Jim. The poor guy stuttered, not his fault, but it drove Harry berserk. Listening to Jim give his report, stammering and halting every few words, Harry felt his blood pressure rise.

Finally unable to stand it any longer, he'd bellowed, "For Chrissake, Jim, get to the point!"—banging his fist down on the desk so hard that hot coffee had spilled all over Jim's trousers. The poor fellow had bolted out the door in a panic, leaving Harry feeling like a damned fool.

Bad scene, he scolded himself. Gotta keep the lid on.

Harry could feel his heart hammering like a bastard.

By now the morning was gone and it was twelve-thirty,

time for lunch. Glancing at his watch, Harry breathed a sigh of relief. He needed the break, all right. Grabbing his coat, he marched quickly out of his office, barely breaking stride as he shouted to Linda, "Back in a few hours. Any calls, tell 'em I'm in a meeting. Except that one from Houston, get me for that. You know where I'll be."

As he did frequently, Harry walked to the restaurant, a diversion he usually enjoyed. Today, however, his pleasure was spoiled by the disturbing aftereffects of this morning's outburst.

Harry liked being tough, but he didn't like losing control. A man wasn't supposed to do that, lose control. It made him feel weak. Soft.

Two months ago, he remembered, Sue had been pestering him when he was late working on a special report. He'd wanted to stay calm, but she'd kept after him, nagging and interrupting, until finally he'd blown. He'd stormed into the kitchen and slammed his fist right into the refrigerator door. Hard. So hard the dent was still there.

Sue had let out an awful shriek, like a wild and wounded bird, as she'd backed away from him in fright.

"Harry," she'd whispered in a very quiet voice, "you act so strange lately. You're so uptight, so explosive, I hardly recognize you."

She'd paused for a moment, the tears welling up in her eyes.

"I just can't stand it when you get so violent," she'd said shrilly. "I hate you like this!"

And then she'd burst out crying and rushed from the room.

Remembering, Harry shuddered. Sue had made him feel like a real bastard that night, and it had sure as hell scared him, exploding that way. Even several hours later he'd been too shaken to concentrate on his work.

That's how he was feeling now, a little shaky, because of the incident with Jim. I need a drink, Harry thought, grinding his teeth impatiently as he waited at the curb for the light to change.

Trying to compose himself, he paused in front of the restaurant to light a cigarette before pushing the door open with a hard shove. Stopping at the entrance mirror, Harry straightened his tie and smoothed his hair, wondering whether this unknown journalist would be pretty.

No way, he decided. But as he walked cautiously toward the table, Harry put on his winning smile—just in case he'd bet wrong.

Sucking in his belly, Harry slides deftly across the banquette and offers his interviewer a firm handshake in greeting.

Not bad looking, he observes, but too skinny for me.

"How about a drink?" he asks, glancing suspiciously at the tape recorder on the table. "That'll make things easier."

After snapping his fingers for the waiter and ordering a vodka martini, Harry grins boyishly.

"This is one of my favorite restaurants," he says. "I really hope you'll like it."

Harry's decided to try a little charm before getting down to business. Why not? He's always had a knack for impressing the ladies. He knows how to flatter, how to be attentive, and it works every time. Makes him feel powerful, too, knowing he can still be seductive.

"That's a marvelous color on you, that red," he says with silky sincerity.

His eyes glowing with admiration, Harry launches into his well-rehearsed act, offering a stream of amusing anecdotes. A good storyteller, he knows he's being entertaining, and for about ten minutes he's even enjoying himself—until, click, he hears the tape recorder being switched on.

Harry stiffens slightly and reaches for a cigarette. Lighting it with a casual gesture, he inhales deeply.

"So you want to know about me?" he asks, shifting his eyes away but still smiling brightly.

"Well, I'm just an ordinary guy, I guess. Forty-three now, getting older, getting a little fat. But I'm still working hard, damn hard, and making a good living, too. Did it all on my own, no rich in-laws, no help from anyone, and it wasn't easy, I can tell you. I've been married nineteen years now, to a girl I met in college. She's been a good wife, Sue, and a good mother. We've got two kids in their teens, two cars, and a big German shepherd. And last year we moved into a terrific ranch house on about an acre of land. I've even been thinking about building a swimming pool. So it's a good life, a real good life. The American dream and all that jazz."

Harry grins, a proud gleam in his pale blue eyes.

"I've worked hard all my life. That's what I was taught. Work hard and you get ahead. Everything I got, I earned, damnit. And now I guess I've got everything I always wanted, always hoped for."

Harry pauses abruptly and scans the room anxiously, as if trying to locate some well-disguised opponent. A haunted look passes fleeting across his face.

"It's strange, though," he says quietly, "because it isn't like I expected, somehow. I'm just not as happy as I thought I'd be, and I don't know why, really. . . ."

Harry frowns, stubbing out his cigarette. He's just finished shredding a book of matches into tiny pieces. "Did I do that?" he asks, surveying the mess. Suddenly self-conscious, he forces his mouth to smile again.

"So what else you want to know?" he asks. "How do I *feel* about my work? That's a funny question. Never thought about it much."

Harry pauses for a moment, shifts his weight around. Reflecting on the question, he looks uncomfortable.

"Well, let's see."

He pauses again and takes several large swallows from the vodka martini, which has finally arrived.

"Okay, I'll tell you. I just got this promotion. General sales manager, right? So I'm an executive now, finally got a job I had my eye on for a long time. I always said I'd get there before I was forty-five, and I did. More dough, more prestige. Terrific, right? But the pressure's something else. I'm up at the crack of dawn, got a long commute, gotta fight the traffic all the way. And then when I get to the office I'm hassled every minute. The phones go like crazy, my calendar is always jammed, and everybody's got problems that should have been solved yesterday!"

Scowling darkly, Harry taps his fingers against the base of his glass and then lights another cigarette.

"I didn't used to feel this way, like the top of my head was ready to blow off, but I don't know, lately I seem to have trouble keeping it under control—my temper, I mean, from all the pressure. And you can't afford to do that in a new position, because everybody's watching you, waiting for you to fall on your ass.

"The thing is, it's different now than when I was a kid.

Years ago you had to start at the bottom, work your way up gradually, and then you'd get security. Be set for life. And that's what I wanted because I saw what happened to my father. He owned a little grocery store and he was always worrying, always sweating. Barely broke even in the best of times, and then the Depression damn near wiped him out. After a while he got it back together, sort of, but he was a beaten man. Inside."

Harry stares off into space for a minute, sipping his drink slowly, and then resumes.

"So I decided to go to college, get a degree, and join a big corporation. I didn't want to get to the very top. I'm not a genius, I know that, but I sure as hell wanted to make good money—and be secure. Well, *nobody's* really secure in a corporation anymore. The heads of some of the biggest companies are getting fired right and left now, and some of them are still in their fifties, for Chrissake.

"Me, I know I'll never even be a vice president. I've gone about as far as I can go, or even want to. But what if one of those hotshot kids moves into my job in the next few years? Then where the hell do I go? You know what it's like, looking for a job in today's market when you're in your forties? It's a fucking ballbuster, that's what."

Harry stabs out his cigarette, giving it a vicious twist. Pointing to his empty glass, he signals the waiter for another.

"Yeah, times sure have changed," he comments bitterly. "The young guys have it so easy today they don't even have to be *good* to get hired. They just have to look hip. It pisses me off, it really does. I'm not saying things were right before, you know, but why the hell should I have to keep breaking my butt at my age just to hold onto my job? Christ, you'd think by this time I'd have earned the right to relax a little."

The veins in his neck bulging slightly, Harry lights up again. Silent for a moment, he fingers his empty glass reflectively.

"I don't know," he continues, "maybe it's not just the job, maybe something's happening to me. A few years ago I loved my work. I loved pushing hard, being on the go, driving myself to the limit. But now I just feel like I'm running all the time, spinning my wheels, and what's the point?

"On top of all this," he says, talking rapidly now, his eyes focused vacantly into space, "my father's got cancer. So after work I have to go racing over to the hospital, visit a little while, try to cheer him up. But it's a terrible strain. I just can't stand seeing him so pale and scrawny, like a fucking skeleton, with tubes stuck in him everywhere. It tears me up, looking at him, knowing he's dying. Knowing I can't do anything."

His jaws clamped together tightly, Harry crushes the swizzle stick with one hand. His drink arrives and he sips it gratefully.

"Maybe I could handle it better, all the responsibilities, everybody pulling at me, if I could go home and really relax. But I can't turn it off like I used to. My nerves are shot anyway by the time I walk in the door, after fighting the traffic and everything. So I have a couple of drinks, watch TV, try to unwind. But lately when I sit down in the den all I can think about is there's another year's payment due on the furniture, and with my father in the hospital it really mounts up. That's no joke."

Harry scowls. Then for the first time he leans back against the cushion.

"To tell you the truth," he adds, "Sue isn't much help either. Used to be she couldn't do enough to please me. Kept the house looking great, organized my drawers and closets perfectly. And she cooked like a dream, even got my favorite recipes from my mother. But now she serves quickie dinners mostly and tells me to take care of my clothes myself. And if I ask her to do something special for me, she usually forgets. Doesn't even hear me half the time, it seems. Maybe she just doesn't give a damn anymore, about what I want."

Harry grinds out his cigarette and takes several large swallows from his martini.

"So the minute I walk in," he continues, "we start fighting. It's always the same old argument, about the things she 'forgot' to do. Or else if we don't fight it's because she's not home yet—and that bugs me too. She's late some nights because she started working part-time at a local boutique. Wanted to get out of the house, she said, keep busy, earn a little money. She doesn't make much, but I don't like it anyway. Her working. My wife shouldn't have to work, damnit, that wasn't the way I was brought up."

Harry sighs deeply.

"She's taking this psychology course now, too, and she's always using it on me. Like when I've had a rough day and I take an extra drink she gives me the fishy eye. Tells me if I'm upset I should *talk* about it instead of drinking so much. Hell, I don't need her lectures. All I want to do is relax and have a peaceful dinner. But she won't leave me alone, especially about my drinking and smoking too much. Maybe she's just afraid I'm going to kick off before it's time to pay for the kids' college tuition!"

Harry smiles weakly, a wounded look in his eyes. Polishing off his drink, he signals for another.

"That's another thing," he continues, "the kids. Eric is seventeen now and Lisa is almost sixteen. I can hardly believe it, they're growing up so fast. But they've changed so much lately I don't know what to make of it. Lisa used to be real affectionate. She'd climb into my lap, give me bear hugs. And Eric and I used to have such fun together. Saturdays I'd take him bowling, or we'd throw a football around in the yard. He was a damned good athlete, too. Fast and spunky.

"But now Eric doesn't do a damn thing except hang around his room listening to records. Or maybe goes to a friend's house and does the same thing there. Smokes pot, too, I guess. It kills me, his being that way. But when I try to talk to him about it he says he just wants to 'groove' on life, get into his own head. Then when I tell him he can't do that forever he says, 'Why not? I don't want to ruin my life with middle-class hangups like you, Dad.'

"Can you beat that? Here I am working myself to death for my family, and my son puts me down for having middle-class hangups! As if that six-hundred-dollar stereo of his fell off a tree!"

Harry cracks his knuckles loudly. His third martini arrives and he takes a long swallow, savoring the sharp, clean taste. The liquor was finally getting to him, loosening him up. He wasn't used to spilling his guts like this, that wasn't his style. But now it felt sort of good.

"The worst thing is," he says, lowering his voice a little and speaking in confidential tones, "sometimes I get jealous of him, my own son. He's seventeen years old and he's getting laid whenever he wants. With great-looking girls, too. Don't get me wrong, I don't blame him for getting laid. Hell, I was making out when I was seventeen too, but it was different then.

"You had to sneak around like a criminal, find some broad who was willing to put out—never someone you really liked—and then do this big snow job on her. And when you finally did get in her pants you were all cramped up in the back seat of a car, feeling guilty as hell. We used to brag a lot, the guys I grew up with, but none of us got laid that much. We were too damn scared, or it was too much of a hassle. Not like today. The kids know how to enjoy sex now.

"So Eric makes me jealous because I wish I'd had that when I was young. Time to run around, screw a lot of pretty girls, really have a ball. But I didn't. And now my own son's a swinger while I'm worrying about how many years I'll still be able to get it up. It bothers me, you know? Does that sound crazy?"

Harry grins, a pleading look in his eyes. Then he shifts his gaze quickly and lights a cigarette. When the waiter appears to tell him he has a long-distance phone call, he jumps up in relief and heads for the phone booth.

"See what it's like?" he says on his return. "They don't even let you eat in peace. But speaking of eating, maybe we should order."

Harry motions for a menu and studies it thoughtfully as he sips his martini. Finally he orders half a grapefruit, broiled sole, no butter, a green salad, and a large bottle of dry white wine.

"I'm always trying to diet, gotta get back in shape," he explains, looking sheepish. Addressing the waiter, he adds, "And bring the wine right away, okay?" Then his face suddenly assumes a pained expression.

"With my daughter it's different," he says softly. "Maybe I'm old-fashioned, but I just can't get used to the idea of her having sex before she gets married. Not that she is yet, at least I don't think she is, but the whole idea bothers me anyway. Maybe because of how she looks. I mean, she's got a great face and figure, runs around braless in skin-tight jeans, and I can tell from the way guys look at her they want to get her into bed already. Just the thought of one of those long-haired kids making it with my daughter gets me furious. But what do I do, lock her up?

"If I even say something about her clothes, hint that they're too revealing, she gives me this suffering look and tells me times are changing, that women feel free about their bodies now. Not even sixteen yet and she's calling herself a 'woman' can you imagine? She's so moody and sensitive I hardly know how to talk to her anymore."

Interrupted by the waiter, Harry tastes the wine he ordered and nods his approval automatically. After his glass has been filled, he drains it quickly before speaking again.

"This sex business," he says somberly, shaking his head slowly from side to side, "sometimes I can't figure it out myself. For a long time I was faithful to Sue, for ten years maybe. You got married you were supposed to be faithful, that's what I always thought.

"Then I went to this business convention in Las Vegas, and it was really an eye-opener. A lot of guys I worked with, guys I knew were happily married, were all lining up girls for the night. I was shocked at first. Then I figured what the hell, Sue'll never know, so I went to bed with a showgirl that night. Didn't even feel guilty afterward. It was just a wild adventure with the boys, something we joked about later. We were all pretty smashed anyway.

"After that it was easy. Whenever I'd go away on a business trip I'd usually get a little action. Pick up a girl at a bar or a party, sometimes even a hooker, whatever the other guys were doing. But I never got involved. Just played around a little, strictly for laughs."

Crushing out his cigarette, Harry pauses to concentrate on his grapefruit, then looks off into space and takes a deep breath. He seems to be poised, awkwardly, on the verge of a confession.

"Then last year something strange happened, like out of the blue," he continues. "And I don't quite understand it myself. I met this girl, a kid really—Brenda's only twenty—and I fell for her. She's a model, works for a guy I do business with, that's how we met. And I've been seeing her regularly ever since. She's sweet and kind of innocent, you know, but sexy too.

"Like the first time I took her for a drink, she sat down and there was this little ripping noise and she started to giggle. She'd split the seam in her slacks and she didn't have any panties on! That blew my mind, really turned me on. No panties, can you imagine?

"But when we finally made it together I was surprised. I thought she'd be wild in bed, but she was pretty inexperienced. Almost a virgin. She'd only been with one other guy, and she'd never had an orgasm before me. Now she has no inhibitions at all. She'll do anything I want her to. Anything. Like she goes down on me all the time, which my wife won't ever do, and she even *enjoys* it!"

Harry beams—and then flicks his Bic.

"So it's great with us, the sex, but that isn't all. I can really talk to Brenda, tell her if I've had a bad day, and I know by the way she looks at me that she's listening. And I can laugh with her and be silly and say romantic things. I even buy her roses sometimes. Corny, huh? But that's how Brenda makes me feel. Young and romantic again. She really appreciates me, too, always tells me how smart and handsome I am. But she never makes any demands on me, never nags. Just whatever I do, whatever I want, that's okay with her. And I need that now, that kind of loving, I guess you'd call it.

"Sometimes I feel like a heel, though, because I've told Brenda I love her and I even talk about leaving home to marry her. But I don't really mean it when I'm saying it, so then I feel guilty afterward. And I feel guilty about Sue, too, because this time I really *am* cheating on her. Then I get angry and think, well, if Sue cared about me more and wasn't on my back so much this probably wouldn't be happening."

Harry knots his brows together, a belligerent look on his face. The food arrives, distracting him temporarily, and he picks at his fish in silence. Then after draining his wineglass again, he resumes speaking.

"I know it's not really all Sue's fault. She's got her own problems, too, and lots of times when she wants to talk I just tune her out. Don't have the patience to listen to her complaining about her varicose veins, or the latest screaming match with Lisa. So I tune out, and she gets hopping mad. Tells me I'm not giving her any help with the things that bother her, and I guess maybe she's right."

His jaws tightly clenched, Harry curls his fingers into fists.

"But damnit, whose fault is it, then?" he continues. "I wonder about that a lot. Maybe marriage is the problem, being married so long. It gets goddamned boring being with the same person for nineteen years, you know? It's got to. And having sex with the same woman all those years, for Chrissake, that's a drag. Sometimes you can't even get it up, period. You've just got to have a change. So I found Brenda.

Is that such a crime? Why do I feel so guilty about it then? I mean, it's not like I want a divorce or anything, you know?"

Crushing out his cigarette, Harry removes a package of Rolaids from his pocket, pops two in his mouth, and chews them thoughtfully.

"Nervous stomach," he comments by way of apology. "Knots up on me when I'm upset. 'Stress' they call it these days, right? Well maybe I'm lucky so far it's only gotten to my stomach, huh?"

Harry flashes a broad grin, which quickly changes into a frown.

"Last year a guy in my office died of a heart attack, and he was only forty-six. Hadn't ever been sick, and then one day he just keeled right over on his desk. That really scared me, happening at the office like that, and so for a while I was always checking my pulse. Finally Sue made me go to the doctor, I was so shook up. No major problem yet, the doc said, but my cholesterol count's too high. So he told me to cut down on fatty foods and try to relax.

"What a joke, relax! I found out I don't even know *how* to relax anymore. When I was a kid I used to read a lot, but now the only thing I pick up is a best seller or maybe a detective story, something I can skim through fast. If I try to really concentrate on a book I get uptight right away. And I don't even enjoy fishing like I did. Years ago I used to love sitting by a stream, all alone, watching the water roll by and daydreaming. But now it just makes me restless."

Harry shrugs and lights another cigarette.

"This is the only way I know how to relax now," he says, raising his glass in mock salute. "And it's gotta be something stronger than wine. Martinis usually, or Jack Daniels if it's going to be a long night. I'm drinking more than I should lately, I guess, and sometimes the hangovers are really terrible. Hell, I feel like my head's been kicked in some mornings. But what else can I do? Liquor's the only thing that really works, gets me to unwind a little, and it's not like I'm an alcoholic or anything. Christ, I hardly ever get *really* drunk. . . ."

As the waiter approaches with coffee and the check, Harry suddenly notices that the restaurant is almost empty. Glancing at his watch, he sees it's three o'clock, much later than he'd thought.

Harry drags on his cigarette and stares at the tape recorder. There's a note of anger in his voice when he resumes speaking, and his face is flushed.

"The way I feel right now, I guess, is trapped. By all the pressures and responsibilities. By my job and the office and Sue and the kids and my father. By Brenda too, sometimes. But what can I do? I can't just quit my job or break up my marriage or go running off to some South Seas island. That's ridiculous.

"Sometimes I think about buying a farm, living out in the country where it's peaceful. I did that one summer when I was a kid, worked on a farm. Had a ball, too. But that's just a pipe dream now. I'll never really do it.

"So I just keep on doing the same goddamned things every day. I run to the office, then I run to the hospital, maybe some nights I run over to Brenda's, and then I run back to the house. Same shit every day. I feel like I'm always running, but I don't even know what I'm chasing after anymore. It's like being on a fucking treadmill. You just feel trapped, you know?"

Harry recalls the nightmare he awoke with, his own words triggering again those frightful images of locked doors and bolted windows. He shudders involuntarily, perspiration breaking out on his upper lip. Stubbing out his cigarette, his hands trembling slightly, he continues.

"Sometimes I want to talk about all this with somebody, but I can't. I mean, who would it be? Some of the guys at work I like a helluva lot, but I'd be afraid to talk to them, you know, because if anything personal got around the office it would sure as hell be used against you. And the guys I bowl with or play golf with, we joke around a lot, but we don't talk seriously. About ourselves.

"And who else is there? The last time I had a really close buddy was in the Marines, that was different, but now there's nobody. With Sue, well, we don't really communicate, not about deep stuff. Sometimes when she knows I'm upset she says I should 'open up' more, let my feelings out. 'That's just your psychology bullshit,' I tell her. But the truth is I don't really know *how* to let my feelings out. They're kind of frozen up inside, you know?"

Harry turns suddenly pale and his fingers start drumming on the table.

"Something's wrong, the way I feel, I know it. And I've got to really sit down and sort things out or I'm going to do something stupid. And I can't afford to do something stupid now, for Chrissake. But I don't have time to just sit around and *think*, either. So what the fuck am I supposed to do? What?"

Harry smashes his fist down hard, upsetting the ashtray and showering butts all over the table. He scowls blackly and then composes himself into a more dignified posture.

"I don't normally sound like this, you know, but I just don't feel like myself anymore."

He sighs heavily, his shoulders slumped in despair.

"I don't know who I feel like sometimes, or what I really feel. I don't know why I'm doing the things I'm doing, and I don't know what the hell I really want. I didn't expect it would be like this somehow. I never thought I'd end up feeling so hassled at work and bored at home and sorry for myself. With nobody I can talk to either.

"Hell, I always thought this would make me really happy: Having an executive job and a house in the suburbs and a swell family, making forty-five thousand a year. That's what it was all about, I always thought."

Harry screws his face into a question mark.

"Now I just don't know," he says quietly. "I just don't know anymore."

Chapter 2 New Hope for an Old Problem

I *A Familiar Syndrome*

Harry probably sounds familiar to you, and so do his complaints. It has long been an item of popular wisdom that forty is a difficult age for a man, and an age when he also makes life difficult for others.

You may have seen men like Harry on TV programs about male menopause, or read about them in articles on the same subject. Or perhaps you've encountered such men in movies like *Scenes from a Marriage* and *Carnal Knowledge* and *Save the Tiger;* or in books like Joseph Heller's *Something Happened* and Alison Lurie's *War Between the Tates*.

Maybe Harry reminds you of someone you know—a friend or colleague. Your husband or lover.

Maybe you even feel like Harry yourself.

If not, take another look around you. You'll discover that a great many men start behaving strangely sometime in the middle of their lives—doing things they never thought they'd do and asking questions they never imagined grown men had to ask. This is the time when careers nosedive, affairs flourish, and marriages flounder or fall apart. Such events are only the tip of the iceberg.

Arriving at the brink of middle age is like being stranded in a foreign country: With few guideposts to direct him, a man feels disoriented by the unfamiliar terrain and the multiple changes jarring his psyche. Suddenly the past seems a humiliating reminder of risks untaken, women unconquered, and chances ignored. And the future seems to be hurtling toward a dreaded rendezvous with old age and death. Meanwhile, responsibilities are mounting and physical energies are ebbing. Children are rebelling or departing, wives becoming assertive and demanding, and parents falling ill or dying. Younger men are scrambling up the work ladder, and job options are shrinking.

With so many altered horizons, a man begins to feel as if he's lost his focus on things. Outward circumstances and inner stirrings now clash in a new way—and something disquieting starts happening.

Most of us will recognize the more common symptoms of mid-life turmoil.

This is the time of life, for example, when a man begins to worry about his body. Suddenly he suffers from prostate troubles and pulled muscles. Suddenly he needs glasses or root canal work. His cholesterol count goes up, his energy level down. His body is less reliable on the tennis court, less resilient under stress. He can no longer work such long hours or travel at his usual hectic pace.

He finds it maddening, this loss of control. He feels that his body has betrayed him.

High blood pressure develops and so do ulcers. Psychosomatic illnesses erupt: A man is suddenly beset by chronic fatigue, acute indigestion, mysterious backaches, painful joints, and migraine headaches. He complains a lot or even becomes hypochondriacal, convinced that every cold is the forerunner of pneumonia, every pain the sign of cancer, and every rapid heartbeat the precursor of a coronary.

Often he panics over his sexual performance and suffers from bouts of impotence. He may become lethargic about sex and cut down his activity. Or do just the opposite, pursuing new sexual conquests with a vengeance. He jokes about sex compulsively, develops a sudden interest in X-rated films, or brags outrageously about his exploits.

To confirm his sexual appeal he may try to regain a youthful image by changing his appearance. He grows a beard or mustache, gets his hair styled or dyed. He buys a toupee, undergoes a hair transplant, or gets rid of his wrinkles and jowls by plastic surgery. He may also change his style of dress:

- A conservative executive trades his dark suits and striped ties for velvet jackets and turtlenecks.
- A diffident accountant becomes a weekend hippie, trans-

formed by French jeans, a shirt slit to the navel, and chains around his neck.
- And a quiet dentist switches to suede jumpsuits and platform shoes.

Habits change, too. A man suddenly becomes serious about dieting or exercising. He gets into Transcendental Meditation, Arica, or EST. He gives up smoking cigarettes, tries marijuana instead. A sedentary lawyer becomes a tennis or jogging enthusiast. A teacher takes up skiing or backpacking. And a salesman goes off to shoot the rapids, hunt deer in the wilds, or learn how to pilot a plane.

Sometimes a man makes a wildly impulsive purchase, treating himself to a luxury item he's dreamed about since youth:

- A newly divorced engineer spends thousands on a racy red sports car, despite his tardiness in meeting alimony payments.
- A computer operator who used to love mountain climbing buys a cabin high in the hills for family weekends, oblivious to the ten-hour drive involved.
- And a store manager who is still struggling to pay off the mortgage on his home splurges on an eighteen-foot cabin cruiser.

This is the time of life when a man often starts behaving in oddly uncharacteristic ways. He ignores his wife and screams at his children. He complains of boredom and fatigue, insisting his life has no meaning. He becomes increasingly detached, withdrawn, and introspective.

He drives himself relentlessly at work, snapping at his colleagues and staying at the office later and later. Or he abruptly loses interest in his job, taking longer lunch hours, forgetting appointments, and dawdling rebelliously over deadlines. The man who was generally calm and easygoing now becomes a demonic whirlwind—always busy, always traveling, always overscheduling himself. Another man, previously cheerful and boisterous, suddenly turns morose and moody. He can't take a joke anymore, hardly laughs at all.

Weekend patterns change, too. The former sportsman and

devoted father now sulks in front of the TV, retreats to his basement workshop, or falls asleep at peculiar hours. When his wife suggests a local movie, or ice skating with the kids, he glares at her reproachfully. And the contemplative man who always relished solitude now fills his weekend with activity—squash, handball, poker, backgammon, anything involving people. Urgently gregarious, he suddenly wants his wife to entertain more, too.

This is also the time of life, as most of us certainly know, when a man is likely to develop lascivious urges. Marriages shake, and sometimes shatter, as men in their forties counter boredom or bickering in the connubial bed with sexual conquests. Suddenly susceptible to erotic adventures, they try everything from intense flirtations to casual liaisons to consuming love affairs. The outcome varies:

- A country preacher refrains from acting on his sexual desires for a young widow with whom he has become enamored. But when he lunches with her weekly he feels terribly guilty nonetheless.
- A timid chemist initiates a furtive affair with his lab assistant, after years of resisting her seductive glances. Six months later he stuns his wife by demanding an immediate divorce.
- A stockbroker begins flirting slyly with the girls in the office, and then graduates to a full-fledged affair with a former high school sweetheart. Unwilling to abandon his children, he settles for a double life instead.
- After years of casual promiscuity, a TV celebrity leaves home because he's found true love at last. One year later he pleads for a reconciliation, confessing that he misses the kids, the dog, and the Sunday barbeques.

Whatever the consequences, mid-life infidelities often involve much younger women, in part because the firm flesh and innocent eyes of nubile girls are particularly enticing to men who are anxious to retain their grip on youth. Such romances may be brief and fanciful, just a rejuvenating interlude, or they may deepen and endure. But in recent years it has become increasingly common for men in their forties to remarry a woman many years their junior. Very successful men especially often flaunt a beautiful young wife like another badge of merit. And a symbol of potency. Today such men are more admired than scorned, and we are no longer so shocked as in the past if:

- A publishing executive who claimed his was the perfect marriage leaves home for a copy editor younger than his daughter.
- A television producer who has just bought a lavish apartment suddenly gets divorced to marry a girl who looks exactly like his wife, only twenty years younger.
- And a travel agent who always seemed devoted to his family divorces to marry an ingenue actress he met only two months before.

Newly critical of themselves, their families, and their whole mode of living, men in their forties often entertain dreams of dropping everything—or dropping out. Some fantasize about living in the wilderness, or on a tropical island; others lust for life in a commune, aboard a ship, or on a farm.

And then there are those who do more than dream. Rather than simply switching women, they change their goals, their careers, and sometimes their entire way of life:

- Tired of the rat race and urban pressures, a corporate executive gives up his high-paying post and moves his family to a farm in Montana, planning to raise sheep.
- Intent on becoming a commercial illustrator, a midwestern car salesman goes to night school, eagerly anticipating the day he can begin a new career in New York City.
- Fed up with the politics of academic life, a biologist abandons his teaching and sells some stock in order to write the comic novel he has been dabbling with for years.
- And a reporter resigns from his newspaper job so that he and his wife can sail to the Caribbean on the forty-foot schooner they've just bought with their life savings.

II *Something Is Happening*

We are all familiar with these symptoms, with the ways in which mid-life men change their appearance, their mood, their women, their work, and their way of life. Whether large or small, foolish or brave, these changes tell us that something is happening to the man in his forties.

Something unsettling.

Something we don't fully understand.

The fact is that nearly all men, extraordinary or ordinary, celebrated or unknown, successful or making-do, experience some depression at mid-life. This is the time when a man begins to realize he is growing older and that someday he will die. Earlier he probably thought about death in abstract terms, but now he is being forced to confront it in a more personal, emotional way.

It hurts, this confrontation.

And it usually causes him to re-examine everything: who he is and the work he's doing; the people in his life and what they mean to him; his past mistakes, present commitments, and future goals. Dismayed by the collapse of youthful dreams, he feels trapped by his own past choices and the rapid passage of time. But he also feels baffled by this newly urgent need to question everything he had previously taken for granted.

"I really feel ridiculous at forty-two asking myself all the same questions I was asking as a sophomore in college," lamented one man suffering doubts about both his marriage and his work. "Earlier I knew what I wanted. Everything was focused, like a tunnel, and I could see where I was going and what I wanted at the end. Now that's all gone. Everything I've been doing seems like bullshit, and nothing has any meaning for me right now. I don't know what the hell I want."

Worst of all, a man is often convinced that he shouldn't feel confused or depressed, and that nobody else feels the same way he does. Why does the life he chose himself now seem so confining? Something must be happening to *him*— but he doesn't understand what it is.

Thrashing around in the turbulent emotional depths of adulthood, most men now in their forties are terrified by feelings they can't account for or explain. More accustomed to dealing with problems that can first be defined, and then aggressively tackled and solved, they are likely to reach frantically for some simple solution.

Some try to drown their mysterious inner fears with liquor.

Some anesthetize themselves with tranquilizers, athletics, or frenzied work efforts. And some seek relief in compulsive sex or the comforting arms of young lovers. Others try to dismiss what they can't fix or flee from by latching onto labels which reassure them that whatever is happening isn't their fault, isn't their responsibility, and can be safely ignored.

Unfortunately, we have all complied in this dismissal by supplying and sanctioning a variety of labels ourselves. Although we have long known that something is happening to men around forty, we still don't really understand it; and we therefore feel disturbed and threatened when the adult men who anchor our society start behaving unpredictably. To ease our discomfort we describe their behavior with denigrating names.

With a condescending shrug we say these men are entering the Foolish Forties or the Dangerous Years. We accuse them of going through a Second Adolescence or a Change of Life. And then, having labeled as sick or silly what we don't comprehend, we file the phenomena away as just a passing phase.

We are all familiar with men like Harry. We have given his problem many names. But we have not yet taken his predicament very seriously.

III *Male Menopause: A Dangerous Diagnosis*

The most popular label for the curious troubles that afflict men at mid-life is male menopause. Unlike the other phrases, it has a scientific ring.

Taken literally, it is of course a ridiculous concept. Men don't have a menstrual cycle, we all know that. Nor do they lose their reproductive powers in their forties as women do. We know that, too. Nonetheless, the question of whether or not there is a syndrome known as male menopause has been hotly debated and widely publicized.

Some doctors use the phrase in a metaphorical sense to describe the psychological reactions that trouble men as they age. Others have focused on the hormonal issue, suggesting that like women, men in their forties also experience devastating hormonal changes. One influential medical popularizer, Dr. David Reuben, claims that because of the menopause all men will become impotent at this time of life—unless they undergo hormonal treatment. Reuben even predicts that without such treatment a man's genitals will shrivel and his breasts enlarge.

This is nightmarish nonsense.

The responsible scientific community overwhelmingly agrees that, unlike the female, the male in his forties does *not* normally suffer from radical hormonal changes. Rather, the decline is gradual and usually too slight to have *any* effect on his sexual functioning. If he is in good health and not victimized by psychic blocks, a man can continue having erections and enjoying sexual relations well into his eighties.

(It is true, however, that a few men will suffer a sharp drop in hormones later in life, in their fifties or sixties. Considered an *illness,* not a normal occurrence like the menopause, this "climacteric" can be treated by hormone therapy. More about that later.)

Given these facts, the phrase "male menopause" only confuses rather than clarifies matters. Why then is this absurd and destructive label so popular? Why do some authorities favor a phrase they must qualify as metaphorical only? Why do women welcome a label with such a castrating bite? And why do men so willingly embrace a concept implying they're on the sexual skids?

The reasons revolve, first, around the profit motive: Male menopause is a syndrome that was originally invented, it has been suggested, by certain pharmaceutical companies to promote the sales of male hormones at a time when the medical community first became enthusiastic about endocrinology.

This in turn resulted in a flood of sometimes lurid literature on the subject inundating the physician's desk. Since there has always been a tendency in medicine to seek a quick cure for psychological symptoms, some bandwagon doctors were only too happy to buy the sales pitch claiming that a hormone injection could "replace the strength of declining manhood"—and to pass this soothing promise on to distressed patients. Besides, it is much simlper for a doctor to whip out a syringe than deal with a man's emotional problems.

Obviously this diagnosis of male menopause did not gain wide currency simply because it was promoted by drug companies and endorsed by some physicians. It also had to be popularized through the mass media. But since the phrase itself is alliterative, and the topic provocative and controversial, it makes for highly commercial copy—which is why in recent years so many magazine articles and television programs have been devoted to this subject.

More important, however, most of us have found it to be a comforting catch-all label. A ridiculous phrase to begin with, it helps us laugh when faced with unsettling male behavior—and lightens our anxiety. Also there seems no limit to its usefulness. It's the menopause, we nod knowingly, when a man in his forties becomes restless and despondent. It's the menopause, again, when he lies brooding in the hammock, drinking too much Bourbon. Likewise when he buys a flamboyant wardrobe, gives up a high-status job for the simple life, or runs off with a much younger woman. Without doubt, we snicker, it's the menopause.

This diagnosis appeals to all of us for the same reason doctors find it convenient: It provides a legitimate excuse to avoid dealing with disturbing emotions.

Women seize upon this phrase for support at a time of life when the battle of the sexes often escalates dramatically. Wife or girlfriend, she wants something to blame when her man glowers at her irritably, provokes arguments unjustly, or leaves a trail of adulterous clues. Attributing his strange behavior to some elusive malady not only lets her off the hook as the possible cause of his troubles, but also eliminates the need to probe too deeply or face shattering realities: like the fact that he is having an affair or that their relationship is over.

For the woman it is surely less devastating to believe her man is sick with the menopause than sick of her.

Moreover, she probably has good reason to use every weapon at her disposal. One of the most common reactions at this time of life is for a man to seek a scapegoat for his problems. Anyone from a secretary to a boss to younger colleagues to welfare recipients will do, but most frequently it is his wife or girlfriend whom he faults. Even otherwise sensible men suddenly grant their mates extraordinary demonic powers during this period.

Subject to such irrational attacks, a woman is likely to become insulting and abusive too. By calling her man menopausal she suggests not only that his sexuality is fading, but also that he is acting like a female. Equally frail and vulnerable. Equally victimized by his body.

What better way to puncture the inflated balloon of male

superiority than this? What more scathing denunciation of *machismo* could there be? After years of being accused by men of bizarre behavior triggered by her hormonal cycles, what sweet revenge for a woman to suggest there is a time of life when a man becomes as loony and unpredictable as a menopausal female.

Seen in this light, it is understandable why women use this label as an epithet, a way of fighting back when they feel put on the defensive.

But why do most men readily accept "male menopause" as an apt description of their mid-life predicament? Many even volunteer the phrase, offering their diagnosis with an earnest air of insight and discovery.

Why should the American male welcome such an insulting label?

The answer is that the insult is mild, and gladly ignored, compared to the vast relief a man experiences when he can stamp all the scrambled threads of his life with this simple tag—meant to excuse everything.

It's the menopause, he sighs as he casually surveys the chaos he's created, the misery he's caused. If his wife is distraught, his girlfriend exploited and his children rebellious, he can now claim it's not *his* fault; rather, the fault of an obscure ailment that has suddenly struck.

There are good reasons for welcoming an escape route: Taught to repress his feelings, the American male now in his forties is poorly equipped to handle the disturbing emotions that fracture his inner peace at mid-life. Beamed into power and performance, he regards emotional upheaval as a sign of weakness. And he has become so used to stoic self-control that by now he has often lost touch with his feelings entirely. Deeply buried, rarely revealed, they represent alien territory.

How then to cope with the frustrations and fears so common at mid-life? How to cope with the doubts and depression? Instead of confronting them, a man often finds it easier, more his style, to seek an external solution: make a major move, find another job, grab a younger wife, leap into an affair—all options oriented toward action.

When this need to run and repress prevails he will do anything to avoid dealing with painful emotions. Anything to avoid plumbing his inner self. And this is when he discovers that wearing the menopausal halo pays off.

Being "sick" has definite advantages: It allows him to be considered slightly incapacitated, mildly indisposed, and therefore not entirely accountable for his behavior. It also provides an excuse to withdraw from the irritating demands of others—and indulge himself instead.

More convenient still, since there is no specific cure available for the male menopause, the diagnosis itself suffices. The phrase implies that mysterious body changes, entangled somehow with the hormones and the aging process, are at the root of a man's predicament. Beyond his control then, certainly. All his problems can therefore be magically disposed of with just a label, exonerating him from the difficult task of having to *deal* with them.

And so the perfect cop-out: If a man is suffering from the menopause, as he might from a virus, how can he possibly do anything but wait to get over it?

In the final analysis, the reason why the concept of male menopause has become so popular is simple: It gives both sexes something to blame during the difficult mid-life period.

Women use it as a damning epithet to retaliate for being made scapegoats, and men capitalize on being called sick to hide from self-confrontation. In these ways both avoid tangling with disruptive emotions.

Despite its appeal, however, the menopausal label is dangerous and destructive:

- It mistakenly implies that aging inevitably destroys male potency.
- It obscures the real problems that a man must recognize and work through during his forties.
- And, worst of all, it perpetuates the notion that the pain and confusion experienced at mid-life are symptoms that mean something is wrong.

IV *At Forty: A Fresh Burst of Growth*

Now there is a new way to look at the strange things happening to mid-life men: not as symptoms of something wrong, but as signs of something right and normal and necessary.

Something promising and productive.

We have always assumed that something must be wrong when a grown man starts making unexpected changes or asking basic questions, like "What do I really want?" or "Where do I go from here?" because we assume that by forty a man should know exactly who he is, what he wants, and where he's heading.

These negative assumptions reflect the bias of our culture: In America we still believe that people finish with the business of growing up in their twenties and never really change in any substantial way thereafter.

But these beliefs are based on a profound misconception of what it means to be an adult. Our tendency to misinterpret and distort the meaning of the middle years was perfectly described some time ago by writer Anne Morrow Lindbergh:

> We Americans, with our terrific emphasis on youth, action and material success, certainly tend to belittle the afternoon of life . . . and therefore this period of expanding is often tragically misunderstood. . . .
>
> The signs that presage growth, so similar, it seems to me, to those in early adolescence: discontent, restlessness, doubt, despair, longing, are interpreted falsely as signs of decay. In youth one does not as often misinterpret the signs; one accepts them quite rightly, as growing pains. . . .
>
> But in middle age . . . one runs away; one escapes— into depressions, nervous breakdowns, drink, love-affairs, or frantic, thoughtless, fruitless overwork. Anything, rather than face them. Anything, rather than stand still and learn from them.
>
> One tries to cure the signs of growth, to exorcise them, as if they were devils, when really they might be angels of annunciation.[1]

Like Lindbergh, our poets and playwrights and novelists have always known that human beings are capable of astonishing transformations even in their later years. But it is only recently that social scientists too have finally discovered the painful trials and joyful possibilities of adulthood.

Today there is ample evidence which shows that, contrary to our popular assumptions, adult life is neither a static state of affairs nor a slow slide downhill. It is a process of continuing development.

Today we are learning that people grow and change throughout their entire life course. Sometimes they go through periods that are relatively calm and stable. But at other times they go through more turbulent and confusing periods—when their life is in flux and their personality is expanding.

These findings have the greatest significance for our understanding of the mid-life period. They enable us to look at an old problem in an entirely new way. A hopeful way.

From this new perspective we can see that what is happening to Harry, and a lot of other men in their middle years, is neither shameful nor peculiar nor symptoms of disease. Rather, behavior that we viewed as strange or troublesome in the past can now be seen as a sign that a man is going through a developmental crisis.

The painful questions that hit around forty signal arrival at a crossroads: A man has reached the point where his internal evolution demands a fresh burst of growth.

V *The Mid-life Crisis: A Normal Developmental Stage*

The idea of a developmental crisis was first proposed by the distinguished psychoanalyst Erik Erikson. Enlarging on Freud's foundation, Erikson suggested that normal developmental stages do not stop with childhood but continue during the adult years.

Life in his view is a continuing series of steps, or stages, each presenting an opportunity for new growth. A developmental crisis occurs, says Erikson, when a person becomes ready to face a new life task, or a new set of choices. He has now arrived at a turning point.

A decisive moment.

The outcome will vary. Here "crisis" means, as it does in medicine, "a turning point for better or for worse." So too in life. When a man arrives at this critical point he can either win a victory or suffer a defeat.

In theory Erikson's ideas had a profound and far-reaching effect on American behavioral scientists long ago. But it is only within the past ten or fifteen years that they have been applied in practice as well. Now researchers across the country have finally begun to fill in Erikson's framework with a wide variety of empirical studies devoted to the problems and possibilities of the adult years.

Increasingly, too, they have begun to recognize that the mid-life period is an enormously important time of change, but also a time of upheaval and distress similar to that which teen-agers experience.

Less well known than adolescence, and certainly less well understood, this mid-life period marks the passage from early adulthood to middle age. It is a time of transition.

And a time of maturing: At forty the American male can finally come of age.

For our purposes the most illuminating study of the mid-life crisis has been done by a team of researchers at Yale University, headed by psychologist Daniel J. Levinson. Begun in 1968, this Yale study of men between thirty-five and forty-five provides a comprehensive framework for understanding the issues we will be exploring, and we will refer to it in more detail throughout.

In general the Yale group offers these conclusions:

- The mid-life crisis is a predictable stage of development that all men go through. Most experience it at around forty, although it may affect some in their late thirties and others not until their fifties. Oddly enough, it occurs even if a man has been successful.
- For some the transition may go relatively smoothly, but it generally involves considerable agitation. Marked by confusion and introspection, it is a time when most men are plagued by fundamental doubts about their work, their family, and their goals. This restlessness and discontent are forerunners of normal personality development, painful but necessary.
- In addition to being predictable, the mid-life crisis is also *desirable*. True, this period has its threats, but it also offers opportunities for new personality growth and life changes never before possible: A man can now move toward greater self-fulfillment in his work, more intimacy in his marriage and other relationships, and a deeper connection with his children.

•Regardless of when it hits or how much distress it brings, however, this crisis is a strategic turning point in every man's life—one that will profoundly affect his future.

During this period of change there is an unsettling feeling of death and rebirth. A man is coming to the end of something known, but also being initiated into something new. With his long struggle to prove himself in the world—to "make it" on society's terms—almost completed, he now feels impelled to find out what he really wants for *himself* and what doors are still open.

A developmental crisis is precipitated, say the Yale group, when a man begins to feel that his old life structure no longer fits his newly evolving self—and this is exactly what happens at around forty.

Embarking on an internal struggle, a period of soul-searching and reappraisal, a man begins to question the choices he made in early adulthood. Forced to abandon some youthful dreams and illusions, he is likely to stir up old, unresolved conflicts—which may intensify his crisis. But there are more positive forces at work as well: New needs and wishes and values have also been evolving.

"Something new begins to perk in a man," says Dr. Levinson, "and I think what perks are other aspects of himself that are not so much reflected in the structure he has built."

The choices a man made earlier allowed him to live out certain parts of himself while others were excluded. Now those parts that were never fully used, that he ignored or repressed, begin to clamor for attention. The Yale group call these stirrings from an inner self "other voices in other rooms." They prompt a man to alter and enlarge a life structure that has now become confining, or even to change it drastically.

The first faint rumblings of these "other voices" are frightening. The loss of illusions is dismaying. And the collapse of an old life structure hurts.

It is agonizing for a man to find himself suddenly unmoored in the middle of his life to battle powerful emotional currents, not sure who he is, what he wants, or where he's going.

But the man who feels as if his life is in shambles can take comfort from the fact that his painful flounderings are probably signs of growth: His world is shaking because he's gotten too big for it.

VI *A Preview of Possibilities*

In the following chapters we will examine many problems that concern men in their forties, problems we all thought were so familiar, and show how when seen as aspects of a developmental crisis they become meaningful and manageable for the first time.

We will listen to the voices of many men, each contributing a unique insight, each willing to share what he has been through and learned so that others may benefit, too.

We will also present the most helpful opinions from medical researchers, physicians, psychologists, psychiatrists, sociologists, and industrial consultants; as well as the most useful findings from studies related to different aspects of the middle years.

And as we look at those areas of life that seem to be causing difficulties, demanding change, or presenting new challenges, we will try to answer a variety of questions:

●What physical changes occur at this time, and what impact do they have? How does a man feel about his altered body? How does he react to the pain of aging and the prospect of death?

●Why are more American men in their forties having heart attacks than ever before? How does their way of life contribute to their premature death? And what can they do to protect themselves?

●How does the masculine mystique handicap this generation of mid-life men? What consequences do they suffer from having been taught to worship the Protestant ethic? Invest their total identity in work and achievement? Be strong and self-controlled at all cost? And why do constricted emotions cause so much trouble at this time of life?

●Why does the meaning of a man's work change now? Why are the rewards less satisfying than he expected? What's happened to his dream? And can he formulate a new one? How does he feel about success? How does he handle failure? And how does he set significant new goals?

•Why are so many men worried about impotence as they age? How does male sexuality change during this period? What can a man do to increase his potency and improve his sex life? And why the extraordinary appeal of young girls?

•Why do so many mid-life men feel lonely? Why do they suddenly become ripe for love? Why do so many long-term marriages fail? And how do others manage to survive? Or be revitalized? What about extramarital affairs? Divorce and re-marriage?

•How does a man feel about his aging parents? The death of a parent, especially his father? How does he feel about his maturing children? And his own changing role as a father? How does he manage if divorced? And why is the issue of fatherhood so important at this stage of life?

•How does a man handle his hopes and fears and feelings during this period? How does he handle painful emotions? Or loving ones? And what does he do, where does he go, when help is needed?

•Finally, how and why do some men alter their lives in their forties? Change careers? Start a new family? Or forge a new self? Why are some changes destructive and defeating, while others are enriching and rewarding? What is the real reason some men self-destruct in their middle years while others expand and thrive?

As we explore these questions in greater depth it will become clear that there are better ways to respond to mid-life challenges than brooding, drinking, chasing girls, overworking, or running away.

It will also become clear that the way in which each man handles himself at this crossroads will determine the road he will travel for the rest of his life. For better or for worse.

At the end of this book we will draw together all our findings and formulate some guidelines to help men and women deal with this difficult time more effectively:

•We will outline specific steps men can follow to make this period pay off for the rest of their lives.

•We will spell out what women can do to help their husbands or lovers.

•And we will suggest ways in which we can improve our

institutions to make them more responsive to adult growth and change.

If dealt with courageously and wisely, the mid-life crisis can be a glorious opportunity for setting new directions.

It can be cause for celebration.

The purpose of this book is to give every man in his middle years the "permission" to change his life that our society still denies him, and to show him how to make the years beyond forty genuinely exciting and rewarding.

Chapter 5
Prisoners of the Masculine Mystique

Chapter 3   Machismo Kills

I *Life Is Like a Clock*

It was a drizzly night in San Francisco, and Enrico's Coffeehouse was virtually deserted. A look of desolation hung over the marble-topped tables as Enrico Banducci sat rapping at the bar with two old friends, relating tales of bygone days. The former owner of the Hungry i nightclub, he is a man of immense vitality. And even when the topic turns to how he feels about aging, his responses are direct and forceful.

Looking in the mirror distresses him, Enrico says. "If you're pale you think about health. You think, 'What's happening to my body?' "

"You start reading the obits," remarks one of his companions, "and anybody dying at eighty makes you feel better!"

"But the worst thing," says the other fellow, "is the subtle onset of hypochondria. I remember running up the stairs not long ago and saying to myself, 'This is heart-attack gulch!' I was suddenly conscious of it."

Enrico nods in agreement, recalling the night he was just about to leave the nightclub when the phone rang. He raced for it, taking the stairs two at a time as usual, and crumpled and fell on the last step.

"From that day on," he says ruefully, "I knew what my father meant when he said, 'Your legs go after thirty-five.' When you're young you can take the steps four at a time, and if you fall you just bounce. But when you fall at forty-four you get hurt."

The next shock came when he was forty-seven and about to close the Hungry i. His secretary asked him what he planned to do next and commented with concern, "You know, you're kind of old to start a new venture."

"Oh, my God, it really set me back," Enrico recalls. "I said, '*Old?* Are you kidding?' My age thoughts had never hit me before.

"I think it's other people who bring you down, more than yourself. I hadn't even noticed I had gray hair before that. What she said really set me to thinking, and I started to count the years I had left. Up to that moment I wasn't counting. But then I started relating it, and I thought, 'Gee, twenty years ago I just opened this place, and that was like yesterday. Now twenty years are all I've got left. Tomorrow I'm dead!' You start giving yourself a sentence."

His first impulse was to jump into something new immediately to prove he could repeat his former success. Eventually, however, he decided he had enough money to get along on and no need to prove anything. Now he spends his days at the coffeehouse, a business he had already owned, but he thinks differently about the time he has left:

"Every single day is important, whereas before it wasn't. I told my son, 'Gregory, life is like a clock. We're born at six o'clock in the morning, and at six o'clock in the evening we die. So I've had breakfast, I've had lunch, and I'm at about two-fifteen on the clock of life. I've got one great big dinner left to order. That's it! When it becomes six o'clock I lower my head with the sun and I'm gone.'

" 'Whew,' my son said, 'the way you put it, Pop!' "

Pausing reflectively, Enrico added, "It's a strange thing when you start counting the years. I don't know if anyone else does that . . . or if it's just me alone."

II *The Core of the Crisis and Its Catalyst: Death*

Enrico Banducci is not alone in his reactions. "You hear so much about deaths that seem premature," one man comments soberly. "Time is now a two-edged sword," another observes. "To some of my friends it acts as a prod; to others, a brake."[1]

These comments reflect a painful reality: The realization that one is mortal is at the core of the mid-life crisis and frequently its catalyst as well.

"The simple fact of the situation is the arrival at the mid-point of life," says British psychoanalyst Elliot Jaques. "What is simple from the point of view of chronology, however, is not simple psychologically."[2] The most disturbing paradox, he explains, is that just when a man reaches the prime of life he is also forced to recognize that this time of fulfillment is limited—beyond it is death.

"The awareness that time is finite is a particularly conspicuous feature of middle age," states Bernice L. Neugarten, who chairs the Committee on Human Development at the University of Chicago, where more than two thousand adults have participated in extensive studies. "Life is restructured in terms of time-left-to-live rather than time-since-birth,"[3] she says.

Significantly, Neugarten found than men talk about this changing time perspective more often than women do, and experience it differently. The onset of middle age is usually perceived by women in terms of events within the family circle, most commonly children leaving home. For men, however, the cues are picked up from the outside world. The first signal often comes, as it did to Enrico Banducci, from the deferential behavior of younger people at work—the door suddenly held open, the package suddenly carried.

Men generally respond to this new awareness of fleeting time by becoming more concerned with their body. They refer to biological changes and health concerns far more frequently than women do, says Neugarten, and regard them as important "age markers." Too, they express their fear of aging by giving anxious attention to their physical functioning—"body monitoring." Women, on the other hand, become more preoccupied with their husband's health than with their own.

"While these issues take the form of a new sense of physical vulnerability in men, they take the form of 'rehearsal for widowhood' in women," Neugarten says bluntly. "Women are more concerned over the body-monitoring of their husbands than of themselves."[4]

III *American Men Die Too Young*

For this generation of men, the normal depression provoked by a confrontation with mortality is compounded by another disturbing fact: Their peers are dropping all around them. No wonder a man approaching middle age experiences a poignant new sense of physical vulnerability: The American male knows damned well that he is likely to die prematurely—earlier than the American female, certainly, and earlier than men in many other countries.

Today the average life expectancy for the white American male is 68.9 years, whereas for the female it is 76.7 years—nearly 8 years longer. And the United States now ranks only twenty-fourth in the world in life expectancy for men, compared to ninth for women.

Such statistics don't surprise us. That women outlive men in this country is a fact most of us now take for granted. We know, for example, that the male is considered the weaker sex biologically. Studies show that although many more males are conceived, they are more fragile than females before and directly after birth. (About 12 per cent more male than female fetuses die before delivery, and during the first week of life the death rate for males is 32 per cent greater than for females.)

We also know that the male's greater susceptibility to trauma and illness continues later in life. Key indexes reveal that heart disease strikes twice as many men as women; that three men die of cancer for every two women; that four times more men than women die of respiratory diseases, and twice as many of cirrhosis of the liver. In addition, men are three times more vulnerable to death from accidents, suicides, and murder.

To explain this disparity between the sexes, some authorities note that men are historically more prone to violent behavior than women, more likely to be killed during wartime. Others point out that excessive male mortality is common to many species—and thus a "law of nature." They therefore blame biology as the primary, if not the only, cause for the American male's dying younger than the female.

Such explanations will not do, however. They ignore the fact that this gap in the life span between American men and women is only a recent phenomenon. At the turn of the century, when infectious diseases were more common causes of childhood fatalities, the average life expectancy was only fifty—but it was the same for both sexes. And among people over sixty-five the male was dominant: There were one hundred older men for every ninety-eight women.

Now, however, women outnumber men in this country at every age level over twenty, despite the fact that more boys are born than girls. There are now one hundred women to every ninety-five men in the population at large; and among people over sixty-five, there are one hundred women to every seventy-two men.

The alarming fact is that this gap is continuing to widen: By 1990 it is expected that there will be only sixty-seven men over sixty-five for every one hundred women.

Thus there has been a steady *reversal* in the life expectancy trends for men, as compared to women. Further, this reversal has been occuring in the United States—but not in other countries.

If the life span of both sexes was the same at the turn of the century, why has the ratio of male to female deaths changed? And why does the American male now die an average of eight years earlier than the female? These key questions cannot be answered by indicting the more fragile biology of the male unless we are prepared to argue that the fundamental biology of the sexes has changed during this period, and that this change has occurred only in the United States—a preposterous theory.

Clearly the untimely death of the American male must be the result of social factors, not natural ones. Just what are these factors?

IV *Stress American Style*

"There has been astonishingly little basic research on the dismal survival record of the male,"[5] states Dr. Estelle Ramey, professor of psysiology and biochemistry at the Georgetown University School of Medicine—and she is quite correct.

But if we look outside the medical establishment toward a dissident minority of scientists who are exploring how social factors influence human survival, we find some important clues. There is a growing body of evidence which shows that social pressures, stress especially, not only cause disease but also lower life expectancy.

By focusing on man's relationship to his environment, and the link between mind and body, these studies underscore the point that it is meaningless to question why the American male dies prematurely without first questioning how he lives.

In America today we have become more vulnerable to illness, these scientists have discovered, because we have lost many old sources of comfort and support, including religious beliefs, while being exposed to increasingly rapid social mobility and changes of all sorts. Change itself is a source of stress, it has been found, and so is the increasingly hurried pace of our lives.

Now recognized as the world's authority on the subject, Dr. Hans Selye first identified the stress syndrome that causes a chemical rallying of the body's defenses, and also demonstrated how stress diminishes a person's natural immunity to many diseases. Stress is a drastic wearing force, he found, and once each man's "adaptation energy" is expended it cannot be replaced.

That the adaptive demands of a man's environment can significantly influence his survival has been confirmed by others. Dr. George Engel and a group of scientists at Rochester University have discovered that the feeling of loss of control over one's life, or a sense of helplessness, can lead to illness.

When a man realizes that all control has been lost, he usually struggles first to regain it—and then eventually gives up. This fierce struggle has a corrosive effect on health, which sometimes results in sudden death. Grief can be a cause for this "giving-up complex," but so can unemployment: Studies show that the loss of work can be so destructive to a man's identity that he gets sick, or even commits suicide.

Similarly, Dr. Thomas H. Holmes and his colleagues at the University of Washington have found that illness inevitably follows when life events require more coping and adjustment than the body can stand; and they have now identified forty-three of the most common stressful life events that lead to disease. Surprisingly, however, not all these events are negative. But even desirable changes—like moving, career change, or promotion—require varying amounts of coping behavior, and are therefore stressful.

"Many of these events are part and parcel of American values—achievement, success, materialism, self-reliance,"[6] says Holmes.

Studies like these are disturbing because they force us to recognize that disease is not really the simple medical concept we once thought it was. But they are more disturbing still when they imply that some of our culture's most cherished values contribute to illness and curb our life span. Nonetheless, there is increasing evidence that our American way of life too often leads to death. And now it is not just social stress that scientists are condemning, but the demands of the male sex role as well.

Today the fact that the American male has more difficulties at mid-life than the female—judging by sex differences in serious physical illnesses, alcoholism, suicide rates, admissions to mental hospitals, and premature coronary deaths—has led some researchers to suspect that our excessively high standards of male performance may be responsible.

One area where suspicions have been raised is that of suicide. Here the difference between men and women is startling: Though three times more suicide attempts are made by women, three times more men actually die of suicide; and the suicide rates increase steadily with age among men only. (We refer here only to whites; suicides among nonwhites is much lower for both sexes.)

Although no completely satisfactory explanation for this discrepancy has yet been documented, some authorities suggest that the need to live up to a strong male image may well be the decisive factor. In her study of adolescent suicides, Boston University psychologist Pamela Cantor found that boys generally choose failure-proof methods, such as hanging and shooting, whereas girls choose a method like sleeping pills, which allows rescue. The boys succeed because they really want to die, says Cantor, observing that because our society "expects" more from males, "boys who doubt their sexual prowess or career prospects may see death as the only way out."[7]

Similarly, Dr. Ewald W. Busse, head of Duke University's Center for the Study of Aging and Human Development, has suggested that older men commit more suicides because the impact of retirement, physical decline, and illness may all be more devastating to a man's self-esteem than to a woman's.

Speculative though they may be, such observations suggest that American men are dying prematurely in the prime of life not simply because they were born male, but because they are pushing too hard to be masculine. The toughest evidence to date for this thesis is the research linking Type A behavior to heart disease.

V *The Lethal Type A Behavior Pattern*

Heart disease is the single greatest killer of Americans—and men in their middle years are especially vulnerable: One American male in five dies of a heart attack before the age of sixty.

Relatively rare in the United States until the 1920s, heart disease is a distinctly "modern" affliction that has increased dramatically in recent years. During the past two decades the coronary death rate for men has risen alarmingly. But at the same time the coronary death rate for women, much lower to begin with, *declined*.

Nutrition experts have virtually convinced the nation that a diet high in cholesterol is responsible for this epidemic. But now this theory has been seriously challenged by two California cardiologists, Drs. Meyer Friedman and Ray Rosenman, who have developed a revolutionary new concept which suggests that how a man lives is more important than what he eats in determining whether or not he will die of a coronary.

Until 1957 Friedman and Rosenman were conventional cardiologists studying the standard risk factors. But they have now built an impressive case for the concept that stress, personality, and behavior account for the high incidence of heart attacks among middle-aged American men.

How did this dramatic transformation in their views evolve? Puzzled by the enormous increase in heart disease in recent years, they first began to suspect that a fatty diet was not the answer when they investigated whether the relative immunity of the American woman to coronaries could be explained by dietary differences.

Although their suspicion was confirmed by cross-cultural studies showing that some groups of people who eat the most fats have little heart disease—the Irish, for example—they decided to test for themselves. Enlisting the help of a Junior League club in San Francisco, they studied what these women ate and also what their husbands ate. Their diets were essentially the same.

What then was protecting the women? these researchers wondered. For years their medical colleagues had argued, and many still do, that female sex hormones are the answer. Not so, Friedman and Rosenman found. Black women in America get even *more* heart attacks than their husbands. And in other countries, like Italy and Mexico, women and men are equally susceptible to heart disease.

So much for sex hormones, and fatty diets too. Since the experts had not yet come up with satisfying solutions, these cardiologists decided to solicit other opinions. They sent a questionnaire listing ten possible causes of heart attacks to a group of businessmen and a group of physicians with coronary patients. The majority in both groups picked "excessive competition and the stress of meeting deadlines" as the primary culprits.

Coming from business types this reply didn't seem startling, but coming from doctors it did. Since the medical literature was filled with studies implicating high-fat diets, their response was clearly at odds with most scientific investigators. And that was news.

Popular folklore had long suggested that people died of heart attacks because of too much stress and strain, but like most of the medical profession, Friedman and Rosenman had always ignored such common wisdom. Now, however, they began to take it seriously.

Aware that the pace of our lives has accelerated rapidly during the years that heart disease proliferated, they began to wonder about the impact of this new stress. Perhaps men were suffering its effects more than women because men were more regularly exposed to such pressure at work. The speculation needed to be tested.

The first indisputable evidence for their thesis that stress—more specifically, an acute sense of time urgency—plays a role in heart disease came from a study of tax accountants. Accountants were selected because the intensity of their workload varies between routine periods and times of pressure when tax deadlines must be met. In this study diet, exercise, and other factors were controlled, and cholesterol levels were measured regularly over a period of several months.

The result: As the April 15 deadline approached, there was a significant jump in cholesterol level for all these men—which fell again in subsequent months when their routine became more placid. Not every man reacted to the tension to the same extent, but the overall peaking of cholesterol level in the blood during a time of great emotional stress meant that these two factors were decisively correlated.

This was the first controlled experiment proving that the amount of cholesterol in the blood can be altered by the *brain*—and not just by the consumption of fat by mouth. Other researchers have since duplicated these results.

The next step was to analyze more precisely the individual differences in how people handle stress. Friedman and Rosenman developed an interview technique for behavorial typing that focuses on work and leisure habits, as well as on attitudes toward time. But it is analyzed more for the intensity and emotional overtones of the responses than for verbal answers.

These interviews led them to define two main behavior patterns, which they called Type A and Type B. (Since most people are mixtures of the two types, the interview techniques were eventually refined to include four subdivisions in each group.) They found that the Type B man, comparatively relaxed and unhurried, at ease with himself and other people, rarely suffers from heart disease before the age of sixty—regardless of whether he smokes, eats fatty foods, or fails to exercise.

By contrast, the Type A man is three times more likely to be stricken by a heart attack; and if he is under fifty, the risk is ten times greater. What is the Type A man like?

The general picture is as follows: Ambitious, competitive, and aggressive, he is involved in a continual struggle against time and/or other people. His sense of time urgency is accute. Almost always punctual, he is greatly annoyed if kept waiting. Delays in restaurants, at airports, or in traffic irritate him; and he is impatient with people who don't come quickly to the point. He tends to talk rapidly and eat rapidly, but usually feels way behind in doing everything he thinks he should—and worries inordinately about meeting deadlines.

Not inclined to spare time for hobbies, Type A likes to do several things simultaneously (reading while eating or shaving, for example), and often engages in two lines of thought at once (polyphasic thinking). He is likely to be an inattentive listener, especially when he considers the conversation insignificant.

Type A regards his home primarily as a place to dress for work, and often his family plays only a small role in his life.

He dislikes doing chores, or getting involved in household matters, and usually goes to bed early. Getting a good night's rest for the next day's work interests him more than family activities, says Dr. Friedman, because, "He values achievement time—and nothing about his home is achievement."

As part of the same pattern, he rarely takes a vacation. When he does, he is likely to combine it with business or choose a competitive activity like gambling or hunting. Seldom away from work because of sickness, he rarely goes to a doctor and almost never to a psychiatrist. He doesn't feel he needs either.

Type A often becomes so mechanized in his responses, so obsessed by numbers, that his life becomes a race in which he is competing against time, against other people—and, ultimately, against himself.

No matter what he buys, only numbers count: how many suits, how many cars, how many cases of wine. It is the same at work: He is concerned about how many clients he has; how many insurance policies he sold; how many articles he published. Likewise during his leisure time: What matters if he travels to Europe is how many cities he visited; in tennis, how many sets he played; in hunting, the number of ducks he shot.

A sense of insecurity about himself and his status usually underlies Type A's tendency to push and strive incessantly. Almost incapable of dealing with people except by setting up a competitive struggle, he often has difficulty in his personal relationships. But because he is always measuring his own value by the number of his achievements, and feels that others are judging him by this yardstick too, he is never content. The numbers must always rise—and when they don't, he feels like a failure.

Despite their drive to achieve, however, Type A's are not necessarily most successful. In fact, they often lose out to B's for the top jobs, because the A's are *too* competitive, *too* driven. Also, being intensely goal-directed, they are apt to be less creative than B's. With an eye always on the clock, A's are unwilling to consider matters they regard as time-wasting; as a result, their decisions tend to be hasty—and often mistaken in the long run.

Though Type A behavior doesn't necessarily lead to success, it bears a startling resemblance to the American ideal, the style that ambitious parents urge upon their sons, the style that most mid-life men have been trained to emulate. Driving and agressive, the Type A man likes to get a lot of things done, all as quickly as possible. He gives the impression of iron self-control. He has *machismo*. He is a composite of many of our society's most admired male traits.

The tragedy is that Type A behavior is also lethal: This living embodiment of masculine ideals is the typical coronary candidate.

Although many questions about coronary fatalities remain unanswered, Friedman and Rosenman have clearly documented that Type A behavior *by itself* generates certain biochemical changes that cause heart disease: Blood cholesterol rises, adrenalinelike substances flood the body, and the normal reserve of life-sustaining hormones is depleted.

Their statistics are coldly convincing because in addition to studying the personalities of coronary victims, they have also studied a large group of healthy men—and successfully predicted which ones would have heart attacks.

Begun in 1960, this study involves 3,500 men, aged 35 to 59, with no known history of heart disease when the program began. They were interviewed and classified according to behavior type, as well as all other standard risk factors. Regardless of whether these men smoked or not, had high blood pressure or not, or exercised or not, those who got heart attacks ten years later were overwhelmingly Type A's. (By 1970, 257 men had been stricken—70 per cent of them A's. And among the younger men 39 to 49, the figure is even higher: Seventy-nine per cent have been A's.)

About half of all American males are confirmed Type A's, say Friedman and Rosenman, compared to relatively few females. But as women become more aggressive, and move into the marketplace on higher levels, they expect this to change—and the heart attack rate to rise. (Heart disease rose sharply among Japanese women after World War II, when they were liberated from wholly domestic duties.) The Type A pattern is common among hard-driving executives, but it also occurs in many other occupations—everything from factory workers to truck drivers to psychiatrists.

Says Rosenman about this Type A condition: "It is a sickness, although it is not yet recognized as such."[8]

VI *An Indictment of Machismo*

Friedman and Rosenman's findings have aroused bitter controversy and antagonism within the medical establishment. Until recently their work was ridiculed or ignored, their federal funding often in jeopardy. Now, after twenty years of accumulating hard evidence, they have finally attained some measure of respectability. But their theories are still phobically resisted by the majority of heart researchers, who remain myopically committed to the standard studies of diet, smoking, exercise, or drugs—which is where the big research money goes.[9]

This resistance is undoubtedly due in part to the traditional reluctance among scientists to acknowledge phenomena that cannot be measured precisely and objectively. But the reasons are more complex than that.

The Type A condition, as Friedman and Rosenman define it, contains both psychological and socio-economic components: Though related to personality and behavior, it depends equally on the challenges and conditions of the environment. And its increased prevalence is due to the special rewards our society offers those who can think, perform, and live rapidly and aggressively.

It is a condition, therefore, that is intimately related to the values of our contemporary American society—a society shaped primarily by men, and now being steered primarily by men. Which means that while the lethal Type A pattern may indeed be an indictment of stress American style, it is even more specifically a stinging indictment of masculine ideals that are deeply engrained in our culture.

*Machism*o kills—that is the key finding and the most threatening implication of Friedman and Rosenman's heart research. No wonder, then, that the mostly male medical community has been reluctant to accept the Type A pattern as a "sickness."

No doubt the day will come when the dangers of this pattern will be widely acknowledged by the medical profession and the corporate power elite. Then values will be changed, and solutions found, to ensure the survival of the American male. But at the moment the concept is still too new—and too threatening—to be accepted on a large scale. Which means that every coronary-prone man in his middle years is on his own.

A great deal can be done to change this destructive pattern, say Friedman and Rosenman, who in 1974 published their advice in a book called *Type A Behavior and Your Heart* (and we will discuss some of their recommendations later). But as a first step, they counsel a man to stop running long enough to take a good hard look at himself, his life, and his goals. And that is exactly what the mid-life crisis compels many men to do in any case.

A sign of growth and a healthy phenomenon, this self-appraisal may turn out to be a life-saver as well.

Chapter 4   Horatio Alger Lied

I Awaiting Society's Verdict

"This is my last chance to have my baby," said one forty-four-year-old man. "I feel as if I've reached the peak of my powers, and now I *have* to make it—because if I'm not successful in the next few years I never will be."

This comment reflects the intense preoccupation with "making it" felt at mid-life by men who are plugged into success and propelled by the American Dream. This is the time when a man comes eyeball-to-eyeball with the issue of his own success or failure. This is the time, he knows, when all his accomplishments—everything he has worked for—will be weighed and measured and judged.

Awaiting that judgment with trepidation, a man often feels as if he is standing on the edge of a precipice: There is a sense of desperation and a feeling that the moment of truth is about to arrive.

The crucial verdict is issued earlier for some men than others. Creative types like mathematicians and musicians are judged early, and so are blue-collar workers and athletes, whose work depends on physical strength; whereas the verdict on lawyers, doctors, engineers, architects—and those at the highest levels of power in government and business usually comes later.

But for the majority of middle-class American males, forty is the watershed age when a man's whole career—his life itself—seems to be on the line. This is the time when society judges him in ruthlessly clear-cut terms: As a success or failure, a winner or loser.

Whether or not he "makes it" at this decisive moment in his life, however, a man is likely to collide uncomfortably with his most cherished illusions and our society's most cherished myths. And for this generation of mid-life men, hooked firmly into the Horatio Alger legend, the collision is likely to be unusually severe. Taught to push hard, compete fiercely, and anticipate continuing rewards for their sacrificial efforts to climb the ladder, they are so heavily invested in work that their identity is in large measure defined by what they do. Thus when the moment of judgment arrives it is not simply a man's job that is at stake, but also his fundamental sense of self.

Ironically, when the verdict is finally issued, a man discovers that it's not an answer but a question. Now he must begin the search for his *own* answers, evaluating what his achievements really mean, and what he really wants next.

II *Myth vs. Reality: When Upward Mobility Stops*

Hard work pays off—that is the essence of the Horatio Alger myth, which strongly shaped the lives of this generation of American men. They were brought up to believe that their manhood depended on becoming a success, and that to do this they must compete ruthlessly, move up the job ladder continuously, and make more and more money. Taught to aim for the Number 1 spot, they learned that their worth was measured by how far and how fast they scrambled up the ladder of success.

The crunch comes at mid-life, when most men discover that the yardstick by which they have always been measured has been yanked from under them. Suddenly the possibilities for continual progress on the job are dramatically narrowed. Suddenly the rewards for striving seem to have evaporated. Suddenly upward mobility turns out to be a myth.

Statistics show that only a handful of highly educated men will continue to move up the ladder after forty, while the majority will merely hold onto whatever rung they have already reached. And some, usually the least educated, will start to slip down. This is the reality in America today, according to a recent study of job problems during the middle years. What this means for most men is no more pay increases or promotions after forty.[1]

This halt in advancement occurs partly because our bureaucratic system organizes workers in a pyramidal form. The higher up the career ladder they go, the more power struggles and fewer jobs there are—with finally just one chief at the top. Only 1 per cent of American workers scale the heights to upper-management positions; and only 5 per cent make it into middle management.

But this is not the sole cause for dismay. Profound social changes and rapidly shifting values have made the American marketplace a much more hazardous arena in which to compete than it was several decades ago. Corporations are much less reliable than they used to be, job security exists no more, and the rewards for working hard are not as certain as they once were.

All these changes are especially hard on a generation of men who were taught that dedication and self-denial would earn them the good things in life—or even the good life. Entering their middle years, they find the payoffs smaller and the pressures larger than expected. The myths they learned to live by and the reality they now confront seem strangely out of sync.

When a man reaches mid-life the demands on him to perform professionally, as well as administratively, are at an all-time high. At the same time, however, the pressures are compounded by a sense of rivalry on all fronts. Younger men are nipping at his heels, competing for his job, and accentuating his anger toward today's youth. Women are entering the labor market in greater numbers and at higher levels, especially during their forties; and blacks and other minortiy groups are also making their presence felt.

For the white middle-class male this invasion of territory he always thought was his exclusively is infuriating. To make matters worse, our culture's premium on youth has become an increasingly ominous threat. "Age discrimination in employment may start as early as thirty-five or forty in some industries and occupations, and begins to take on major dimensions at age forty-five,"[2] states the National Institute of Industrial Gerontology.

To ease this "older worker" problem a federal law against age discrimination in employment was passed in 1968. But it has been poorly enforced at both the federal and the state levels. Countless middle-aged job hunters have testified to the continuing prevalence of discriminatory hiring practices, reporting that employers generally regard these laws as a farce and ignore them completely, or else simply tell the older applicant that he is "overqualified."

Said one forty-six-year-old man about his humiliating job hunt: "I'll never forget getting off the train at Grand Central Station every morning for weeks, and looking up at all those tall buildings and *hating* them. I knew they were filled with people who didn't want me to call them for lunch because they didn't know what to *do* with me. They thought I was too old."

Four million American males were unemployed in 1975—and the situation is expected to worsen. For men with technical skills or professional knowledge there is a threat of occupational obsolescence.[8] Within the corporate world there is the increasing trend toward early retirement, both voluntary and involuntary. Although belatedly some manpower experts, economists, and sociologists have begun to doubt the wisdom of this trend, corporations are providing continuing impetus for it. The number of companies whose pension plans now contain liberalized early retirement benefits has doubled in the past decade.

Today even chief executives are discovering that their working life span is shorter than it used to be. The turnover rate among corporate presidents is now 20 per cent a year—twice what it was in the 1960s. And although a growing number of bosses are quitting voluntarily before the traditional retirement age to begin another career in public service, or to pursue some personal interest, more than half of those who leave are being forced out.

This exodus is largely due to future shock: Chief executives are being fired faster because the accelerating pace of change in our society makes running a corporation tougher than ever, and more unpredictable. Marketing cycles change rapidly. Rules and procedures become obsolete almost as soon as they are set. And dissatisfied workers as well as aggressive consumers are clamoring for more response from top management.

All these intensified pressures make the men in charge increasingly vulnerable. But the shock waves reverberate insidiously throughout the entire corporate structure, imposing a distinctly unsettling feeling of dis-ease on men raised to value job security above all else.

Their distress is justified: Today workers at the middle-management and supervisory levels are competing more intensely and being judged more harshly than ever before. Thus they are actually being "defeated" at an earlier age than ever before.

III *A Sense of Disillusionment and Defeat*

This mid-life crunch in the American marketplace can be shattering for men who regard upward mobility not only as a basic goal but also as a measure of their merit. Conditioned to believe that their identity depends on what they do, this generation of men cannot help feeling that business failure means personal failure. Thus the man in his forties who is fired, or who loses his job for any reason, is likely to experience a devastating loss of self-esteem.

But men who lose their jobs are not the only ones to suffer at this stage of life. Those who have failed to meet their own goals, or who have simply stopped moving up, must also wrestle with a sense of defeat—and despair. Feelings that bewilder them.

While working as a management consultant and career counselor, a clinical psychologist from Michigan, Dr. Benjamin Shumaker, saw so many discontented men in the thirty-five-to-forty-five age range that he coined the phrase "career menopause" to describe the phenomenon.[4]

"At first I thought there was something wrong with these people," he explains, "because they had all set a good track record. They were doing very, very well. And then suddenly they say, 'I'm not happy in what I'm doing.' But they don't say it that way. They project the blame on the lousy company, the damn boss, or something else related to the job.

"Of course you immediately say, 'What's bugging this guy?' 'What's wrong with him?' That was my initial reaction. Except there were so many of them that it dawned on me that this was *normal*. A normal part of career development."

The root of the problem, in his view, is that American men have been told all their lives that it is possible to be Number 1. "We've been led to believe Horatio Alger is it," he says, "and we approach our career *à la* Horatio Alger. You get into the race and initially you move very well. You get promoted. You get recognized. And then the movement becomes slower, and it may stop, and you begin gradually to feel that something is wrong.

"Suddenly you start asking, 'Am I in the wrong field?' 'Am I doing the wrong thing?' And in our culture that's *terrible*. You're supposed to *know* what you want, get an education, get started, and that's it. You're supposed to be set for the rest of your life.

"So why are they having trouble? Well, they're having trouble because they've been led to believe they shouldn't have these kinds of feelings."

What happens to men in their forties who realize they are not going to be Number 1—and then feel like a failure? Stuck in the middle, doing work they deplore or have tired of, they retire on the job psychologically. Or, embittered by a sense of worthlessness, they sabotage their bosses and savage their families.

Though no figures are available, it is now common knowledge in the corporate world that many workers, those in middle management especially, feel thwarted and defeated.[5] Blocked in their ambition to reach the top, they often fault themselves for having "peaked out" when they stop moving up.

For these men the American Dream has turned into a nightmare.

Surprisingly, however, a similar sense of disillusionment often attacks the men who do succeed in making it. When the golden ring of recognition is finally within their grasp, they too feel severely disappointed. The fact of success, they discover, cannot match the fantasy. The dream fulfilled loses its luster.

"When I turned forty I had everything I wanted," said one prosperous businessman. "I had interesting work. I was making more money than I expected to as a kid. I had a nice family. My kids were healthy and intelligent, and I was fond of my wife. But still, I was miserable.

"I suppose in society's terms turning forty is symbolic. You start questioning what you've really achieved. And sometimes I'm proud of what I've achieved and other times I feel it's absolutely nothing. Actually my life changed a lot because of being successful, but not much was changing within *me*. I keep wondering why I'm not happier, but I haven't found any answers."

Though usually unanticipated, this feeling of depression that follows in the wake of success is a common reaction. Something paradoxical occurs when the executive gets his promotion, the banker his raise, the salesman his franchise, and the teacher his tenure. The battle won, each man expects to feel victorious. Instead, there is a sense of loss. Is this all there is? he wonders.

Sometimes the letdown comes from a man's sudden perception of the sacrifices required by his ambitious ascent. What he has gained doesn't seem worth what he gave up. Like Babbitt, who at forty-six exclaimed, "I've never done a single thing I've wanted to in my whole life!" he feels cheated.[6]

Having reached a long-desired goal, many men experience "feelings of having been had, or exploited," explains Dr. Robert N. Butler, the director of the National Institute of Aging, who also has a psychiatric practice in Washington, D.C. "Some men reorganize and go on without much clinical noise. But then there are those who wind up in the doctor's office, like mine."

A typical example, he says, is the man who "worked his heart out" to become a Representative to Congress. He made all the right compromises, like marrying the right woman in the area where he lives, and he took all the right steps in his legal career and touched bases with all the right organizations. But when he finally gets elected and comes to Washington, he discovers he doesn't have as much power and influence as he expected.

"He comes into my office with a raving depression," says Butler. "He feels as though this is not really the woman he loves—and that everything he's been doing is really a hollow zilch."

A similar sense of letdown is often felt by men who harbor no regrets for the sacrifices they made to build a career. They too experience distress when they arrive at the place where they have long been heading.

"A lot of men have lived until they were forty with the myth that if they work hard and move up the ladder, they will find at the end of it some satisfaction," says Dr. Ian Alger, a Manhattan psychiatrist. "But a great deal of disillusionment comes when they reach a kind of stabilized position. They feel as if they have to settle down to die at that stage—or else try to make some big change in their lives and start looking again for their dream."

An accomplished thirty-nine-year-old physicist describes this feeling of frustration vividly:

I'm at the stage where I'm taking stock of myself, my professional life, my family life—*everything*. It started, I guess, about a year ago when I had reached a certain plateau where I was established.

And that's when I started to say, "Well, this bugs me, or that bugs me," or "This isn't good enough, or that isn't." Maybe it was one of those long rides on the turnpike . . . you know, starting to ask, "What the hell am I doing here? Why am I in this car? Why am I bucking this traffic jam? Why am I going home to Patty?"—all that kind of thing. You know, "Why do I teach? Why do I write papers? Why am I in this field?"

I ask myself, why should this guy who has the world by the tail, who is an associate professor in a department with an established reputation feel so dissatisfied? I wish I knew why, but you are always seeking and searching for something better.

I think it has a lot to do with the realization of the limits of your profession. In other words, you have defined what your goals are, what your position is, and what the importance of your job is in terms of the overall Universe. Eventually, I'll be a full professor here, and I *know* what a full professor at this University is all about.

I've been to many international conferences, and given papers I've written. I know the feeling of people coming up and saying to me, "Joe, that was terrific, that was great." I know the feeling of getting reprint requests. I know the feeling of getting gallons of papers published. I know what it's all about. *I know where the walls to the room are.*

You say to yourself, "Jesus Christ, I don't want to live in these walls all the time." When you start to look around and see the limits, the walls of the room, any intellectual, any dynamic, any responsive guy would say, "This is great"—"Now what else is there?"

Like an undergraduate I thought, "Gee it would be so great if I could be a professor somewhere in some college." Why? Because I was in awe of professors. I thought, "Boy, he's really made it." They represented the end of a long, academic, intellectual trek. There they were, with all those students lapping up their every word. I *admired* them, I *worshipped* them. They represented something just phenomenal.

And then suddenly when *you* become it you say to yourself, . . . "So what!" It loses its meaning, because you know yourself it isn't so great. I mean if I were stupid and had an IQ of about 60 I could think, well, this is a magnificent achievement. But anyone who is reasonably bright, and has a reasonable sense of his field, can do what I've done.

There are guys who would give their left ball to be where I am. I really don't know why I feel this way—it's part of the machinery of my head, I guess. If I became President of the United States, I'd wonder why I wasn't President of the *World!*

It's like the concept of the house. The guy who gets the house, and all of a sudden he says, "Jesus Christ. What am I doing here? I'm going to be living here for the rest of my life! I'm like dead already."

As this physicist makes clear, the disappointment experienced by the man who gets what he wants is not too different from the disappointment felt by the man who doesn't. At mid-life the man on top, like the man who realizes he is stuck in the middle, must also confront the fact that he has stopped moving up.

In our society lack of continuing progress feels like failure—especially to men in their middle years who have become accustomed to constant climbing as a major source of gratification. Trained to get somewhere, they feel defeated when they finally arrive.

IV *The Work Ethic at Mid-life: A Disabling Addiction*

Men of this generation have made a heavy investment in hard work, and at mid-life they are forced to come to terms with what that means. In large part their difficulties stem from a gigantic gap between myth and reality: Taught to expect more from work than it could possibly deliver, they find themselves waiting for rewards at a time when work itself is less rewarding than ever before. Jobs today are more impersonal and pressured than in the past, less satisfying in terms of providing a sense of human worth. Moreover, the rules for playing the game—and winning—have also changed.

"What it takes to get ahead in the organizational structure is almost directly *opposite* to what we've been taught," claims Shumaker. Working hard and being loyal—basic tenets of the Horatio Alger myth—are not enough. To be successful, he says, a man must be more concerned about his boss's needs than his subordinates. He must be self-centered, manipulative, and totally committed to his career—sparing almost no time for his family.

Businessmen themselves are gradually becoming aware of this. In a recent survey they agreed overwhelmingly that "pleasing the boss is critical to success" and that "a dynamic personality and the ability to sell oneself" is more important than "a reputation for honesty or firm adherence to principles."[7]

But if striving and hard labor are not enough to get to the top, neither are they enough to lead a fulfilling life. The trouble is, however, that many men of this generation don't know how to do anything else but work. In response to disappointments and anxieties on the job, pressures that push them to re-evaluate the meaning of their pursuits, they toil even harder. Many, in fact, become work addicts.

Still largely unrecognized as a sickness, work addiction has only recently been identified as a neurotic syndrome, a syndrome that is peculiarly American and primarily male. Professor Harrison M. Trice of Cornell University's School of Industrial and Labor Relations describes it this way:

"Like addiction to alcohol or food, addiction to work develops as a means of managing heightened anxieties and tensions, whatever their source. Work addicts become attached to work as an expression of neurotic conflict and obsession. . . . They are not the employees who simply work hard, but rather individuals who work all the time. They live, eat, and breathe their jobs. They stay late at the office, take work home with them, work all weekend and on holidays, and refuse to take vacations."[8]

What happens to the work addict when his job responsibilities are curtailed, or when his value to the organization diminishes? He becomes anxious and depressed; and then—Catch-22—responds to these feelings by working even more. The neurotic quality of his addiction becomes still more apparent when he is formally demoted or fired: "Separation from work can bring on feelings of worthlessness and inadequacy that reach such extremes as chronic depression and suicide," says Trice.[9]

Other alternatives, both for men who lose their jobs and those who continue working at jobs where they feel useless, include giving up their aspirations or sublimating them into nonjob activities. However, since these choices are generally repugnant to men who feel compelled to achieve, they more commonly resort to drinking—and the reasons are understandable.

"If you become addicted to work and then become obsolete, what the hell have you got left?" says Trice. "You don't know how to play. You don't know how to enjoy leisure. Drinking is pretty easy to learn. You just drink the stuff—it goes down real easily."

Today an estimated 4.5 million American workers are alcoholics, and physicians and psychiatrists report that countless more men are excessively heavy drinkers. Evidence is mounting which suggests that the responsibility falls directly on corporate shoulders: Alcoholism is caused primarily by job factors, especially the specter of obsolescence, according to a study of drinking pathology conducted by Professor Trice and his colleague, James A. Belasco.[10]

The majority of men they questioned, 82 per cent, had no drinking problem until they moved into a period of competitive career effort and upward mobility during their mid-thirties. Typically, alcoholism began when the older man felt forced to keep up with younger, more recently trained competitors; and it accelerated when he felt increasingly worthless—when his work role was diminished, or his responsibilities reduced.

To put it more bluntly, men become alcoholics when industry treats them like expendable objects. Despite the evidence linking alcoholism to work pressures, however, and despite the cost in sick pay and absenteeism now estimated to total a whopping $8 billion a year—industry has, with rare exceptions, refused to accept responsibility for this huge problem. Moreover, the few corporate programs that do exist to rehabilitate alcoholics almost never cover executives or professionals.

At mid-life when the scramble for success accelerates, the man who has become addicted to work finds himself in a double bind: Even if he doesn't turn to drink to ease the pressures, he will probably wind up as a coronary candidate. Compelled to overperform in his job role, the addict tries to manage his anxiety by pouring all his energies into his work—withdrawing from his family, shunning leisure time, and suppressing his feelings. But he never really escapes anxiety; he merely passes it on to his heart.

Horatio Alger's disabled offspring, the work addict, is really the psychological counterpart of the Type A man. Unfortunately, however, both patterns are rarely seen as sicknesses in our society because, despite being harmful to the individual, they are valuable to the organization.

V *The Verdict Reversed*

Seduced since boyhood by an alluring ode to achievement, this generation of American men were programmed to meet society's needs by aiming for success. Trained for a world that no longer exists, they discover at mid-life that the values they believed in have either disappeared or been discredited: Job security is a thing of the past; climbing up the ladder becomes impossible after forty; and hard work gets you nowhere today. Worse still, in the middle years excessively hard work often produces anxiety, depression, ulcers, alcoholism, and heart attacks.

It is time to face the facts: In America today some of our most prized values are poisonous, and some of our most beloved legends are lies. The standards we have imposed on men as the yardstick by which they must measure their masculinity are crudely based on economics. They serve the national interest—the growth of our country and our corporations—but not the individual.

The success ethic may have been valid, even personally rewarding, when America was on the frontier of industrial expansion. But in our technologically advanced society, the idea of dedication to production and progress as a national virtue is rapidly becoming obsolete. As an individual virtue it has already become destructive.

Today the imperatives of the work ethic twist men's lives into a combative, competitive struggle, leaving little time or energy for pleasurable pursuits that cannot be measured. The traditional male role, which says a man must be a superachiever, striving incessantly for power and success, leads too often to the death of the human spirit. Or to death itself.

In this age of dramatic social change, marked by growing malaise and discontent among American workers, it is becoming increasingly clear that our corporations will have to respond to these facts—and revise their values. Success at any cost is becoming too costly, in human lives and ultimately in business dollars.

Until that day of enlightenment dawns, men in their middle years face a solitary challenge. Goaded by a sense of defeat, they are being forced to reconcile fantasy and fact, and come to terms with an unreliable marketplace that no longer delivers on promises implicit in the American Dream.

Their disillusionment is prodding them to reappraise their frenzy to achieve, and to reorder their priorities. In the process they are abandoning their dedication to goals that society has imposed on them—and beginning to ask what they want to achieve for themselves.

This reshuffling represents a significant reversal: Though many men begin the mid-life period by waiting for society to pass judgment on them, they often end up to their own surprise passing judgment on society. Their verdict? Horatio Alger lied.

Chapter 5   Prisoners of the Masculine Mystique

I *The Handicapped Generation Comes of Age*

There are no rites of passage to guide the American male across the rocky threshold of middle age. Our culture provides a man with motives for climbing and clawing toward success, but once the scorecard of his wins and losses has been issued, then all social prescriptions stop.

With no established norms to follow and no sanctioned sources of support available, a man is suddenly all alone.

Now the realization that things which were "supposed" to make him happy are not doing so in fact triggers off a great many questions: Were the beliefs he based his life on really his own? he wonders. What do the myths he's lived by really mean? And what good are the rules he's always obeyed? Why has there been so much discipline in his life—but so little enjoyment?

In asking these questions about his relation to the external world, a man transforms the nature of the battle: At mid-life the combat zone becomes internal and the focus turns toward the self.

This is a generation of men who grew up strongly influenced by the Horatio Alger myth and the masculine mystique. But at mid-life they are severely handicapped by both.[1]

Taught to worship money and success, to be good providers and responsible husbands, they had great ambitions for the future, and even greater expectations: Self-sacrifice would be rewarded, they were sure.

Poured into a rigid male mold, they learned to keep a stiff upper lip and maintain a stoic mask. There was no permission, once programmed on this path of duty and achievement, for a man to play freely or cry freely or complain freely. No permission to be gentle and loving, or show weakness, or ask for help.

American men now in their middle years are a transition generation: Much of what they have been taught about striving and success and masculinity no longer works at mid-life. And when they discover, in the prime of life, that the promises and prohibitions from their past suddenly backfire, they have good reason to feel angry. Nobody warned them:

- That after doing everything they were supposed to they would feel cheated and disillusioned.
- That working hard wouldn't nourish their egos forever.
- That adults as well as adolescents go through periods when they are plagued by profound self-doubts, burning dissatisfactions, and a violent need to question everything.
- That they would still be growing up at forty, and that this coming of age would force them to face their feelings and explore their inner self.

II *A Crippling Heritage*

The handicapped generation is coming of age burdened by a crippling heritage: They were taught that their manhood depended on living up to the masculine mystique and maintaining a *macho* style. But it is a style that usually self-destructs at mid-life.

Based on biology, the masculine mystique inflated the obvious fact that potency requires a hard penis into a definition of masculinity that dictated that a man be hardheaded and hardhearted as well. A real man must be aggressive and tough, according to the mystique, because male superiority insists that he compete, perform, achieve—and win. Not just once, but repeatedly. Based on values that obtained in the frontier days, this *macho* style has in recent years been transferred to the sports arena and transformed by athletic metaphors, but the element of combat is still essential: How, after all, can a man prove he is the toughest gun in town unless he is always ready to challenge his competitors, defeat his opponents, and destroy his enemies?

Manhood becomes a compulsive concern with potency and power, according to this code, and a man must prove his masculinity again and again. Therefore the mystique demands that a man be cool and in control, his fears disguised by a cock-sure swagger, his feelings concealed beneath a menacing mask.

At mid-life, however, this *macho* commandment to keep cool and hang tough becomes increasingly impossible to sustain. It is a style that never worked very well, except on the frontier or in the movies. But even at its best, glorified by heroes like Billy the Kid and John Wayne, by flashing guns and fiercely set jaws, it is a young man's style, a style that ultimately becomes exhausting and futile.

The injunctions on masculinity were just as treacherous as those imposed on women by their traditional sex role. Narrow and constricting, the feminine mystique taught a woman to be childish, passive, and dependent—a servile homebody, a submissive wife, and a sacrificial mother. It was the golden rule that all girls growing up in the 1950s or earlier were supposed to follow.

In essence the feminine mystique required women to be subhuman. But there was a golden rule for boys, too, which was simply the other side of the coin: The masculine mystique required men to be superhuman.

The frustrations felt in the middle years by American men who modeled their lives on the traditional male sex role are comparable to those felt by women once their too-narrow role began to pinch.

When Betty Friedan wrote *The Feminine Mystique* in 1963, identifying a problem that until then had no name, she described masses of women who had done everything they were supposed to do, everything they were programmed to do; dedicated mothers and loyal wives sitting in their split-level houses, surrounded by the most modern conveniences—and in despair.

They were dying of boredom, dying of depression, dying of alcoholism. Miserably unhappy with their lives, they felt guilty and lonely and puzzled. They wondered what could possibly be wrong.

What was wrong, said Friedan, was the myth: The myth which insisted that a woman be confined to the home, her whole life centered on marriage and motherhood. It wasn't enough, this rigid role prescribed by the mystique. By prohibiting a woman from using her skills in the larger world, by prohibiting her from seeking satisfaction in the work arena, it was stunting her development as a complete human being—in the name, supposedly, of femininity.

The mystique stopped a woman from growing and left her with a forfeited self.

Like the women Friedan described, many mid-life men today are dying of boredom and depression and alcoholism. Or dying of heart attacks. Like Harry, they feel as if they're running all the time, just running—but they no longer know what it is they're chasing.

They are beginning to discover that striving and competing are not enough, that achievement at work is not the answer, and that even success does not bring happiness. They are feeling guilty and lonely and puzzled. They are wondering what could possibly be wrong.

In part their dissatisfactions are related to the mid-life crisis: This is the time when a stabbing recognition of mortality and the limitations of time spontaneously trigger new questions about life's meaning.

But for this generation of men, the painful nature of the crisis is intensified by their particular heritage. The masculine mystique has stunted their development just as the feminine mystique did with women, and they too have been left with a forfeited self. Based on distorted definitions of what it means to be a man or a woman, these traditional roles have prevented both sexes from realizing their full human potential: Women were cut off from the outer world and deprived of a working self, while men were cut off from the inner world and deprived of a feeling self.

At mid-life the amputation begins to ache.

III *The Pain of Impacted Feelings*

As he grows older, the *macho* male finds himself increasingly isolated—cut off from his inner being, incapable of intimacy, and dangerously ill-equipped to handle the inevitable assaults of aging.

Brooding strong and silent behind his invincible mask, he may try to disguise his pain by appearing perpetually cheerful or by translating psychic suffering into sardonic jest, a time-honored masculine defense. But now the jokes are etched in acid, the laughter laced with bile, and a man discovers that comic detachment and cold-blooded denial are feeble weapons to use at this critical stage of life. After forty impacted feelings take their toll.

During this turbulent period women have an important advantage over men: They are allowed to admit their dissatisfactions without censure and seek comfort when they feel troubled, confused, or ill. Our society not only encourages women to express their feelings openly but also supports them in doing so.

By contrast, since male superiority requires forfeiting the right to be merely human—human enough to admit weakness—men are sternly prohibited from confiding their troubles, confessing fears, or seeking help.[2] And that is why, some researchers suggest, women have less difficulty aging than men, less difficulty surmounting major life crises.

The masculine mystique dictates that a "real" man be self-sufficient. A male in our society is therefore trained from childhood to follow the cult of toughness. Little boys don't cry or complain, he is told. They take it on the chin. Little boys are supposed to be brave and bold, strong and sturdy, fearless at all times. Sentimental outbursts, he soon discovers, are for women only.

Because of this conditioning, a man learns early to suppress or deny these forbidden feelings. He learns to conceal his pain, bury his anger, and clamp the lid on all emotions. In time he gradually becomes dulled to his own inner responses, detached from his feelings, and finally in some cases incapable of feeling.

This schizoid separation occurs because traditional sex roles pit male against female by defining masculinity and femininity as polar opposites. Thus, the man who fails to conform to the masculine mystique—who fails to obey the commandment that he be in charge of his emotions—does so at great peril: He is automatically accused of being like a woman—soft, weak, and foolish.

Feelings are dangerous, according to this polarized logic, because if you rely on feelings rather than facts, you lose control. And if you lose control, people take advantage of you, and then you get screwed. Which means being passive, feminine and manipulated.

But this masculine ideal of keeping cool is based on a monumental fallacy: The assumption that emotions can really be "controlled" by pushing them aside. There is now much medical evidence which suggests that buried emotions backfire, either physically or psychologically. Thus the more a man tries to control his emotions, the more they actually control him.

The reason for this paradox is that suppressed emotions don't go away. If concealed or denied, they smolder underground until they finally find some devious route for release. Contrary to the masculine ideal, then, repressed emotions are more dangerous than those that are openly expressed.

A good illustration of this is seen in the man who regularly suppresses his anger. His rage builds up gradually until he finally explodes. "I don't know how to express my feelings aggressively without being violent about it," confessed one mild-mannered man whose life experiences all seemed strangely muted. "When it comes to dealing with anger I can't stop the escalation. If I start to scream and yell I'm likely to throw things, bang walls, even smash you in the face. Of course, it takes a lot of provocation to bring this out, so mostly I just clam up."

His experience is typical. Many men who pride themselves on rarely losing their cool oscillate between these two extremes: Their emotions either remain buried—or else break out and go berserk.

Such violent outbursts are frightening, of course, because the man who blows up after overly long periods of repressing anger is indeed "out of control." Moreover, such explosions often have devastating consequences: A man gets fired; he loses a good friend; or his wife walks out on him. Surveying the mess he's made, he resolves to exercise even tighter controls in the future.

The result? The next time he turns his anger against himself, infecting or inflaming the body. He gets sick, stricken by ulcers or colitis or hypertension or migraine headaches, to name but a few among the many diseases that authorities now agree are caused by stifled emotions, anger especially.[8]

It is the body that finally pays, because if emotions are not expressed in words or actions they must find release through physical illness. This is the basic explanation for what are now called psychosomatic diseases. And in our society men who take pride in keeping all their problems to themselves are especially prone to this psychosomatic response.

But at mid-life the stoic injunctions of the masculine mystique cause psychic pain, too. Emotionally armored to do battle against the world, men who have been taught to deny anger and pain have also closed off other, more positive feelings.[4] With age they become increasingly unable to express or respond to affection, tenderness, or warmth. Rigid and out of touch with others, they have learned to substitute guarded, mechanical responses for spontaneous, felt action.

As a result, many men are indescribably lonely as they enter their middle years. They complain that life has lost its meaning. They feel bored and restless. Nothing excites them or gives them joy.

The emotional juices that provide pleasure, that give life meaning, that inspire action, have dried up. Their lifelong habit of discipline and self-control has taken its toll, sapping their energies, muting their emotions, and leaving them cruelly isolated. They have become detached from other people and their authentic self, a self so long concealed behind a cool cover, a false *macho* mask, that it has been stripped of all passion, stripped bare. A self sacrificed in the name of masculinity: outwardly strong, inwardly sterile.

Such a man feels hollow, empty, dead inside. He laments like the character in *That Championship Season:*

> I'm so bored half the time it's killing me. Watching the same old faces get old, same bullshit, day in and day out. Bored. Sometimes I get on the turnpike and just drive until I feel like getting off. Alone . . .
> What's left? Hit a few bars, some music, drink, play old basketball games over in my head. Pick up some strange pussy now and then, here and there, you know. Always need something young and juicy sitting beside me. Mostly sit and replay the good games in my head, believe that? . . .
> Sometimes I think that's the only thing I can still feel, you know, still feel in my gut . . . that championship season.[5]

This lament comes from a man who has made his million but lost the capacity to feel anything except the ancient thrill of a high school basketball game. Like many mid-life men, he complains he is dying of boredom, but he is really suffering from a terminal case of impacted feelings.

IV *Cracks in the Male Mask*

American men haven't had as much opportunity to explore their lives as women have. But now, largely influenced by the feminist movement, men too are finally beginning to ask whether the role society places on them is valid.

When *The Feminine Mystique* was first published, Friedan's insights exploded like a bomb in this country, dynamiting women out of their despair and inspiring them toward action. And though the feminist movement is but the beginning of a major humanist revolution that will radically alter America's power structure and values, it has already started to change our definitions of what it means to be a man or a woman.

As a result, some men are beginning to realize that they have been victims of a distorted definition of masculinity. They are discovering that men pay a high price for their exclusive claim to power and supremacy, and that they have been deprived of a basic human right—the right to reveal and express their feelings.

This new awareness has led to the publication of books like *The Liberated Man* and *The Male Machine,* and to the teaching of courses on the masculine mystique at colleges and universities. It has also led to the formation of a men's liberation movement, which aims to free men from a dehumanizing sex role.

Members of this movement have been holding consciousness-raising sessions that focus on the ways in which they have felt oppressed in their own lives by society's demands. And they have strongly criticized the standard male image, which insists they be aggressive and competitive breadwinners, but prohibits their being nurturing and vulnerable human beings. To correct this imbalance they advocate replacing obsolete sex roles with a fuller concept of humanity, a concept that recognizes that both men and women can be either strong or weak, active or passive, cerebral or emotional; and that these qualities are not the province of one sex only.

To date the men's liberation movement is still comparatively small and composed primarily of men under thirty. But they do not have an exclusive claim to critical awareness or to feelings of having been cheated. Some men in their middle years are also beginning to feel uncomfortably confined behind their male mask.

Not long ago, for example, a group of ten men in their forties enrolled in a course entitled "Communication Skills and Personal Growth Workshop for Men" at an adult education center in Michigan.[6] Their experience led to some startling new discoveries about their old ideals of masculinity. Here are two reactions:

●Dave B., forty-six, is a junior high school teacher who has been married seventeen years and has three children. Plagued by the feeling of being "stuck" at work, with nothing to look forward to except retirement, he joined the group because he was "looking for something":

> The sessions were an eye-opener to me. It was quite a revelation because I always suspected I had some of these walls around me—and that's why I couldn't relate to people.
>
> My parents were very strict, very moralistic. No emotional feelings. I wasn't allowed to cry if I got spanked. And I remember when I got drafted, one of my biggest concerns was whether I should give my mother a goodbye kiss or not! Because I never recall kissing her except as a very small boy. There was no close touch—it was all tight, traditional, controlled.
>
> Well, anyway, this feeling of rigidity has been with me all my life and, in fact, it's been getting worse as I've been getting older. I was unable to get out of it. My relationship with other teachers was always kind of aloof, and I found it difficult to be warm and close to the students. My discipline was always, "I'm the dictator. The boss!" That kind of thing. No warmth, and I couldn't break through.
>
> Now for the first time I can see daylight! I'm not saying I've resolved it, but I felt I was worse off than a lot of other people, and this kind of proved to me that I really wasn't. Some of the guys really went through torture to be able to get out this expression of themselves.

Some cried, some got completely angry and stormed out. But afterwards there was even a physical change. Henry is a good example—he used to have such a tight fist. And, boy, he smiles so easily now and talks in a flowing, relaxed way.

But the thing that amazed me in the group was how everybody has this kind of problem: *The wall.* It's not just myself.

●Ray W., forty-one, is a manager in a General Motors printing plant, who has been married eight years and has two children. He joined the group hoping to improve his relations with co-workers:

What really impressed me was how when we first started everybody in the group seemed so cool and calm and collected. But as it progressed I began to see that most of us had some sort of problem where we couldn't get any sort of feeling out. It had never dawned on me how important it is to get some of these feelings out.

Everyone was completely different after just one episode of opening themselves up. You remember how Bob was—very stoic and stone-like? His facial expressions never changed. And yet inwardly he was just being torn apart. But of course, we didn't know that. Later, after he had quite an emotional experience, he would sit in on the sessions and his whole face was just glowing. Just one quick glance, and you knew he was a different person. He had sort of a glow from inside.

There was this release of emotion. I think we all got in touch with some feelings we aren't afraid to show anymore. I think men have a tendency to hold back a show of exuberance—or a show of sadness. But after the course I don't think any of us is so afraid to show a happy feeling or a sad feeling, or even an angry feeling. I think you can see it on our faces now, whereas before there was a *mask* there.

And none of us was aware of how much under control these things are. There was one incident where I was furious. I was so worked up I thought anybody could see it—but they could barely tell. And the same thing happened with the other fellows. Our controls were so tight that although we thought our feelings were showing, the controls hid them.

Before I would have thought it was an admirable trait—keeping this coolness under pressure. But I'm not so sure it's admirable anymore. I think it's a mistake.

These Michigan men are not alone. Other mid-life men are also beginning to perceive, if only dimly, the anguish caused by their own emotional constriction. Some make the discovery in a similar way, by attending a sensitivity or encounter group; by embarking on psychotherapy, analysis, or marital counseling; or by joining a human-potential organization like EST, Arica, or Scientology. In other cases a man is nudged toward a new awareness by a barrage of accusations: when his colleagues insist he is arrogant and remote; when his children denounce him as cold and critical; or when his wife berates—or abandons—him for being incapable of love.

In these and other ways men in their middle years are discovering that the masculine imperative to keep cool has chilling consequences. And they are beginning to question whether keeping a stiff upper lip is a mark of manhood after all.

V Mourning: A Mid-life Imperative

This new criticism of old taboos is not only healthy but vital: The fact is that no man can withstand the major mid-life stresses unless he can dislodge and disgorge his feelings.

This is so because the mid-life crisis is, first and foremost, a period of mourning.[7] Marked by discontinuity and depression, it is a time of change and challenge—but also a time of loss. And to weather the storm successfully, a man must be able to ventilate the painful feelings of anger and disappointment that accompany all loss experiences.

He must, in other words, learn how to mourn.

Some of the losses which occur at this stage of life are undeniably devastating: the loss of youth and youthful dreams; the loss of an illusion of immortality; and the loss of physical and sexual energies—to mention only the most obvious.

But there are many other changes that take place during this period, and all of them, even changes for the better, involve an element of loss: the loss of familiar supports and old sources of gratification. Combined with the pressure of new demands, this sense of loss is what makes all change stressful: When the new displaces the old, we experience this change on the psychological level as a loss; and the experience is accompanied by feelings of abandonment and helplessness and sorrow.

"All change is a loss experience," explains psychologist Harry Levinson, a management consultant who heads the Levinson Institute in Cambridge, Massachusetts. "Whether you change jobs, or change families, or change relationships, something is ripped up. Something is taken away from you. And if one is going to adapt to change—personal change or organizational change—there has to be some opportunity for disgorging the feelings of loss, the negative feelings, and doing the mourning."

In our society loss experiences tend to be denied, especially by men. At mid-life, however, such denial is dangerous and disabling. It causes depression and also increases a man's susceptibility to illness.

The only effective way to counter loss experience is to openly express the feelings of pain, anger, and sorrow. The process is similar to the mourning done for the death of a loved one. By talking about the person, and expressing feelings of grief, a survivor gradually relieves his burden and heals his wounds, thereby recovering the strength and vigor to go beyond the loss and begin life anew.

"When feelings are put into words, they can be dissipated or acted on with conscious intent," explains Levinson. "If they cannot be verbalized, there is no release from anguish and people are compelled to act on impulses which they only dimly perceive."[8]

Alien though it may seem to men who have developed a long-standing disdain for expressing emotions, this prescription to ventilate painful feelings—to mourn—is a vital imperative at mid-life.

VI *Reclaiming the Forbidden Self*

Impacted feelings are a form of imprisonment as well as a source of pain. The man who fails to become more open to his emotions and his inner self at mid-life will become weighted down by an overwhelming sense of loss, thereby losing the vitality needed to meet new challenges and make new choices. Unable to surmount his depression, he will suffer instead from a feeling of boredom and stagnation.

But this need not happen.

There is a natural tendency at this stage of life for a man to be turning inward, to be moving away from the outer world of work toward the inner world of self.[9] This shift is normal in terms of adult development and necessary for future growth.

It relates to a man's outgrowing the life structure he built earlier, according to the Yale group's theory mentioned before, and to his new readiness to listen to "other voices in other rooms." The parts of his personality that have been silent or unexpressed now begin to clamor for attention.

To achieve at work a man has usually had to emphasize "the rational, consciously intelligent, tough-minded aspects" of his personality until he reaches his mid-thirties at least, explains Charlotte Darrow, the Yale group's sociologist. Therefore: "He simply has had to sacrifice, to neglect or suppress certain parts of his self. This often meant defending against another whole area, having to do with more emotional, softer, less masculine wishes and feeling."[10]

But in his forties, when the battles with the outer world have been either won or lost, there is a basic shift marked by an upheaval of those parts of the personality that have been ignored. Now the crucial issue becomes the degree to which a man can listen to these "other voices" and respond to this other side of himself—the side that our society has traditionally labeled "feminine."

Threatening as well as challenging, this developmental shift brings every man in his middle years face-to-face with all taboos rooted in the masculine mystique.

And as we shall see in more detail shortly, men react in very different ways: Some will experience this shift consciously; others will not. Some will be alarmed; others will be delighted. Some will let their feelings erupt dramatically; others will keep them simmering just beneath the surface; and those who are most rigidly controlled will force their feelings even further underground.

What a man actually does depends on many complex factors, according to Dr. Braxton McKee, the Yale group's psychiatrist. It depends on his particular background, character structure, and personality development, as well as on his response to social roles and society's expectations—all of which enables some men to be more in touch with themselves than others.

As an example of a man courageous enough to follow these mysterious inner voices wherever they might lead, McKee tells the story of a forty-year-old man, a personnel manager, who changed his whole life as the result of new feelings that had first surfaced during an extramarital love affair. McKee describes what happened after the other woman broke off the relationship:

This man was very upset when the affair ended, but then he said, "The strangest thing happened. I started getting interested in writing poetry and painting." Not only did he get interested in it, but he got *into* it. He had some stuff published and a couple of exhibits. Not only that, but he got very much more interested in being with people.

He and his wife and some friends, all in their 40s, opened a commune so they could be with one another more. And he left his job because he wanted to get into something that allowed him to work more intimately with people.

He was involved in a search for intimacy, and he was absolutely explicit about it.

Not only was he aware of what he wanted, but he said, "You know, as a result of my experience with that woman I discovered there is something down there that I didn't know anything about! I just want to listen for awhile and find out what I hear."

Observing that this man was an unusual person, one who had already been fairly open to his feelings, McKee points out that a different sort of man might have done just the opposite:

"Another guy who has not been in touch with himself, for whatever reasons, might experience something like that in a way where he would say, 'Jesus Christ, I'm queer!' It would make him anxious and frightened, and lead him to cut it off even more. And perhaps drive him into even more frantic, phallic, hypermasculine kinds of things. It's very tricky and complicated."

The Yale group regards a man's getting more in touch with the caring and nurturing part of himself as an important developmental step during the mid-life period. But their point is understated.

How well a man succeeds in dislodging impacted feelings—and dealing with his evolving emotional self—is undoubtedly the single most important issue facing every American male during the mid-life crisis.

In the next section of this book we will see more specifically how this issue is at the heart of all the major changes and challenges that occur at this stage of life.

Whether related to work or sex or marriage or fatherhood, there are losses to be faced and worked through, new problems to be confronted, and new choices to be made. And though these choices may differ greatly in scope and significance, they all have one thing in common: They force every man trying to decide what he wants—in his job, his marriage, or his lifestyle—to get more in touch with his emotions, because no man can decide what he really wants until he has discovered what he really feels.

And in the following section of this book, which concerns new directions, we will see that the men who succeed best in making meaningful life changes are those who are courageous enough to shed obsolete prescriptions about success and masculinity, listen to their inner voices, and reclaim their forbidden self—their feeling self.

For members of the handicapped generation this is what the mid-life leap from boy/man to man is all about: daring to revolt against the taboos and prohibitions of the masculine mystique.

'Chapter 6   A Life-cycle Perspective

I *Beyond Freud*

There is no cure for time. But there are different ways to view the passage of time, different ways to look at the cycle of life. And the view we adopt dramatically reflects how much reverence our culture has for the individual and for its own humanity. In this respect we Americans are still savages: We worship the young, abhor the old and disdain the middle-aged.

Impressed by power and productivity, we have not yet separated the virtues we most admire from youth itself, nor abandoned our illusion that the young have a monopoly on all the best things in life. A dangerous form of innocence, our idolization of youth causes us to mutilate each other and ourselves. It causes us to resent our children, recoil from aging, and deny the reality of death.

Rather than identify with the elderly as human beings who mirror our own future fate, we keep our distance from them—or renounce them as worthless relics. Nonpersons. But our blindness backfires inevitably as the first subtle signs of our own aging register, and we begin to sense that we will soon be condemned to the same trash heap. Terrified, we run to gyms and cosmeticians and plastic surgeons to retain that precious aura of youth which we consider the essential hallmark of our humanity.

It is a vicious trap: By victimizing the elderly we guarantee we will become victims ourselves. Our fear of aging stunts our own growth as human beings.

This predicament occurs because we have never endorsed a concept that embraces the whole life cycle. Unlike many Eastern cultures, where life is regarded as a series of stages to be savored, we Americans still see life as a ladder to be scaled. Rooted in the Protestant ethic, our "world image is a one-way street to never ending progress," says Erik Erikson, which means that "our lives are to be one-way streets to success—and sudden oblivion."[1]

Perhaps this world outlook worked reasonably well at the turn of the century, when fifty was the average life span, but it fails miserably today when that span is closer to seventy. Today men in their forties are justified in finding the moment when upward striving stops, frightening. Those leftover years ahead seem like empty years of oblivion because our culture has failed to dignify them with new meaning.

Given our long-standing love affair with youth, it was no accident that the ideas of Sigmund Freud found fertile soil in America. His obsessive concern with childhood matched our own, and we readily embraced his concept that our lives are largely set and determined by the early years.

Today we can choose from an astonishing array of therapies, including Gestalt, primal scream, EST, hypnosis, Rolfing, sensory awareness, and meditation. Nonetheless, our Freudian heritage continues to exert a powerful influence over the way in which we view our own life, and the amount of responsibility we are willing to assume for its evolution. When things go wrong and we want someone to blame, someone other than ourselves, we fault our family and rage ferociously against that classic psychoanalytic scapegoat: Mom.

"We saw our purpose of enlightenment perverted into a widespread fatalism, according to which man is nothing but a multiplication of his parents' faults and an accumulation of his own earlier selves," says Erikson about this misuse of Freudian principles. "We must grudgingly admit that even as we were trying to devise, with scientific determinism, a therapy for the few, we were led to promote an ethical disease among the many."[2]

Until recently this static view of ourselves was perpetuated by behavioral scientists who generally failed to bring a life cycle perspective to their investigations, who failed to acknowledge that the human personality grows or changes in any substantial way during the adult years. On the whole they have preferred to study children rather than adults, and to view the personality in terms of continuity rather than change.[3]

True, their methodology imposes limits. If these researchers have acted as if nothing significant happens after twenty-one, it is partly because children are much easier to study than grown-ups, and because the subtle changes of adult life are more difficult to measure. But that is not the only explanation. Even behavioral scientists are not immune to the predominant values, and persistent taboos, of the culture. They too have been intrigued by the young, repelled by the elderly, and fearful of a confrontation with aging.

Today, however, some of our most destructive myths about aging are gradually being proven false. Growing old does not necessarily mean becoming senile, sexless, or incapacitated, say many experts now. Contrary to popular wisdom, they have found that most older people suffer no dramatic loss of intelligence, agility, creativity, or sexual response. And to the extent that such decline does occur, it is now thought to be caused by the lack of activity, or lack of hope and purpose. But not by the aging process itself.[4]

This means that most of us can remain vital and vigorous in our later years, if we continue to be purposefully engaged in the world: working, learning, playing, and loving.

This burgeoning exploration of the human potential has led a number of researchers to ask some long-overdue questions about the degree of flexibility in the adult personality; the ways in which people grow and change in their later years; the different stages and stresses they go through; and the kinds of situations that help foster growth.

In the process they are discovering that Freud was wrong: that the human personality is not immutably set in childhood, firmly fixed forever. Too, they are discovering that mid-life difficulties are not merely replays of old conflicts but signs of new growth and development.

These findings make possible a more encompassing vision of the middle years than was available before. By putting many fundamental issues into a life-cycle perspective, they also help to illuminate what is happening to American men during the mid-life crisis—and why. And since in order to manage this period successfully a man must first understand it, we will now consider briefly the basic theoretical framework in which the potentials of the adult years are currently being explored.

II   *Jung: Striving Toward Wholeness*

Today many psychologists dedicated to the idea of adult growth are turning for inspiration to Swiss psychiatrist C. G. Jung. Long forgotten or ignored, Jung, unlike Freud, saw life as a continuing series of metamorphoses.

"Personality is a seed that can only develop by slow stages throughout life," Jung stated. "And it is not the child, but only the adult, who can achieve personality as the fruit of a full life directed to this end."[5] Such an achievement, he insisted, is both an ideal to strive for and a task requiring effort and courage.

Jung believed that the roots of neurosis are found in present situations rather than in the remote past. He and Freud differed radically in other ways as well. For example, Jung did not accept the equation of libido with sexual drive, nor the concept of the Oedipus complex. And he regarded the unconscious as the seat of universal primordial images, or archetypes.

The central archetype is the Self. Jung viewed the Self not merely as the conscious ego, however, but as a psychic totality that comes from unification of the conscious and the unconscious. This unification is achieved by "individuation," he said: a process that leads a person toward wholeness, toward becoming more fully what he really is, over the course of an entire life.

Jung described forty as the "noon" of life, and he considered this period "a time of enormous psychological importance." In fact, he referred to this mid-life period as "the moment of greatest unfolding." But he also warned that embarking on the second half of life is painful, a warning that came from his own personal experience.

In 1913, when Jung was thirty-eight, he entered a six-year period of decisive change: He broke with Freud, whose devoted disciple he had been; he resigned from the International Psychoanalytic Association; he severed his ties with Zurich University; and he began what he called his *Nekyia,* a painful journey through the unconscious.

Curiously, Freud himself also went through a period of

mid-life change that was remarkably similar. Beginning in 1894, when he too was thirty-eight, Freud embarked on a six-year period of turbulence: His father died; he broke off an intimate relationship with his mentor, Wilhelm Fliess; he abandoned his interest in neurology to begin formulating the principles of psychoanalysis; and finally, he initiated his own self-analysis.

Describing the mid-life crises of these two great men and the astonishing parallels between them, Dr. Henri F. Ellenberger writes: "Both suffered symptoms of emotional illness: Freud spoke of his 'neurasthenia' or his 'hysteria'; Jung spent long periods brooding by the lake, or piling stones into little castles. Both men underwent self-imposed psychic exercises, each according to his own method: Freud by free association, endeavoring to recover the lost memories of his early childhood; Jung by forced imagination and the drawing of his dreams. In both men these exercises worked as a self-therapy, although in the beginning they increased their sufferings."[6]

When this critical period ended, both men emerged dramatically transformed and strengthened. At the age of forty-four each was now ready to lead rather than follow, with his basic ideas more sharply formulated. Freud's focus was on the past—childhood and sexuality. Jung's focus was on the present and future—evolving adulthood. But it was Jung alone who drew universal truth from his personal transformation, incorporating his own mid-life metamorphosis into his thinking about the development of the human personality.

When a person begins to look backward and take stock of how his life has developed, "real motivations are sought and real discoveries made," said Jung; but the insights that follow "are gained only through the severest shock."[7] He accounted for these shocks by pointing out that we tend to regard every experience forcing us to greater awareness as a curse—just as the biblical fall of man, which began with the bite of the apple, presents the dawn of consciousness as a curse. Thus we tend to turn away from such insights, or deny them, because our increased awareness "separates us even further from the paradise of unconscious childhood,"[8] he said.

Nevertheless, Jung felt strongly that mid-life was the time to renounce this unconscious paradise, because the second half of life had a purpose quite different from the first. The first half of life should be devoted to making our mark on the world by earning money, extending conquests, and raising children, he said. But in the second half of life there should be a contraction, an end to getting ahead, in order to concentrate on exploring the self.

Jung believed that many neuroses are rooted in flight from one's life tasks. Thus, he suggested, the difficulties that men in their forties experience are often caused by fear, and their resistance to growth and change. "The very frequent neurotic disturbances of adult years all have one thing in common," said Jung. "They want to carry the psychology of the youthful phase over the threshold of the so-called years of discretion."9

In the Jungian framework psychotherapy begins by bringing a person back to reality and making him more aware of his present situation. Even more important, however, since Jung believes that every human being is always striving for wholeness, striving to be well. many symptoms that in Freudian terms are seen as pathological are viewed, in Jungian terms. as healthy signs of growth.10

This distinction is absolutely crucial to our understanding of the process by which the growth of the personality proceeds over the entire life course, and equally crucial to our understanding of what the mid-life crisis is all about.

To illustrate the significance of this difference, Dr. David Hart, a Jungian analyst, explains that if a man is working at a job that no longer stimulates him, he may begin to suffer from disturbing symptoms like anxiety or fear. But that does not mean that he is "sick."

"If you analyze what is going on," says Hart, "the man may really be trying to repress tendencies towards greater realization of his personality, which might lead him into a different kind of life, or to different activities, or even different relationships. In other words, for the development of his personality he might need to expand beyond the narrow life which he is now leading, which, of course, produces a lot of fear."11

In Jungian terms disturbing symptoms like anxiety, fear, or pain generally mean that a man is being challenged to grow and change. If he resists, if he is unable to tolerate this distress long enough to see where it might be leading him, he will have thrown away an opportunity to enlarge his life.

III *Erikson: The Stages of Life*

Despite Jung's suggestive ideas on adult growth, he did not attract many disciples, largely because his outlook was metaphysical and spiritual rather than scientific and sexual. Instead, Erik Erikson became the most influential psychoanalytic thinker on this subject as he built on Freud's foundations, and then forged beyond the early years to show how development proceeds throughout the entire life span.[12] Erikson's concepts have influenced scores of social scientists now exploring the problems of adulthood.

Perhaps the most important departure is that Erikson sees the mind *in its essence* as always developing, whereas Freud saw the mind as largely structured and set in childhood. This fundamental difference led Erikson to regard the life cycle as a continuing series of steps, each presenting possibilities for new growth, in contrast to Freud's view of the adult years as a mere unfolding of events whose direction has already been determined.[13]

Erikson took another step forward with his concept of identity, which links man's internal psyche with the external world of culture, history, and society. And by now many of us are familiar with this concept, and also with his formulation of the Eight Stages of Man.

Outlining these stages, he suggested that psychosocial development proceeds by critical steps, or "crises": decisive turning points where a shift one way or another, for better or for worse, is unavoidable. Erikson underscored this aspect of a developmental crisis by assigning double terms to each life stage, thereby emphasizing the either/or nature of the outcome.

"A new life task presents a *crisis* whose outcome can be a successful graduation, or alternatively, an impairment of the life cycle which will aggravate future crises," he explains. "Each crisis prepares the next, as one step leads to another; and each crisis also lays one more cornerstone for the adult personality."[14]

In Erikson's scheme the first five stages correspond to Freud's stages of psychosexual development; and the next three, it has been suggested, seem to have been inspired by Jung's concept of individuation. During the identity crisis of adolescence, development becomes more complex than it was in childhood, says Erikson: A restructuring of all previous identifications occurs, which often means having to fight some earlier battles over again.

The complexity increases even more as a person proceeds through the adult stages of this hierarchy. Each of the next three stages adds either a "blessing" or a "curse," says Erikson, and at the same time makes "a new ensemble" out of the preceding steps in development. When a later crisis is severe, earlier issues are likely to be revived. And despite the identity crisis having been resolved in adolescence, later stresses can precipitate its renewal.

The crisis of young adulthood concerns intimacy vs. isolation, and if resolved favorably results in the capacity to love. Love in its truest sense cannot evolve until this stage of life because it must be preceded by the forging of an identity, says Erikson, and it also requires a capacity for commitment. Whereas the earlier sex life was really a form of "genital combat," intimacy can now transform that combat into closeness. In turn, this new capacity for loving sexual relations makes the need for sex less obsessive.

The crisis of the middle years, which begins around forty, centers on generativity vs. stagnation, and results in the ability to care if resolved favorably. At this stage a widening concern with the younger generation is necessary in some form if development is to continue. "Generativity" means becoming more responsible for younger adults, besides one's own children; and it also relates to products, ideas, and works of art.

"Adult man is so constituted as to *need to be needed* lest he suffer the mental deformation of self-absorption, in which he becomes his own infant and pet,"[15] states Erikson. Teaching is a perfect example of generativity, he says. Teaching also illustrates the way in which the life stages interlock within a total life cycle: By lubricating the turning wheel of the generations, it benefits and connects the adult, the child, and the culture.

The eighth stage of life is the culmination of everything that has preceded. This final crisis pits ego integrity against despair, and if resolved successfully leads to wisdom. Fortified by matured judgment, the wise man is able to accept his "one and only life cycle as something that had to be and that, by necessity, permitted of no substitutions."[16] Despite being well aware of varied lifestyles, he defends the dignity of his own.

"Only such integrity can balance the despair of the knowledge that a limited life is coming to a conscious conclusion, only such wholeness can transcend the petty disgust of feeling finished and passed by,"[17] says Erikson. Because he sees the life cycle as a circular, interlocking bond between the generations, the successful resolution of this final crisis is of vital importance. Infantile trust, the first ego strength, depends on adult integrity—the last ego strength.

As they rotate, then, the generations nourish and enrich each other. Or at least they should. In fact, however, this reciprocal enrichment can exist only when a culture respects the old as much as the young.

IV *The Yale Group: Adults in Transition*

Today an increasing number of researchers are following Erikson's leads in their investigations of adult development. But the most provocative ideas, as we mentioned earlier, come from Daniel J. Levinson and his team of researchers at Yale University. Moreover, they are the only group to have studied the male mid-life period in depth, and to have placed it in the life-cycle framework.[18]

This study was inspired by their personal mid-life churnings; by the theories of Erikson and Jung; and by novels and plays. Levinson explains that his making a major career move at age forty-six prompted him to investigate this period in order to better understand his own evolution. His team includes: Charlotte M. Darrow, a sociologist; Braxton McKee, a psychiatrist; and Edward B. Klein and Maria H. Levinson, both psychologists.

The Yale group began their study by assuming that this decade was an important developmental period in its own right: A time when a man faces new tasks and dilemmas, but also has new opportunities for growth. To find out more about this decade in relation to the whole life span, they decided to use an intensive case-study method, in keeping with their view of themselves as biographers rather than statisticians. Now they have studied forty men, aged thirty-five to forty-five, and have reconstructed their lives in detail. These men come from four occupational groups, ten in each: business executives; blue- and white-collar workers in industry; academic biologists; and novelists.

Basically, the Yale group wanted to know more about the process of change in individual lives. But they also wanted to discover why this crisis period led to a constriction in some men's lives, and an expansion in others. Thus their initial focus was soon enlarged to consider what had happened during the preceding years, and they began to ask questions about how adult life evolves over time. Now they have concluded that a number of age-linked developmental periods exist between eighteen and forty-five.

Levinson says that they have deliberately tried to be very specific about age in order to counter the conventional wisdom that no age-linked development occurs during the adult years. They see the life course divided into several major eras: Early adulthood, twenty to forty; middle adulthood, forty to sixty; and late adulthood, sixty and over. They also see life as consisting of some periods that are relatively tranquil and stable, and others that are marked by change and discontinuity. Rather than use the word "crisis" to describe a critical point, however, they prefer the term "transition."

To clarify what happens during the mid-life period, the transition between early and middle adulthood, they offer the following description of how the male's development has proceeded until this time:

Leaving the Family, Eighteen to Twenty-two: This is the transition between adolescent life and full entry into the adult world. During this period a young man is usually half in and half out of the family, but trying to separate himself from their support and authority. This involves moving out of the family home, becoming financially independent, and assuming new roles that make him more autonomous.

The major developmental task of this period is getting across the boundary between the family and the adult world. This period ends when the balance shifts and the young man has begun to make a place for himself outside. The Yale Group caution, however, that further work on separation from the family continues for many years—or in some cases, forever.

Getting into the Adult World, Twenty-two to Twenty-eight:
A young man now tries to establish an occupational direction and form more mature friendships and sexual relationships—including, perhaps, marriage. The developmental task of this period is to arrive at a preliminary definition of himself as an adult, and fashion an initial life structure based on his interests and goals. This is a time for exploration and for making tentative choices.

Many men, but not all, enter this period with a dream of their personal future. Usually related to work, this dream might revolve around winning the Nobel prize, becoming president of the company, or writing a great novel. Such a dream is considered a vitalizing force for further growth. Without it, in fact, life can be oppressive and bland. In later years the reactivation of this guiding dream, and concern with its failure, may become a key issue. Major shifts around forty are often caused by a man's feeling that he has betrayed or compromised his dream.

An especially significant finding: The Yale group discovered that a man's having a mentor during this period is highly correlated with his future growth—and his success. Eight to fifteen years older, this mentor may be a teacher, boss, editor, or experienced co-worker who represents a level of achievement to which the younger man aspires. He invites the younger man into his world, shows him around, and—most crucial—gives his blessing to the dream. In this way the mentor not only helps foster the younger man's development, but also reinforces his sense of manhood.

"Generally speaking," says McKee, "it is assumed that once a person separates from his father, and leaves home, he is independent. But that's simply not true. What seems to be consistently overlooked is the parental function of the organization the man becomes involved with—and also the fact that, despite his newfound 'independence,' he starts almost immediately to seek out these semiparental mentor figures. And develops much farther, by the way, if he succeeds in finding them."[19]

Age Thirty Transition, Twenty-eight to Thirty-two: During this period a man generally questions whether he should continue in his chosen occupation, or make a change while he still has a chance. Pointing out that there are wide variations in the course chosen during the twenties, the Yale group found that the most frequent pattern around thirty was for a man to remain in the occupation initially chosen and reaffirm his existing marriage—or get married now.

In some cases, however, when a man decided that his first choice was not the right one—perhaps because it was too constraining, or a violation of his dream, or because he lacked the talent to succeed—he then made a major shift, which sometimes included breaking up his marriage. In still another version, the man who lived a transient, unsettled life in his twenties often began feeling a desperate need around thirty to put some order and solidity into his life. Like other transitions, this one may cause considerable turmoil, or simply involve reassessment and intensified effort. But it is usually marked by some significant changes, and is a prelude to a calmer stage in development.

Settling Down, Thirty-two to Thirty-nine: During this period a man generally makes deeper commitments to his work and his family. He "joins the tribe," as the Yale group puts it. One keynote of this period is order: building a nest and working for security. Another keynote is "making it": moving upward according to an inner timetable about the age when certain goals should be reached. By forty, for example, the executive wants to be earning fifty thousand dollars; the assistant professor desires tenure; and the professional man aims at becoming a senior partner.

One of the most pernicious myths about adulthood is the notion that once a man has established a stable life pattern, it can continue more or less indefinitely—without any major problems ahead. This is simply not true, say the Yale group. No matter how satisfying the life structure created during this period, it cannot possibly fulfill all of the self—and must therefore be enlarged, or radically changed, later.

Another reason for future change is that this structure is inevitably based partly on illusions about the importance of work goals, relationships to others, and what a man truly wants in life. And later on, letting go of these illusions will be vital for further growth.

The Mid-life Transition, Thirty-nine to Forty-two: Just as some adolescents move into adulthood with relative ease, so some men pass through this period with little apparent stress. But the Yale group suspect that most men have some difficulty. And those who don't, or say they don't, may just be deceiving themselves. For example, several men in their study described themselves as happy, content, and on top of the world. But their psychological testing revealed unconscious themes of despair, humiliation, and disintegration.

"These are men who haven't yet been able to confront the nature of their fantasies and their unconscious experience," says Levinson. "There is a crisis in their lives, but they are not yet ready to face it, take responsibility for it, and meet it at a conscious level."[20]

A major crossroads, this transitional period bristles with threats as well as promises. The man who feels hopelessly trapped in his life pattern, with no imaginable escape, may thrash around wildly—anesthetizing himself with excessive liquor, frenzied work efforts, or compulsive sex. But if he cannot make a meaningful step to enrich his life, and grow further as a human being, he will probably move numbly and mechanically through his remaining years. On the other hand, this period offers an opportunity for personal growth never before possible. The real dividend that comes from a man's having had a hard time at forty is that his life will be better and richer in the future.

"This transition is not just a little upset, like a cold that you get over," warns Levinson. "The fact is that there is something very profound happening here; or at least there is that possibility. It is important how much you do change your life. I mean: Take it seriously, man! Don't just say, 'If I can hold out I'll be alright; now that you tell me everybody goes through the same thing I can relax a little bit and I'll survive it.' There is more possibility here than just survival—in your job or whatever. And if you try for big changes, you may fail miserably. On the other hand, if you don't try for changes, you'll feel dead in a few years—because you'll be stagnant."[21]

Restabilization: The Beginning of Middle Adulthood, Forty-three to Forty-seven: Somewhere around forty-five a man is ready to move into the next life stage, hopefully having formed a new life structure as the basis for living in middle adulthood. Some men will have made destructive changes, while others will have refocused their energies around new commitments. But even if a man has remained in the same groove, his life will now have a different meaning for him, say the Yale group, because he will have changed internally to some degree.

To dramatize the fact that the mid-life transition is a time of great threat to the self, as well as a time of great possibility, the Yale group point out that men like Dylan Thomas, F. Scott Fitzgerald, and Sinclair Lewis destroyed themselves because they were unable to handle the crisis. By contrast, men like Freud, Jung, Frank Lloyd Wright, and Gandhi all went through a profound crisis around forty—and made tremendous creative gains as a result.

It is becoming urgently apparent that we Americans need to revise our priorities within a life-cycle perspective. Our present view of life as a ladder to be scaled, as a one-way street to success, is causing widespread human obsolescence not only among the elderly, but among the middle-aged as well. Today too many men are entering middle adulthood resigned to emptiness and despair. They seem burned out already, burdened by a crushing sense of loss but lacking any sense of what has been gained.

In order to develop some cultural wisdom about the years after forty as a season with its own rewards, we need to alter our thinking about the development of the human personality and the meaning of life's stages. We need to abandon our stubbornly held, but grossly mistaken, conviction that aging means not simply wrinkled skin and waning physical energies but also a monumental loss of all human potential.

Today the evidence needed for such a revision of our attitudes is already in. Many social scientists, including those at Yale, have clearly proven that adults are more flexible than we ever suspected; that the self is too complex to be contained by a static identity; and that growth can occur throughout the entire life span.

These are the principles to keep in mind as we look more closely at the changes and challenges that take place during the mid-life period. If every man in his middle years will also heed these same principles, remembering that the keynote of this turbulent period is growth and development, he will have taken a major step forward in managing his own mid-life crisis and triumphing over it.

Chapter 7   Penis Angst and the Balm of Nubile Girls

I *Sexual Fears and Failures*

On the brink of middle age a man can no longer nourish dreams of great new conquests in the working world. Even more fundamental to his sense of manhood, he can no longer count on asserting his masculinity with an instant erection. Time, he feels, is castrating him.

Earlier in life women seemed to be suffering from penis envy, but now the tables have turned: After forty men suffer from penis *angst*—a condition which, as we shall see, has many ramifications. This anxiety is aggravated, certainly, by our attitude toward the elderly. Our culture endorsed the fiction that sex is reserved for the young (and beautiful), while the old (and ugly) are relegated to rocking chairs and celibacy. This prophecy is so pervasive that even men who had dismissed it in their youth are suddenly beset by doubts when they discover that their penis doesn't harden as quickly as it used to, and sometimes to their horror doesn't harden at all. No longer able to respond automatically, like a superb athlete or a *macho* superstar, they become preoccupied with their waning sexual prowess—and harbor deep-seated fears for the future.

"The conventional male fantasy of being ready to perform anytime, anywhere is wholly neurotic and impractical," says Dr. Alex Comfort, author of *The Joy of Sex*. "Only the totally insensitive are all-time fucking machines like a stud-bull and stud-bulls too have their off-days."[1] But the fantasy persists, causing havoc at mid-life. Which is why impotence begins to trouble many men, sporadically at least, and even those who do not yet have serious problems worry that they will.

In response to these anxieties, Norman C. King, a media consultant and selfmade millionaire, has decided that the problem of "obtaining and sustaining an erection" is so enormous that a national solution is required. In 1969, he recalls, "I was sitting around with a very famous broadcaster, a very famous comedian, a couple of banker friends, and a movie producer, and a couple of guys indicated they weren't performing like they used to and were very concerned about it. But no one knew where to go to *solve* the problem—including me. And I'm supposed to be an expert in everything!"

This conversation led King to gather information, consult physicians, and research the market for a potency clinic. When he sent a mailout on his projected clinic to fifteen hundred executives making forty thousand dollars a year, he received over three hundred phone calls. When another mailout to men making only twelve thousand dollars elicited the same number of calls, he concluded: "It has nothing to do with money. The need—the desperate need—is there." Thus he plans to open a chain of clinics, the Male Potency Centers of America, in the near future.

"I really believe I'll make a billion dollars out of this deal," says King, who sees himself becoming "the Oral Roberts of the genitals."

King claims to have found the magic formula that will get the sexual athlete performing again quickly, simply, and relatively cheaply. The treatment at his clinics, to be staffed with a doctor and a psychologist, will be mostly chemotherapy (male hormone shots, or pills) and will cost five hundred dollars for ten visits. Best of all, in his view, no partner is required. Scornful of sex therapists who treat couples only, he says: "You have to make an appointment to go with your wife, or go with your girlfriend and pretend she's your wife, and be prepared to give four weeks of your life. One wonderful thing about *my* clinic is the man goes by himself, like to treat a sore finger or a cold or a pain in his side.

"What he really has here," King says of his future client, "is a pain in his heart, generated by the fear that he can no longer get a hard-on. I plan to solve this by chemotherapy. You know, marketing an erection is no different from marketing a lipstick."

Can impotence really be cured by hormones? As we have seen, there is no "male menopause." There is a syndrome called the male climacteric, which affects only a small percentage of men, and then usually in their fifties or sixties. Characterized by a sudden failure of the testes to perform, and a sharp drop in hormone production, it does indeed lead to impotence. But it is a relatively rare condition: Only 15 percent of older men will ever suffer from the climacteric, say most authorities. An illness, not a natural event, this condition can and should be treated by hormone replacement therapy.[2]

Such disorders aside, however, what are the ordinary hormonal changes that occur with aging, and how do they affect a man's sexual response? In the male the testes are the sex glands that produce testosterone, the hormone that makes a man aggressive, virile, and sexually active. Testosterone production begins in puberty, continues to increase until a man is in his twenties, and from then on decreases very gradually as he ages, too gradually in most cases to interfere with sexual activity or account for impotence. This means that the average man in his middle years will not suffer any symptoms that can be attributed to a radical change in hormone production. Nor will the aging process itself prevent his having a vigorous sex life—ever.[3]

When impotence troubles a man at mid-life the problem is usually in his head. Consequently attempts to counter sexual fears and failures with chemotherapy are likely to do little good. In fact, the attitudes of men like Norman King—that sex is simply a matter of physical performance, and sexual problems a matter of technology, best solved in secret—are part of the problem, not the basis for a solution.

The male is not "a push-button sexual performer,"[4] as Masters and Johnson have often stressed. To the contrary, his sexual response is influenced and inhibited by many factors—his attitudes, expectations, feelings, and past experiences.

One of the most important recent advances in the field of human sexuality is this discovery that the male's sexual response is as complicated as the female's. The theory used to be that impotence was always a sign of pathology, but now there is ample proof that it has multiple causes.[5] In general, say the experts, erectile failures are produced by anxiety—

and this anxiety can spring from many sources: anticipation of failure, a stressful sexual atmosphere, criticism from a hostile wife or lover, guilt about sexual pleasure, and grandiose performance expectations are among the most common.

But the anxiety can also be totally unrelated to sex—a finding that has special relevance during the stressful mid-life period. It has been shown, for example, that sporadic impotence can be caused by anxiety generated at work, when a man's job is in jeopardy or he feels under extraordinary pressure. It can also be caused by depression, mental fatigue, excessive alcohol, marital tensions, or psychological conflict of any sort. Moreover, recent studies have shown that depression, defeat, and chronic stress can themselves product a sharp drop in the level of testosterone production, thus documenting the impact of emotional states on the hormonal system.[6]

Too, the sexual attitudes of this generation of American men exacerbate their penis *angst*. Thanks to our puritanical heritage, most men now in their middle years were poisoned from an early age by taboos suggesting that sex is sinful and disgusting. The worst result of this training, says Dr. Helen S. Kaplan, a psychiatrist who heads the sex therapy program at the Payne Whitney clinic of New York Hospital, is that "the erotic impulses are not acknowledged as part of the personality. They are dehumanized, relegated to the alien realm of 'dirty' and pornographic. Sex becomes a conquest or a submission instead of a beautiful integrated aspect of the self."[7]

Our society encourages this schizoid split primarily in the male. Traditionally women have been conditioned to integrate their sexuality with their feelings, to regard sex as permissible only when accompanied by love, or at least affection. Men, on the other hand, have been taught to separate the two.

The double standard is slowly dissolving, but that is of little help to men over forty who remain sexually muddled by the madonna/whore dichotomy absorbed in their youth. This dehumanizing code ignited a ferocious adolescent battle in which boys gained status according to how much sex they got, while girls became desirable according to how little they gave. It has also promoted a marital mentality in the adult male, inciting him to prove his masculinity through conquest, while viewing women as the enemy to be vanquished and bed the battlefield where orgasms are won.

Other cultures have taught that sex is sin, or war, but the American male is further sabotaged by the application of athletic metaphors to sex: Having been trained to compete aggressively, perform perfectly, and score frequently, he often participates in sex like a quarterback intent on plowing toward the end zone—proud of his feats but oblivious to feelings.

The tragedy is that while this gung-ho approach can provide erotic calisthenics for the younger man, it stops working at mid-life when athletics are no longer so easily performed, nor high numbers so readily scored. Too, it reinforces the profound split between sex and emotions that the double standard encouraged, a split that can eventually short-circuit a man's sexuality.

II *The Mid-life Itch*

There are many responses to the first attacks of sexual distress, but the most common is a heightened desire to seek out sexual adventures, a heightened susceptibility to romance. Freud called it *Torschlusspanik*—the panic before the closing of the gates, meaning the time when men feel compelled to have a final fling before it is too late, the time when philandering seems to be the perfect salve for penis *angst*.

Some men play on the fringes of erotic temptation, while others embrace it fully. But at the least all men in their forties dream about an abandoned fling, because the temptation itself is universal. To begin with, there is boredom, now rendered intolerable by a dawning awareness that life is poignantly brief. Anything new or novel entices, simply because change itself means relief from oppressive ruts, but the most accessible adventure is often sexual: Another woman means another world to explore and conquer.

At the same time, a man is probably re-evaluating the Spartan code that guided him in the past. Suddenly aware that he missed out on many pleasurable experiences, he is beginning to shed his youthful inhibitions and question his dedication to getting ahead. Moreover, his longings are bound to be further inflamed by the freer sexual attitudes of his younger colleagues at work. "These kids are it, these kids know

how to live," exclaimed one forty-two-year-old man, surveying a singles bar. "They're balling all the time—and we didn't
ball until we were over twenty-one!"

Men of this generation frequently feel that their struggle
for success has entitled them to have some fun. They want a
reward for the years of disciplining their desires and sacrificing their sensuality. Thus among businessmen, professionals,
and politicians, in the higher ranks especially, sexual interludes are universally regarded as an obvious and well-earned
payoff.[8]

Some men want more than interludes. They feel deserving
of a whole new way of life, more pleasurable, more playful.
Said one man when criticized for divorcing his wife after
twenty-two years: "Look, damnit, I was never part of the
swinging scene. I've been working since I was eighteen, and
it's only *now* that I can afford to do the things I've always
wanted to do—go to the track, travel to Europe, blow five
hundred bucks in a night if I feel like it. And I don't have to
worry about spending all my time in the office, either. I want
to run and do and see. Live it up! I couldn't have converted
my wife even if I'd wanted to. She thinks I'm going through
my second childhood. Well, maybe I am. But for the first
time I can afford to *enjoy* life—and I damn well plan to!"

At this stage of life a man also discovers that a measure of
success makes him newly desirable to women. He doesn't
even have to be seeking an affair to become the object of
seductive approaches. Suddenly he finds himself surrounded
by scores of admiring young women—secretaries, students,
researchers, lab technicians, journalists, and production as-
sistants—who are openly turned on by his power or status or
money. Such female flattery is often irresistible to the man
who never fancied himself as a lover in his youth, or who
had little sexual experience before he married. This is particularly true, of course, when he feels unappreciated at home.

"The trouble is that as you grow in your job people there
look upon you differently," explained one man, "but back in
your home life your wife doesn't see these changes. And so
she reacts to you in the same way. 'That's old Joe, he's the
same old guy. He'll take a lot of shit, you can pile another
ton and a half on him.' Then suddenly, because you've
evolved in one situation but are treated the same as you were

ten years ago in another, you want to stand up and say, 'Fuck you!' So you start screwing around. It's easy."

Just how easy is described by a woman familiar with both sides of this situation:

> In any large city the offices are staffed with single women who are intent on quite blatantly attracting these older, intelligent, successful men for whom they work. And so he sees all these women preening, spending much more time on themselves than his wife does, and sitting on his every word.
>
> The wife who married him when he was twenty-one, and wasn't sure of himself, doesn't really see him fully formed. She doesn't realize that a man who can't decide what pair of undershorts to put on in the morning is capable of saying "Yes" or "No" to a half-million-dollar proposition!
>
> She's still living with the boy who once existed, and she's treating him the way she always did. I've heard many women whose husbands I knew were having affairs say, "Oh, Dick, he wouldn't do anything even if he could. Dick likes young girls, but what would they see in *him?* He's getting potty and gray, and God knows he's not the greatest lover!"
>
> In the meantime he has unlimited possibilities in the office. The women there are feeding his ego and offering him *another version of himself,* which he believes and responds to. And that's very powerful—because they're reflecting back to him a much more mature, grown, confident, whole man!

Bedding nubile girls is nothing new. When Groucho Marx remarked, "A man is only as old as the woman he feels," he was endorsing ancient folklore. In bygone days many Near and Far Eastern rejuvenation efforts were based on "gerocomy," the belief that a man absorbs youth from young women. King David in the Old Testament is said to have subscribed to this belief, as did the Romans and many other societies.

But in America today liaisons between older men and younger women are conducted more openly than ever before, and it is no longer assumed that they depend on a financial arrangement, like that of the Sugar Daddy and his chorus girl. Still, disapproval lingers. At mid-life a man's involvement with a young girl has become the archetypal symbol of his aberration, proof positive that he is hopelessly bewildered—or menopausal. Accused of trying to recapture his youth or prove his virility, he is regarded as foolish, desperate, or lecherous. Or he is dismissed with contempt as a dirty old man.

The truth is neither so simple nor so pat. Although individual reasons invariably exist to explain the large age gap, relationships between older men and young girls are not necessarily neurotic nor a sign of immaturity. Often the attraction is related to a man's need for something different from what he has at home. If he is feeling overwhelmed by rebellious teen-agers or complaining in-laws, he may choose the nubile girl as entrée to another world: frivolous and unfettered. A no-strings-attached fling offers the married man, resentful of heavy financial and familial responsibilities so common at this stage of life, a way to break out and have fun without incurring further obligations.

Similarly, many recently divorced men in their forties go through a phase that includes dressing youthfully, prowling singles bars, and pursuing promiscuous sex. This behavior may look like a return trip to adolescence, but it is usually only a temporary means of regaining equilibrium. Typically the man in this situation married early and devoted his life to supporting his family. When his marriage breaks up he feels that, having been overburdened with demands from his wife and children, he now wants to be carefree and uncommitted. Women over thirty insist on being taken seriously and, worse still, remind him of the wife/mother he just left. But the young girl is different. She too relishes her freedom and is not yet ready to settle down. And her apartment is enticingly romantic, a haven without kids or other domestic trappings.

"With older women you have to be too responsible," explained one forty-seven-year-old man. "The younger woman is a lot easier to get along with. She can afford to let the game lead her wherever it leads. She doesn't care whether it's productive or unproductive, she doesn't evaluate it. To me the younger women are just the free spirits, is what it amounts to. The ones who can play and can afford to relate to you casually—and that's the appeal."

Some men prefer a youthful playmate because she is acquiescent and untutored. They satisfy their Pygmalion proclivities by shaping her ideas, molding her tastes, and introducing her to new experiences. The man who is extremely high-powered may choose her primarily because she has the energy and vigor to match his pace and accommodate herself to his schedule.

"Undemanding" is the quality many mid-life men say they value most in a younger girlfriend, especially if they perceive their wife, or ex-wife, as aggressive and overbearing. Describing his affair with a twenty-one-year-old, one man summed it up this way: "She was the first female I knew on an intimate basis who made absolutely no demands on me. Absolutely *none*. Everything I did was all right, anywhere I wanted to go was fine. I was made to feel like I was the center of the relationship."

III *A Soothing Balm: The Nubile Girl*

Whereas Kinsey enlightened us about the wide range of variations in sexual behavior, social scientists today have begun to emphasize the wide range of *meanings* that such behavior has. And in contrast to Freud, who said all human actions were shaped by sexual needs, they now suggest the opposite: that sexual activity is often motivated by other needs. Nonsexual needs.

Thus a careful observation of the erotic adventures of men in their middle years reveals that their penis *angst* is usually related to larger mid-life anxieties, and is best understood as one aspect of a shifting sense of self.

In response to wrenching changes, a man at this stage of life is struggling to revise his own self-image and find dignity in the face of undeniable limitations. More than ever, he needs the confirmation of being seen as a powerful and desirable man—a need that the nubile girl is uniquely suited to satisfy. Our culture's most obvious symbol of hot-blooded sexuality, she can meet the aging male's intensified need for reassurance both in public and in private. Even when appearances are deceptive, she still has something special to offer, as one connoisseur testifies:

I've known a lot of young women, and I find that they're full of sexual problems and fuck-ups. My experience is that they always have to be taught and initiated. It's *labor,* not paradise! It's not some marvelous, highly sexed, steamed-up, ready-to-go honey that you're getting! It's more than likely somebody who's insecure and frigid and inept.

One thing that's true, though, I think you can get a younger woman to respond to you very strongly. She's going to be less appraising than an older woman. She's had less experience. There are fewer men in her life to which she can compare you. You can dominate her more, sort of impose your myth on her. And you can feel you're initiating her into all sorts of things and blowing her mind and enslaving her—or whatever the hell it is that you want to do with a woman.

The younger woman has a virginal imagination. After all, what was the whole appeal of the virgin ultimately? That you could mold her and shape her and do this trick with her—that's why men wanted to marry virgins. They didn't want any comparisons with any other men. So I think that is a great emotional kick.

During the mid-life period men of this generation often have difficulty separating the two intertwined elements that define their sense of manhood: work and sexuality. It is common, therefore, for a man to suffer first from a feeling of impotence at work, and to then seek compensation through sexual conquest. This is especially true when he despairs of having failed to meet his own standards.

In *The War Between the Tates,*[9] Alison Lurie describes this situation perfectly. Previously disdainful of colleagues who dallied with students, Brian Tate is a college professor who sees himself as "a just, honorable, and responsible person." At forty-six, however, he painfully recognizes that he will never become what he had always aspired to: a great man.

His dream demolished, he derives no comfort from knowing that others consider him successful, or that he is blessed with a beautiful wife and two intelligent children. And so he gradually succumbs to the persistent advances of his young student, Wendy Gahaguan—a move that puzzles him. Perhaps, he speculates, his descent into adultery was caused by "the realization that all this solemn self-regulation had been for nothing."

Despite Brian's confusion, it is obvious that Wendy provides a powerful antidote for his feelings of failure. To her Brian is a hero and a great man. Basking in the nourishing warmth of her admiration, he feels increasingly exploited at home by rebellious adolescents and a scolding wife. Why shoud he continue living in "a hostile camp," he wonders, when Wendy—who "never judges him, withholds nothing, cares for him more than for herself"—offers unconditional love?

Thus Brian separates from his wife to frolic with Wendy, until the frenzied chaos of her life exhausts him and he finally returns to his familiar domestic comforts. But something significant has happened in the meantime: Having retreated to a hospitable harbor during a stormy period, he returns with his self-esteem restored.

Surprising though it may seem, this same magical act of restoration and reassurance is often performed just as skillfully by a call girl as by a college girl. That at least is the finding of a study entitled *Lovers, Friends, Slaves*[10] by Martha Stein, a Manhattan social worker. Based on the direct observation of sex acts involving 1,242 men, this study shows that for men in their middle years even sexual liaisons involving cash are not motivated by simple sexual desire, but by a special constellation of factors related to the mid-life crisis.

The majority of these men came to the call girl to seek relief from overwhelming performance pressures, says Stein, who concluded that most of them were having difficulty working through the problems related to their stage of life. (Described as top-level businessmen and professionals, 42 per cent of these men were in their forties, with the rest roughly divided between the thirties and the fifties.) Generally they regarded the call girl's apartment as a haven where they could escape their worries. And more than half imposed on her a therapeutic role—for ego support, sexual counseling, airing their troubles, and reducing anxiety. Some men confided fears or feelings that they had never shared with anyone else—including their wife, or even their psychiatrist. Others increased their visits during times of crisis, when the tension at work or at home became acute. Better than tranquilizers, they said their visits helped them unwind physically and also provided much-needed emotional comfort.

Ambitious and self-denying, these men often described themselves as feeling harassed, overworked, and lonely. Over and over again they spoke about having no one to talk to. They complained about physical health problems; ambivalence about their chosen lifestyle and the value of monetary success; and feelings of estrangement from their wives and children. In turn, these tensions were expressed through excessive drinking, which was very common; depression; stress-related illnesses such as heart conditions, ulcers, and high blood pressure; and a high incidence (25 per cent) of sexual dysfunction.

Equally revealing, in this setting where a man was under no obligation to satisfy his partner or to conform to social standards, half these men chose to abandon their prescribed role as an "aggressive" male. Sexually passive, they wanted to relax and let the call girl direct the love play, rather than "perform." They also preferred the female-superior position to any other, and frequently requested fellatio.

Thus, says Stein, the call girls provided therapeutic benefits—which a man could accept without seeing himself as maladjusted—by fulfilling emotional needs that were not being met in his marriage or dealt with by the helping professions. That is, in addition to sex these men used their sessions primarily to bolster their own self-image—by choosing roles that brought praise or reassurance.

According to their preferences, they fell into nine categories. The "Lovers," for example, approached sex in a highly poetic way and often fantasized romantic scenarios of escape, which might include vacationing with the call girl. Anxious to be considered special, the "Lovers" also demanded much flattery. The "Friends" wanted, above all, to ventilate their problems and anxieties. They complained about the stressful aspects of their work or home life, and needed to be listened to in a supportive, sympathetic manner. The "Guardians," on the other hand, rarely talked about their own problems because they wanted to appear strong, wise, and protective. Concerned about impotence, they preferred very young girls who giggled, got confused, and needed their help. Another group, the "Adventurers," were interested in becoming liberated swingers and in experimenting with different techniques and postures. Attracted by the counterculture's notion of playful sex, they wanted to combine sex with drugs and rock music, or arrange scenes with several girls.

Adept at responding to the particular role chosen by each man, the call girl became the fantasy woman who was paid not merely to provide sex, but also to be totally devoted to his needs and wishes. Eager to please, utterly accommodating, she was a welcome relief for men who felt both over-pressured and underappreciated.

And so it is for other men: Seeking refuge from the harsh assaults of this mid-life period and release from the heightened anxieties that haunt and perplex them, they confirm their manhood through the worshipful gaze of a nubile girl—who mirrors back an image of their most potent self. Contrary to popular wisdom, men in their middle years are generally drawn to younger women not because they want to recapture their youth, but because they need to reconfirm their maturity. One man explains:

A lot of people have said they see me as someone who is interested in young women because this contradicts my own age or makes me feel young, or something of that sort. I don't really believe that at all.

I don't think I have any particular prejudice in favor of youth, but I do feel that after a certain age—and it isn't a very advanced age, maybe something like twenty-eight—women become very difficult to deal with because they have been through the mill. They're like a damaged, fractured vase, and if they get one more knock they'll fall apart. Or else they're sort of a shrewd appraiser of male horseflesh and they just want a good deal. It's either defensiveness or canniness, but it certainly makes a big problem for men.

Another thing: As you grow older you more and more prize the quality of sweetness in a woman, and I find the word "sweet" a very important word in the middle-aged male's vocabulary. "Isn't she sweet?" "Such a sweet girl!" It's part of the escape theme—away from harshness, away from reality, away from contests of ego strength with mature women. You want that sweetness, that sense of—I don't know—tenderness, affection. It's

a childlike quality as balm, as relief, as comfort,
pe from this endless power struggle that you always live in.

Earlier in my life I don't think that quality would
have been recognizable to me. I wouldn't even have ar-
ticulated it. Women were either good-looking or intelligent or very stylish or sexy. Today I'll look at a woman
and I'll say, "Well, she's attractive and bright, but she's
just not a sweet person, so what good is it?" That's really
the master quality, I find, at this stage of my life. It's a
quality of innocence, or yieldingness, of no hostility, no
combat, and no rivalry.

I think younger women are more romantic and more
tender, and sort of sweeter. Older women tend to be
maternal and sympathetic and understanding, but it's all
turning into your mother—which is *not* what you're after! A mature woman is in the same situation you're in.
She wants her pleasure, and you're going to contribute
to it. She's not going to be your slave, and she's not going to be your adorer, and she's not going to fall down
and collapse in front of you!

The young woman can enhance your ego by reflecting
back on you the image you want to have reflected. You
want to be taken for a big man or a generous man or a
sexy rogue or a great fuck—whatever image you're trying to promote, you can get it back from her a lot easier
than you can from an older woman.

So I don't think it's trying to recapture your youth, or
trying to be young. It's just the *opposite*. It's an attempt
to assert your true maturity, your true masculinity, your
true power. I think the young woman provides the
measure of ourselves that we think *we've earned*, and
which mature women withhold from us. They won't give
us the respect, and they won't give us the surrender, and
they won't give us the ego-flattering imagery we crave.
That's it, man, they won't give it to you!

This, then, is the single most seductive reason for the appeal of the nubile girl: A yielding innocent on whom a man
can project whatever fantasy he craves, she makes him feel
not merely potent, but also omnipotent. A soothing balm
indeed. Where else, after all, can the aging male find a sex-

ual partner who will offer applause and adulation without demanding reciprocal attentions? Who will satisfy his emotional needs without requiring him to cater to hers? Only the young can afford to be so selfless.

IV *Changing Sexual Responses*

Applied to sexual matters, numbers have caused much needless misery. Most of us are familiar with the statistics which show that the male attains his sexual peak at eighteen, and declines steadily thereafter. But does this mean that a man's sexual functioning is really impaired by the time he is in his forties?

The answer is No. This somber emphasis continually placed on the male's inevitable "decline" has been extremely misleading. It is more accurate to talk about the sexual *changes* that occur with aging, and it is vital that they not be misinterpreted.[11]

What are these changes? First, a man's energy and vigor normally diminish as he ages. Therefore just as he does not expect to run as fast now, so he should not expect his sexual performance to be characterized by the same physical energy as it was earlier. Once a man is past forty his erection will take longer to achieve—minutes perhaps, as compared to seconds in his youth. It may not be as full or firm as when he was younger, and at the end of intercourse his penis will return to a relaxed state much more quickly than it used to. Also, it will probably take him considerably longer than in the past to obtain another erection. There will be a reduction in seminal fluid, and some men may notice that they ejaculate with less force.

All these changes are quite natural, and none should be cause for concern. True, the force and frequency of the male orgasm is affected by aging, but the erective response is not. A man should know that he need *never* lose his ability to attain an erection. Equally important, he must understand that his responses now resemble those traditionally considered feminine: After forty his sexual pleasure changes from a strongly genital sensation to a more sensuously diffused experience, and he will require greater and more prolonged stimulation to achieve an erection.

Kaplan points out that cultural conditioning plays a role in the way both male and female sexual patterns shift over time. A woman's responses have generally been determined primarily by psychic factors, a man's by physical ones. Thus, while the double standard victimizes both sexes, it does so at different times of life. Women are scarred most severely in their youth, when they are more strongly prohibited than men from obtaining sexual satisfaction. Their apparent sexual flowering around forty merely reflects a long process of shaking off old inhibitions. Men, on the other hand, were allowed more sexual freedom in their youth—but only on the condition that they regard sex as a strictly physical urge.

Therefore, just when women are recuperating from the double standard, men begin to feel its devastating effects: At mid-life they must adjust to the fact that their sexuality is becoming more dependent on psychic factors and that they now need more erotic stimulation, more emotional reassurance.

If a man suffers from penis *angst* when he can no longer perform like "an all-time fucking machine," it is not because aging has destroyed his sexual ability or caused a "decline." It is because he has been taught to value performance over pleasure and to detach sexuality from self—which handicaps him severely at this stage of life when he must rely increasingly on fantasy and feelings to excite his sexual desire.

Ask an American male what turns him on, and he might say, "big tits, long legs, a well-rounded ass." Or "a fresh young face, a firm body, a braless bounce." But unguarded emotions? Few men would call that sexy. At mid-life, however, adjustments should be made. Those men who continue to regard sex as genital combat will be grief-stricken by their physical losses. They may even arrange their own erotic death, by gradually withdrawing from sex or retreating into impotence. Others, even those determined to enjoy their sexuality in full, must learn to break down the barrier of emotional constriction. One man candidly describes the difficulties:

I think in our day we have promoted fucking from a dirty and sort of secret pastime to a publicly endorsed indoor sport or health exercise, but we haven't accompanied this with any particular release to the fantasies.

Most men are just too embarrassed to do it. To take

out your cock and stick it in somebody, *that's* not too hard to do. But to go through this whole thing where you insist the girl has a blindfold on, you tie her up, put her in weird clothes, or whatever the fantasy demands, it's embarrassing. It's idiotic. It's crazy. See, it doesn't belong to this sophisticated, conscious, moral good guy. You feel *vulnerable*. You don't want to expose it.

That's typically what they did in whorehouses. They went in and made all these crazy demands, right? Because you couldn't face it with anybody you "respected." In quotes. It's that whole thing of the girl you respect and the girl you want to fuck. The girl you *respect*, you can't imagine putting her through the paces of your fantasy life—that's all. In a whorehouse you never see them again, and even if they didn't like it, who the hell are they to complain?

Anyway, a fantasy doesn't want simply to be *indulged*, because that's childish—which is why a whorehouse wouldn't appeal to me. The goal is to find someone who wants the same thing you want. It's the locking together of these mutually entertained fantasies where the real satisfaction and excitement lies, I think. It isn't in frequency or technique. What's that? Nonsense. I think it's the image. And when you hit that erotic image, just thinking about it can get you excited.

Like when women lose control and go completely out of their head, it's very exciting to a man because he feels he's *produced* that effect in her—and it can also help release some of his inhibitions. But men don't lose control like that very often. It's happened to me very rarely, and it's frightening. Definitely frightening.

I remember one time I was with a girl who said, "Well, what do you want?" And I said, "Well, I guess what I really want you to do is suck me off." And she said, "That's the simplest thing in the world," and she got down and put her mouth on my penis and started sucking me. And suddenly I began to feel this unprecedented sexual sensation. Like a tremendous stirring that started down in my feet, and it seemed to be rising up my legs, up my diaphragm, up my whole body. Like a tremendous force, a tremendous energy. It was just . . . it was *alarming*. It was loss of control, and I remember I began screaming. I was just panicking.

It only happens, I think, when defenses aren't up. Like with this girl the fact that we hadn't taken our clothes off was very significant. I'm much more relaxed in my clothes, and when I get naked I get clothed on an emotionally defensive level. So it was a combination of being dressed, and it was in the morning—which is the "wrong" time!—and there was no preparation. It was totally spontaneous. There hadn't been a chance to get the whole context of "Now we're going to screw" into play. And so before I could get all my emotional rivets in the holes, the sensation got too strong for the restraints. It was a fantastic thing, a very strong sensation. But it was also a fantasy. An image. Here was this girl kneeling down sucking me off!

There's no question that women are much more abandoned than men. That's the most impressive thing, sexually, about women. They get much more out of screwing than men do. I believe that. They experience it deeper, longer, and are much better able to deal with it. You don't see a lot of men moaning and raving and flailing, you know what I mean? I know a lot of guys who have tapes of women they're screwing, and the women are screaming and talking and babbling, but you don't hear one word from the guy. You don't hear one sound. They're just busy grinding away there—the little pile-drivers at work!

My feeling about most men is that they have a very impoverished emotional life. And their sexual life is basically a lot of physical rubbing and grunting and fucking away—but they're not getting off at all. On the intellectual and achievement level, I think they're quite formidable. But when it comes to the sensual and the emotional, they're cripples.

People confuse the fact that most men can easily attain an orgasm with potency. But just being able to ejaculate—*that's* no measure of any emotional thing, you know? You can pop off and hardly feel anything.

A carry-over from the work ethic, the idea of the sex act as a disciplined performance is destructive. Controlled efficiency in corporate boardrooms produces cold-blooded fucking in suburban bedrooms. It can even lead to impotence.

Despite some liberating changes in our society, Masters and Johnson confirm that our sex lives remain contaminated by the principle that work is virtuous, whereas play is wasteful and sinful. The consequences vary. Religious persons tend to view work as redemptive while regarding sex as intended more for procreation than pleasure. Others, less religious, may claim to value sex as an important dimension of their life, but actually treat it like work—as a task in which performance can be measured and mastered.

Contrary to popular belief, these researchers claim that a couple's sex life improves during vacations not simply because they have more time and energy, or are less distracted by routine worries, but because they are freed temporarily from our culture's demand to put productivity before pleasure. It is the spontaneous expression of feelings—doing whatever they feel like at any given moment—that dramatically changes the erotic atmosphere.

The toll taken by excessive self-discipline is "the most insidious element carried over from the work ethic to the sexual relationship," say Masters and Johnson: "Let a man at the office keep his emotions under tight rein eight hours a day while he concentrates on getting his work done . . . and the transition to becoming an individual who acts according to spontaneous and authentic feeling becomes difficult. For some persons it becomes impossible."[12]

But in their view it is precisely the part of themselves that men are conditioned to control at work—"their true emotions at any given moment"—which must be free of discipline for a sexual relationship to flourish. This conviction is shared by other authorities, Kaplan among them. Speaking of her work as a sex therapist, she comments, "It is heartbreaking to see the unnecessary pain and constriction suffered by couples who cannot shed their defensive armors."[13]

Although it is true that the quanity of a man's orgasms is somewhat reduced by aging, it is also true that the quality of his sexual pleasure can be increased. Shedding his defensive armor is the most important task facing the mid-life male struggling to adjust to his changing sexuality. Now he must reclaim both the fantasies and the feelings that society has taught him to deny, and summon the courage to become emotionally vulnerable—for this is the key to his enriching his sexuality as he ages.

In other words, the way for a man to stop feeling penis *angst* is to start feeling other things. Sexual potency after forty depends on renouncing the need for conquest and surrendering the heart.

Chapter 8   The Quaking Marriage

I *Existential Divorce*

Mid-life is the time when marriages frequently quake or break, the time when husbands behave strangely and wives need more than epithets to survive. "You start itching from a rash of sameness," complained one restless husband. "I guess anytime your life gets too predictable there's something like death about it."

In recent years the divorce rate in America has been rising steadily, and even long-term marriages are no longer immune. Today, in fact, the middle years are being identified as a major crisis point for marriage: One quarter of the marriages that have lasted fifteen years or more now end in divorce.

The men most likely to be immune from marital traumas in their forties are those who married late in life, including those recently remarried for a second or third attempt; and those who have first marriages that are still thriving—either because the two people have remained warmly in touch with one another, or because they have worked out a coolly pragmatic arrangement to which both partners subscribe. (Men who have never married or remained single after a divorce have other problems during this period, as do homosexuals, who face their own sort of mid-life loneliness and desperation.)

In general, no simple formulas exist to predict what turn a marriage will take at this stage of life. Adultery is certainly no predictor since, given the ubiquity of philandering in our society, the man who has been monogamous until now is probably the exception, not the rule. Moreover, extramarital affairs have strangely varying consequences: Some couples wind up divorcing because of infidelity, either the husband's or the wife's, while others transform their relationship into a close and truthful one for the first time after an affair.

At mid-life, however, men and women change, and so do the dynamics of their relationship. Suddenly the old and familiar, the tried and tested, are no longer enough. Both sexes want something different, something more—a desire that dramatically increases the likelihood of an affair's becoming more emotionally consuming, and therefore more disruptive, than it might have earlier.

Adultery aside, when a marriage of long duration falls apart, the most common cause of conflict is different rates of growth. In time some people outgrow each other, or grow in opposite directions. Each needs more room to experiment and stretch. The third person in the triangle is not another man or woman, but an evolving self, which now feels suffocated within the confines of traditional marriage.

"Existential divorce" is the phrase used to describe the break-up caused by one, or both, partner's concluding their marriage no longer has meaning. This sort of rupture is usually devoid of dramatic clashes: no violent fights, no intrusive lovers, no major differences in background. Rather, the choice made at twenty just doesn't seem valid, or rewarding, at forty.

In the classic situation it is the man who starts to chafe and stomp. After years of dedicating himself to working hard and getting ahead, he has tasted power, won recognition, and changed in the process. Suddenly he takes his eyes off the brass ring and spies a stranger in his bed: his wife. She's somwhat frayed now; cranky too, perhaps. And why not? Enlisted as an adjunct to his career, she has been confined to cooking, cleaning, and raising the kids—preoccupations that rarely promote growth or glamour. But that, of course, was the bargain they made in the 1950s, when marriages were based on conventional roles: The little woman was meant to stay at home, while the big man conquered the world.

Ironically, this bargain often backfires at mid-life when a man dumps his wife for precisely the reason he first desired her: because she subjugated herself to him. Earlier he adored her being docile and devoted, but now he finds her merely dull. He has grown and she hasn't. Suddenly he wants a different kind of woman—someone less dependent, say, someone with more pizzazz. A playmate, peer, or partner—but certainly not a Mom.

How does a man in this situation feel about the marriage he used as a bridge between childhood and maturity? And how does he account for its collapse? Consider the case of Michael B., the president of an industrial conglomerate who divorced his wife after fifteen years. These are his reflections:

When Shirley and I got married we were just too young. She was nineteen and I was twenty-one—and we hadn't really been formed as people. What happened is that we grew up *after* we were married and moved in totally different directions. On the surface, the whole relationship was terribly simple. Underneath is what's complicated.

Shirley's drives were all centered about me. She had some solid creative drives, but she put them down because she felt exercising her own life ambitions would be taking away from what we had together. She became a nonperson, essentially. And so it became an enormously selfish way of life for me. Whatever I wanted was okay. Whatever I determined was the way it was, and there was never any resistance.

And what happened over the years as we grew up was that we had no communication whatsoever. I became lazy. I never communicated anything about my own thoughts or about business—unless I chose to. I didn't share anything in that sense. And my work was my life because I *loved* it.

Actually I remember almost all the years as being content. Till the day I walked out we never fought—because we didn't communicate. After about eight years I started to have an occasional affair. None of them were that important, but they were *all* with bright, intelligent working girls. They were people I could talk to and there was an honesty in the relationships.

So I was living a life which some men would think is the best of all possible lives: a happy home life, two lovely children, and being able to manipulate with the least amount of guilt. Shirley may well have suspected, but she would never have acknowledged my affairs.

But I slowly became aware that I wasn't going to be

able to keep this up, that I wasn't really happy. It was guilt, I guess, and a feeling it wasn't fair to her or to the children. And the pressures had built up. She would want to come on trips and I resisted her. Things like that. And we weren't talking much. She knew something was wrong.

I don't really know what led up to it, but finally there was just so *nothing* to talk about at home that I told her I had tried, and it wasn't working, and that I was leaving. I said we had no common interest except her interest in our home—and my being happy. But we *shared* nothing. It was very difficult when I told her, and it came as a shock. We talked it out, but I have never really been able to satisfy her as to why. I didn't dislike her, and I don't to this day. But she simply turned out to be a person I couldn't open up with. I couldn't share. There was no intimacy whatsoever. None. And that's hard to explain to someone.

Because of the children I stayed for another three months, and we got some advice on how to handle them. It was very depressing for a while, and there was a lot of upset with the kids, but we finally got the divorce about six months later.

Now when I look back on my marriage, I feel regret mostly—regret that I wasted my life like that. Coldly. Those were fifteen years of growing and learning which should have been shared. I just didn't have the right person to share them with. And what I really did was run away from my *life* to my *business*, which fulfilled all the appetites I had to have filled.

Except it left me less than a whole person.

II *An Explosive Sexual Reversal*

Today many other American men in their middle years are discovering that having devoted all their energies to work has left them less than whole. Michael describes himself as a man whose business was his life, a man who earlier refused to communicate his thoughts to his wife. But, approaching forty, he complains about the lack of intimacy, sharing, and openness in his marriage. Now his needs have a new dimension.

His is a common reaction, related to the mid-life phenomenon of a man's evolving to a new emotional place, a place where he is likely to be confronting his own repressed or atrophied feelings, a place where he suddenly feels lonely and in need of love. This new yearning for intimacy occurs because in the normal course of development men are beginning, as the Yale group suggest, to discover the softer, more sentimental part of themselves—the part that was ignored earlier.

But what is happening to women?

There is a growing body of evidence from social scientists which suggests that a sexual reversal takes place at this stage of life, a reversal that is likely to be explosive. At mid-life men and women seem to be switching gears and heading in opposite directions. Intent on living out the potentials and pleasures they had relinquished in earlier years, men begin to move toward the passivity, sensuality, and tenderness previously repressed in the service of productivity. Women experience the opposite: Now that their nurturing function is no longer needed, they often become more autonomous, aggressive, and cerebral.[1]

Jung claimed that their reversal entailed a fundamental psychic shift whereby men become more "feminine" at around forty, women more "masculine." "We might compare masculinity and femininity and their psychic components to a definite store of substances of which, in the first half of life, unequal use is made," Jung stated. "A man consumes his large supply of masculine substance and has left over only the smaller amount of feminine substance, which must now be put to use. Conversely, the woman allows her hitherto unused supply of masculinity to become active."

Pessimistic about the consequences of this shift, Jung predicted trouble: "Very often these changes are accompanied by all sorts of catastrophes in marriage, for it is not hard to imagine what will happen when the husband discovers his tender feelings and the wife her sharpness of mind."[2]

Despite having been formulated some years ago, Jung's metaphor is oddly apt today. Many couples now in their forties are clashing in precisely this way. What this mid-life switch means in contemporary terms is that men of this generation are trying to break out of the masculine mystique at the same time that women are seeking to break out of the feminine mystique.

Having come of age at a time when the division of labor implicit in conventional sex roles dictated that men and women be "halved," prohibited from cultivating traits traditionally labeled masculine or feminine, both sexes begin to discover a forfeited self they now want to develop. At mid-life men are groping toward increased self-awareness and more meaningful personal relationships. They are trying to get in touch with impacted feelings and develop the emotional side of their personality, an effort that sometimes leads to creative expression, sexual experimentation, or even to love affairs.

At the same time, a counterpoint to that struggle is occurring among women, who are trying to forge a more complete identity by going back to school, getting a job, or acquiring money and influence. Having been imprisoned too long in a role that restricted them to nurturing their husband and children, they are seeking validation in the outside world.

With rigid sex roles breaking down rapidly, younger men and women will probably develop less narrow ways in the future and not awaken later to find half a "self" badly neglected. But couples now in their forties, caught in the middle of confusing social changes, are likely to find their marriage threatened as each partner struggles to grow and change.

Since two people rarely manage to self-actualize in total harmony, one or both partners sometimes feel that to grow whole they must split. Propelled by the illusion that they can become free of internal shackles by breaking away from external commitments, they insist on leaving the incubator that sheltered them in earlier years. Divorce becomes a necessary rite of passage into full adulthood.

Even if a split does not occur at this stage of life, however, both men and women often feel an urge to break the stranglehold of a well-ordered life, at least temporarily, an urge to relieve the dreariness of dutiful behavior and dutiful sex. Such wishes are understandable. Having been brought up in the conformist 1950s when rules abounded, this generation of men and women were never encouraged to be free, spontaneous, or playful. When they begin to realize that they have spent a lifetime doing what others want, they suddenly yearn to express forbidden impulses and follow where they lead. Mid-life is the time when both sexes become more concerned with pleasing themselves than with placating others.

III *Women at Forty: A New Toughness*

Today there is a new marital scenario that centers on women who feel less than whole, women who are discovering that they too want something "more." Influenced by the feminist movement, women are becoming increasingly assertive, and their demands are causing additional problems for the American male at a time when he may feel that coping with his own mid-life turmoil is quite enough.

Today women are insisting on having their needs and desires satisfied in totally new ways, and they are doing so in unprecedented numbers, with unprecedented force. Even in their forties women are throwing down the gauntlet. They are saying, "Don't put me down" or "Stop criticizing me" or "Don't treat me like a child." They are insisting that their men be more passionate lovers, more affectionate mates, more giving fathers. They are pushing them into marital or psychiatric counseling, marching them to sex clinics, and pursuing extramarital affairs for their own pleasure. They are forcing their husbands to grow emotionally—or else.

Today women are leaving home to travel, lecture, attend conventions, find a job, resume their education—or enjoy time alone. They are asking for separations to "do their own thing." They are initiating divorces because they are unhappy, or want their freedom, or simply no longer wish to be married. And they are doing so without another man waiting in the wings, and despite their inexperience as wage earners. Some women are giving their husbands custody of the children. Other women are leaving their families to join the swelling tide of "runaway wives."

Today women are risking themselves and their marriages for what they want, and their grown-up growth spurts are challenging many an astonished husband. The first dislocation that seems to threaten the male often occurs when a woman moves into the world of work, no matter how slight her first step. Though a husband may couch his objections in reasonable terms, his opposition may actually be quite arbitrary.

"A lot of guys resent losing the service," observes Dr. Ian Alger. "They are so tyrannical and used to being served that they hate making it possible for somebody else to live a little more fully."

Or a man may be afraid that once his wife enters the larger world, a whole Pandora's box will burst open and she'll go wild sexually. Alger tells of a professor who sought therapy because he felt anxious about his wife's returning to school. Since she was meeting more people and forming new friendships, he was convinced she would soon start having affairs—and he would lose her. But after he worked through his own insecurity, the marriage actually improved. "When he stopped pressing her and just let her be as free as she wanted, she felt much closer to him," says Alger.

Many comparable situations are not resolved as happily. The issue of a woman's infidelity is still an inflammatory one for men who have the "good girl/bad girl" syndrome embedded in their psyche. Determined that their wife be forever monogamous, they become outraged if she is not. When a man's sense of being violated is so intense that he is unable to surmount his anger, a woman's infidelity can become the trigger event that destroys the marriage. As an example, Beth and Ernie are divorcing after sixteen years of marriage primarily because of his horrid reaction to her brief affair. Beth describes what happened:

Ernie was from a lower-middle-class Jewish family, and became an executive who moved up very fast—and that kind of scared him. He was vice president of one of the largest furniture companies in the country. But he was so intent on earning money and being successful that he would just come home and collapse. There was nothing left.

I've never had a career, but I was always doing something. I worked in an office, and a nursery school, and I studied dancing and singing and acting. I was constantly going to classes. Gradually the marriage bit got very boring, and I was very unhappy. Our sexual relationship had been pretty good when we first got married, but then life got to be such a bore that the sex wasn't very exciting.

I had an old boyfriend who kept reappearing in my life, and I finally decided to have an affair with him. I had fantasized this mad, passionate affair and built up a big thing in my mind. And then I saw him twice—and I was sorry I had *bothered* with it. What I wanted was some intellectual companionship and a change from a boring marriage, but that wasn't it—and I didn't pursue it.

But I told Ernie about it. Kind of as a danger signal. "Look at what's happening!" It shook him up tremendously, and *that* is what started the ball rolling.

Within a month—although I didn't find out about it until later—he started sleeping with a young hat-check girl. That summer I went to Spain to study dancing for a few weeks, and when he came to meet me I barely recognized him. He had gained forty-two pounds, and he was very distressed and upset. He told me about this girl, and said he was going to *leave* me. That it was all over! And I was just in a state of shock. We spent a month together in Europe, but it was really bad. He was drinking most of the time, and I just couldn't respond to him. We had no sex at all during that time.

Anyway, when we got home I became very sick. I got a period that didn't go away and an inflamed ovary, and I was bedridden. He stayed with me for about seven weeks, and it was *terrible*. We hardly spoke, and he was running back and forth between me and this girl. And I was bleeding all the time, and terrified.

He said to me, "I'll never love anyone the way I love you. But I can't go on in a marriage where I'm constantly worrying that you're going to find someone else and run off." And I said, "Ernie, I'll never forgive you if you leave me like this. I love you and I care about you—but that will be a breach that can never be repaired."

But he said he couldn't help it. He was so insecure about me that when I had first told him about having the affair, he had said he was going to *kill* himself. Imagine—because I slept with somebody *twice!* I don't believe for a minute that he really meant it, but he just couldn't *deal* with the whole issue. He couldn't cope with it.

I think he had arrived at a point in his life where he had to take care of himself—no matter what was happening to me. He just had to get away for his own survival. He was at a stage where he suddenly didn't know what was happening anymore. He was re-evaluating.

And of course I couldn't understand it then, and I still react to it emotionally.

We've been separated for six months now, and Ernie comes to see me and our daughter once or twice a week. He cries, and tells me that he's a fat old man. *Old*—at thirty-nine! But he won't really talk to me. He says his life is miserable, that he's sick, he can't sleep. He's not concentrating on his work the way he should, and his business is suffering tremendously. He's totally disoriented.

All he says is that he wants to live peacefully, and he doesn't want any pressure. So after we get divorced, he'll probably get married again and live a quiet kind of life. But I don't have very much hope for him in the sense that he's going to open up. Or change.

Ernie's reaction is not unique. All hell is likely to break loose because of a woman's infidelity when a man has not yet matured emotionally. Stuck in old insecurities, Ernie was so tightly controlled, his feelings so deeply suppressed, that he couldn't even express his rage appropriately. Terrified of facing painful emotions, or engaging in open conflict, he simply withdrew from the relationship. In turn, despite his having found a new girlfriend, he became increasingly despondent, developed physical symptoms, and finally sunk into a kind of muted despair.

Now on the verge of divorce at forty, Peter K. tells an even more melodramatic tale of a break-up caused by a husband's inability to forgive his wife's adultery. Unlike Ernie, Peter handled repressed feelings by exploding. Equally damaging and equally immature, his style was to rage, shout, and bully like a self-indulgent child. The trouble began shortly after he and his wife moved to Darien, Connecticut, having been married thirteen years. It was a big jump for them. Peter had just been promoted to sales manager for a chemical company; and Jill, who had done some art work earlier, was now in search of a career. She began designing desk accessories and trying to sell them, an effort that upset him:

She was calling up people for help—always men. And her work was thrusting her into the creative world of New York City, into a *man's world*. I'm just a pragmatic businessman, and I always had a strong insecurity that I wasn't the artistic, creative type I thought she preferred. I really felt threatened.

Several months later, Peter discovered that Jill was having an affair. His fury and condemnation set them both on an increasingly destructive course, as he explains:

I caught her in some outright lies—and she's not a very good liar. When I stepped on her and sort of browbeat her, she finally admitted she'd been seeing someone, and that she was in love with him. I got very upset but reacted fairly normally by saying, "*Bullshit!* You're *not* going to see him anymore. You're going to cut it out!" As I said I was going to be *very* ugly about it if it continued. I guess I was sufficiently angry to make the point, and so she said she wouldn't see him anymore. It stopped soon after that.

During our marriage I had been Joe Straight all the way. I was satisfied with our sex life at home, and though I traveled a lot I wouldn't go down to the bar and see what developed. It was a lot easier not to try than to risk being rejected.

Anyway, after I found out about her affair, things were very tense for about eight months, and there were a *lot* of recriminations. We sort of coexisted. Jill would never say she was sorry—and that really bothered me. Her explanation was that I drove her into the affair because of my insensitivity to her needs in the way I treated her. In that respect a lot of what she says is probably true, because I was very much a male chauvinist.

We probably should have gone to see someone about working on the marriage—but we didn't. I wish, in retrospect, that I could have been that grown-up about it. But I was very immature. I had always trusted her, and I took it very personally. I couldn't understand how she could do it—and I was *very* vengeful.

Their unresolved tensions soon led to a brief separation, a tenuous reconciliation, then another separation a year later. Despite having now begun his own affair, Peter started spying on his wife and discovered that she too had a lover. "I confronted her with it and really blew my cork," he recalls. "I said I was through and wanted a divorce."

Their situation then became desperate. Jill went into a depression and begged Peter to come back. After another unsatisfactory reconciliation, she attempted suicide and had to be hospitalized. Though she was treated successfully with shock therapy, Peter was unable to surmount his sense of self-righteous indignation. "She went into the hospital saying *I* was wonderful and *she* was wrong," he remarks. "But she came out as if nothing had happened, and she *hadn't* done anything wrong. I was flabbergasted and became terribly antagonistic. From then on it was downhill all the way."

During the next year they tried going to a marriage counselor, but too much damage had been done, and so they finally decided to divorce. In retrospect, Peter still cannot understand Jill's need to grow on her own terms, unrelated to him, although he recognizes how he himself has changed:

When I look back and try to see what happened, knowing a little bit more about myself now, I think we both satisfied some neurotic need in each other—and as long as that was in balance we could continue being "the happy couple." I think moving to Darien and my starting to be successful upset the balance. It made Jill feel insecure and in need of a career. And I think she had the affair because I started developing some confidence in myself.

She thinks I treated her very badly, but most of it goes back to a period when I admit I was being a shit. I wasn't doing it intentionally, but I didn't know any better. I didn't start to grow up until I was thirty-five. And yet I still want to be married to the person I *originally* married. And I still feel deep down if she could just straighten herself out we could have a great life together.

I'm just happy I found out that I was heading down the wrong path—a path of more of the same. More attempts to be successful, more competition, more anxiety. But no goals and no self-awareness. Somewhere along the line I lost a lot of my ambition. Maybe I suddenly realized that without a family, what the hell does money and position mean? I was success-oriented, but I didn't have any goals. I *still* don't, but I'm hoping to find some.

One of the things that has changed is that for the first time in my life I feel I have *friends*. Before I just had people I was friendly with. Now I have close relationships—male and female. And it's a genuine interest and caring, which at this stage of my life is very important to me.

I don't think people ever really mature until they've had some hard times. Now I feel as if I've been going through a soap opera for the last five years. And I think all the pain has caused me to grow and to change.

IV *Men at Forty: A New Tenderness*

Like Peter, many men become more interested in meaningful relationships at mid-life, less preoccupied with success and achievement. Their values become more humanistic, more expressive. They develop a deeper rapport with their children, warmer friendships with both men and women. Some switch careers, change the focus of their work, or get involved with philanthropic or political causes that bring them into closer contact with people. Others begin to paint or sculpt or write. All these changes relate to the natural evolution of a man's inner self, an evolution that frequently generates a new tenderness.

At the same time, however, these emotional stirrings can threaten the old détente between marriage and adultery. Before, if a man had affairs he was generally careful to prevent their jeopardizing the life structure he had built for himself. But now he is questioning that whole structure, and after years of harnessing his emotions in order to realize his ambitions, he is beginning to discover that he has an improverished inner life with needs and fantasies that have never been nourished.

The result? Suddenly the man who had previously engaged only in detached, perfunctory extramarital affairs, or juggled two lives calmly, or never even considered cheating at all, finds himself at forty yearning for something romantic and consuming, something more rewarding than mere fucking around.

The mid-life man is ripe for love. Ironically, if he finds it he often panics. Accustomed to self-discipline and denial, he is terrified by the loss of control and the feeling of vulnerability that accompany unbridled passion. Falling in love can be a disturbing experience for the aging male who has always kept his feelings under wraps, his affairs under control. The new emotions are sometimes too hot to handle for the man taught to preserve his cool.

The case of forty-year-old Edwin Gottesman, profiled in Morton Hunt's *The Affair*, is a good illustration of this phenomenon. The son of uneducated immigrant parents, Edwin was a shopping-center developer in Washington, D.C., who had been married since age twenty-two. Wealthy and successful, he was living contentedly in a lovely suburban home with his wife and two children until he began doing business with a group of Philadelphia investors. When he discovered that these men were all having affairs while away from home, he was shocked at first—and then jealous. After several months of fantasizing, he began to cautiously romance a young secretary whom he had met through a client.

From the first, this liaison both delighted and disturbed Edwin. He regarded Jennifer as an "ignorant low-class girl" who failed to match his wife, Betsy, in looks, intelligence, or sexual responsiveness. But Jennifer enchanted him nonetheless. And although he had always regarded money, self-development, and his family's welfare as his primary concerns, these were all put aside after he met Jennifer. "She became the most important thing," he said, "because I liked the way I acted and felt when I was with her."[3]

During the next year their affair intensified. But as Edwin's behavior became increasingly impulsive—leading him to cancel business appointments to be with Jennifer, or rush out to call her from phone booths late at night—he realized he was dangerously possessed. "For a man like me, the whole thing was crazy, absolutely crazy. I had the best wife you could want, a good life, and I had been making a hundred thousand a year, and here I was letting my business fall apart and making only a half or a third that much, and ignoring my kids and my wife, and taking more and more chances. . . . But I wouldn't look at the facts; I felt I was living the best and most exciting life possible, and I didn't ask myself any questions because I didn't have any answers."[4]

As Jennifer grew more petulant and demanding, and as

their fights became stormier, Edwin resolved to get out—but with only half a mind. And so their affair, marked by blow-ups and reconciliations continued for a second year. When Jennifer finally announced she was moving to New York, Edwin was furious at first, then relieved. But his relief was short-lived. Interviewed a year later, he seemed restless and dissatisfied, still puzzled by what happened:

> Betsy herself is much happier these days, but I'm not. I'm contented—but I'm never *happy*, the way I used to be when I was seeing Jennifer. . . . The things I used to do! Rushing around playing tennis, taking sailing lessons, hiring airplanes! The fighting, the drinking, the love-making. The lies, the chances I took, the loving things I did that I never knew I had in me. I would have done anything for her, and yet she was no good—a total mess, a complete misfit, not even a great lay. But she made my heart beat fast, she made something happen in me. . . .
>
> But if my wife is so marvelous, why isn't she enough for me? I wish I knew. She loves me and I love her, and it's very nice, very comforting. But it leaves me feeling middle-aged and settled, and I'm not willing to accept that. Yet I don't want anything like the Jennifer business again, so I run after women I don't care about. I play the game, I chase them, I get laid, I go home feeling good for a little while. . . . But the truth is, I'm not as happy as a man should be who has everything I have. Go figure it out.[5]

The reasons for Edwin's confusion become clear when his predicament is seen in terms of the mid-life crisis. At forty he had already achieved success, but with no new goals in mind he was ready for adventure, also ready to release the softer parts of himself, which had lain dormant during his years of "making it." Despite his failure to understand why he fell so deeply for Jennifer when she was neither beautiful nor bright nor sexy, it was never really *her* qualities that had attracted him, but the qualities she brought out in *him*.

Reflected through Jennifer's youthful eyes, Edwin was transformed from a plodding businessman into an ardent and protective lover. She helped to release his spontaneous, tender side, long buried in an excessively rigid personality. Elated with his new self, he then ignored the responsibilities that had always consumed him and gambled recklessly with everything he had worked so hard to achieve.

The tragedy is that Edwin was unable to grow or change after his affair ended, unable to draw on his new capacity for feeling to revitalize his marriage or alter his direction. Instead, he seems to have entombed his loving, playful self, retreating into joyless sexual pursuits and a constricted way of life. And although his choice may not have been conscious, it was clearly influenced by the terror his dramatic shift inspired: Having changed from an overly controlled man into an overly impulsive one, a temporary metamorphosis that is common among men who have never been in touch with their emotions, Edwin was eager to put the lid back on his feelings lest they cause more trouble. Beneath his middle-aged mask he mourns, not Jennifer, but the death of his own fleetingly awakened emotional self.

V *Letting Each Other Grow*

Whether or not a husband and wife hurdle the stresses imposed by the mid-life sexual reversal will depend on many factors: How strongly are they still bound together by loving feelings? Is their sexual relationship mutually satisfying? How deep is the hostility between them? Equally important: How much loyalty do they feel for each other and for family life? What does each expect from the marriage and from a marital partner? What does each imagine is possible in another relationship? And how much is one, or both, willing to risk to get something better?

In general, however, the survival of a marriage at this stage of life hinges on this key question: How much can each partner let the other grow without feeling unbearably threatened?

With the exception of couples who are emotionally disengaged from each other, and therefore relatively indifferent to their partner's changes, one person's growth will usually cause some disruption in the marital relationship. This is to be expected. What really matters in determining a couple's success or failure in letting each other grow is the extent to which they are neurotically dependent on one another.

Those who are not so neurotically intertwined can usually ride through this decade fairly easily, despite their mutual changes, and then establish a new equilibrium in their fifties that will enable them to live out the remainder of their lives as close companions. The crucial factor is that "they don't push and they don't squeeze," says Dr. Ian Alger. "For example, some women realize their husbands may be having affairs, but they aren't threatened by this. And it isn't necessary they confront the husband and make him feel guilty. On the other hand, if a man is able to accept his wife's having an affair or starting a new career, then the same thing may happen in reverse."

Nonetheless, such tolerance is often more easily preached than practiced, which means that in some situations a couple may need outside help in order to handle the perplexing changes made by a partner. Today, for instance, a man may find himself challenged by his wife in a peculiarly subtle way: She goes into psychoanalysis and then uses her therapist's perceptions to attack her mate for his emotional and sexual inadequacy.

Husbands who have gotten this double whammy are called "victims of psychotherapy" by Dr. Melvin B. Goodman, a psychiatrist who has treated many men in this dilemma. Reporting his findings on sixty-two men from the New York/Philadelphia area whose average age was forty, Goodman describes them generally as very successful businessmen and professionals.[6] Despite their ability, however, these men wind up in his office needing treatment for depression because they are being attacked so relentlessly by their wives that they have begun to see themselves as complete "failures."

Having largely withdrawn from family involvement to dedicate themselves to work, these men were all suffering from impacted feelings, says Goodman: "They were out of touch with their emotions, detached from them, constricted. You have to get them to see that they are not really so insensitive, that they *do* have feelings, and that it's not unmanly to have feelings—which most of them believed."

And how did he accomplish this? First by developing a relationship that helped to neutralize their antipsychiatric attitude, and then by encouraging them to be more emotionally expressive. "Some of the energies that have been channeled into business can be channeled into feelings," says Goodman.

"They have to *work* at it. But once they start becoming more insightful, and more sensitive to their own feelings and their wife's feelings, then it's carried over from the treatment into the family."

In order to improve their marriages, however, Goodman also found it necessary to use couple therapy and to help the wives as well. The woman's becoming a person in her own right was essential to reducing her rage against her husband and making their time together as a couple more gratifying. By and large, says Goodman, these upper-middle-class women were discovering that neither cars nor country clubs, furs nor jewels, could compensate for their lack of self-esteem. Thus his efforts were aimed at reducing the woman's total dependency on her husband for intellecutal and emotional gratification, and helping her find her own identity, which often meant returning to school or going to work.

Goodman's findings are significant. What he is suggesting, and what other authorities in the helping professions confirm, is that mid-life marriages need not be destroyed when men and women begin to move in opposite directions. To the contrary, as each partner grows and changes in an effort to become more whole—the man by becoming more expressive, the woman more independent—their relationship is actually strengthened. Without such movement, in fact, both persons will stagnate and so will their marriage.

Which is not to say that the road toward transforming a long-term marital relationship is smooth or painless. Achieving a new balance that accommodates the changes of both partners can be a searing experience—especially when it is precipitated by a major crisis, like the revelation of a love affair.

As an example, Jonathan B. talks candidly about the months of turmoil, fighting, and confusion that he and his wife, Lily, went through after sixteen years of marriage. His going into psychotherapy led to the birth and evolution of his emotional self, and then to his falling in love with another woman. In the meantime Lily was changing too, becoming more serious, intellectual, and intent on a career.

A classic case of mid-life reversal, their separate changes led to some violent clashes and then to a totally transformed relationship. Jonathan describes what happened:

Two years ago Lily and I were still maintaining a superficially placid relationship, but underneath we were really getting more and more estranged, and anguished. Finally we both recognized that we weren't communicating with each other. There was no fighting, and we loved each other, but we couldn't get across to one another. So we decided together to seek psychiatric help. After a few false starts, I got involved in group therapy—which was extremely helpful in opening me up, and getting me to recognize emotions and problems within myself that I had refused to see or deal with before. I also started to realize how much of a sham my marriage was.

I became much more able to open myself and talk to people—and it was very noticeable to everybody. My personality changed on the social level. Where I had been uptight and hard to approach and snobbish, I became very free and easy. There was also a definite change in Lily. In her twenties she was a bubbly, vivacious, gregarious young girl. But in her thirties, although she was an extremely attractive woman, she wasn't so approachable. Also, she had begun working for a graduate degree—and was very serious about her career.

We reversed—and it frightened her, I think. We made commitments to work on our marriage, but I never really followed through. Instead, my opening up in the group was almost directly related to my becoming emotionally involved with another woman for the first time.

Nora was an enormously sympathetic woman who made me feel very comfortable, very successful as a man. The main contrast I felt was an overwhelming emotional vibration. She was very, very obviously in love with me, and very demonstratively so, and I began to feel very strongly about her. I was telling her I was in love with her, but I was also telling her I wouldn't leave my family. And at home I didn't feel that I *didn't* love my wife, but I didn't feel the same emotional pull. I became much less attentive and more distracted.

It finally came to a crisis after about six months when I felt just unable to handle the two situations anymore. I found myself in a turmoil—and I couldn't continue carrying on what was developing into a real double life.

The normal thing might have been to say to my wife,

"Hey, it's just all over between us, and I'm leaving. Good-bye." But instead I went to talk to my therapist, and she said, "I can't really advise you. But if you think you might still possibly want to save the marriage, go home and tell your wife the truth about everything." And I said that was quite a tall order, and the therapist said, "Yes, it *is* a very tall order, and it's very dangerous. It might kill the marriage."

So I went home that night, and after some fencing I unloaded the whole thing! My wife's initial reaction was that she still wanted to be married to me, and she would give me time to work out my feelings, and be patient. My feelings were I didn't know *what* I wanted, and I was in love with another woman!

That talk precipitated her coming back the next night and saying that since I had been honest with her, she would be honest with me. And she told me that she had had several affairs—all with men who were our *friends*. One was even a close friend, and that was a very tough thing for me to take. These talks were extremely emotional, extremely packed. But I always walked away with the feeling—and so did Lily—that, well, we've unburdened all this. Let's start to build something that makes sense now that we're really telling each other how we feel about the most difficult and intimate parts of our lives.

That was in May. During the summer I was very confused and ambivalent. Extremely confused. I told Lily I wanted to see Nora again until I could figure out where I was at, and that maybe we should separate. But she said No. So while the kids were at camp we went into a period that was extremely painful for me, and I'm sure for both women, where I would with Lily's knowledge see Nora several times a week. It became untenable for everybody. It was *impossible*.

By this time, too, Lily and I no longer had a placid relationship! That was broken by those few nights of unburdening ourselves. After that we had some actual *physical* fights, and we were much quicker to criticize each other and be emotional. Also, our sex life had improved immediately after that. Immediately. But during those months of going back and forth I was feeling like I didn't know *where* the hell I was.

Finally I stopped seeing Nora. I sent her on a trip, to get her away from me. But I resented myself for doing it, and I resented Lily for pressuring me to do it. And after the kids came home from camp, the resentment was there to be seen. It was very oppressive. I also realized I had a lot of unresolved problems with Lily's past, and I hadn't really accepted it, whereas she had decided the marriage was what she wanted, and that whatever she had done before was either a mistake—or at least she was *through* with that phase of her life. And now she was looking for a real commitment and a real relationship on a mature level.

So when we hadn't progressed after a few more weeks, we decided mutually that I should move out of the house until I made up my mind. *Really* made up my mind. I didn't know what I was doing at that point, except I hadn't solved anything and I was just hurting everyone by living there. And I felt that if I got out and separated myself from it, maybe I could come to some decision.

I moved into an apartment, but I didn't publicize the fact that I was separated. I didn't really *act* like a free man. And although I saw Nora I told her I was trying to sort things out—and it would be a very rough period. I started withdrawing into myself, and I decided I was acting very immature. That I had let the cat out of the bag in the first place, so it was my responsibility to make a definite choice. And I painfully came to the conclusion that I belonged in the marriage, and I should commit myself to it. The main thing was I really couldn't make a clean break of it. I saw myself covering up things, and I thought, hey, if that's the way I'm acting I don't really *want* to start again and make a new life.

I also realized that I definitely had deep feelings for Lily. I realized I was very uncomfortable leaving my children, and that being with them a lot wasn't the same as living with them. Although I could bend it, and cheat on it, when it came right down to breaking the marriage structure, I *couldn't*. And so I decided—after about six weeks—to go back home. Not just to try, but to *make* the marriage work.

I've learned a lot about myself. I've learned to be a little more honest about what my real motives are, and what's driving me. And I've learned that I'm capable of real emotion. I haven't been able even to this day to sort out all my emotions, but I think they're *real* for the first time. Before I never had deep feelings that really, really troubled me with regard to other people—and that's a very maturing thing.

I spent the supposedly best years of my life working to attain what is nothing more than material success—and when I got it, I frankly didn't think it was worth what I paid. I paid ten years of being miserable—being a nonperson. When I got to that plateau it was very empty, and yet I didn't know how to turn back to Lily. I didn't know how to reach out to her. I was afraid to, just as she was afraid to reach out to me.

One of the answers I've come to in being able to handle her past is that she didn't just go out and find some other guy and start screwing. It involved *me* in those early years, too. My strivings and my directing my life the way I did—though I might not have been able to help it—were in large part responsible for the way she acted. She has said she has no excuses for what she did—but that I just wasn't "there" for her.

In many ways Nora represented a simpler solution. Cutting away all the past, not having to carry it forward with me. Starting new with someone I cared about. A *much* simpler solution! Lily represents building amidst a lot of ruins, and doing a lot of work on my own feelings in many areas that are painful to me. Just the fact that we've opened up all this, and lived through it, and come out of it *together* and able to say, hey, we went through this and we're going to take a shot at it—I think that's probably healthier than 99 per cent of the marriages I see!

In contrast to Jung's pessimistic prediction that marital castastrophes are inevitable when men and women begin to veer in opposite directions, what many quaking mid-life marriages seem to need is for the husband to discover his tender feelings, and the wife her sharpness of mind. Despite being explosive, this sexual reversal can be a blessing in disguise for couples who want to continue growing and also want to restructure a more honest, loving relationship for their middle years.

Chapter 9   Double Bind: Generation in the Middle

I *The Pressure of Responsibilities*

"I feel like a drowning man with all these people clinging to my neck," sighed one forty-six-year-old man. "My father died of a brain hemorrhage last year, and my mother has been helpless ever since. Then my ex-wife ran off to England a few months ago, leaving our three teen-age daughters with me, which doesn't exactly thrill my present wife, since we have two small babies ourselves. And now my brother-in-law is dying of leukemia, and my sister is leaning hard on me. I feel as if I have to be a father to *everybody*, and the truth is I've never been a very good father."

This man's complaint is not a cry of self-pity but an accurate reflection of reality. For most men the responsibilities that come with being in the prime of life are truly staggering. This is the time when a man must father two generations, the young and the old. His children are becoming adults, and his parents are approaching death or dying. Suddenly he has to take care of everyone, but nobody is there to take care of him. Moreover, the challenge to become a father in the fullest sense comes not only from within his own family circle, but from the rest of society as well.

This sense of being overburdened, even overwhelmed, affects men in all economic groups. Alex R. is a forty-one-year-old lawyer who, despite his prosperity, feels deeply ambivalent about his accomplishments. "You know all the things I've always wanted to happen only started happening in the last couple of years," he said at first, describing the heady rewards. He had just realized a childhood dream by moving his family out of the city to a twelve-acre farm, still within comfortable commuting distance. His law firm's income had increased dramatically, as had some of his own investments, allowing him to become involved in new areas of work. And, seeing his knowledge and experience come to fruition, he had finally acquired a strong sense of self-confidence.

After completing this sunny summary, however, Alex switched abruptly to the darker side of his life:

> I don't want you to think that everything is pie in the sky, or sweetness and light, because that's not true. One of the things that happens to you, as your business gets more successful and you get more successful, is that you get to the point—I know I have—where you say to yourself, "I've had it with responsibilities."
>
> You get *tired* of it. You are responsible to your office, you are responsible to your wife, you are responsible to your children, you are responsible to your parents, you are responsible to your in-laws. You are responsible to *everybody!*
>
> My whole life is a series of responsibilities. Especially in my profession—you're responsible not only to your business, but to every one of your clients. And you really get to the point where you would love . . . you know, you have this little dream, wanting to go to some little island somewhere and just get *rid* of everything. Just let everybody worry about themselves, and you *stop* it.
>
> And I think that is a real problem I have. That's the other side of the coin: You have the power and you have the achievements—and you don't want them.
>
> This was a very, very difficult year for me in that, first of all, we bought the house. And moving from a 6½-room apartment where you've lived for 12 years to a farm, with the renovations and everything, is very traumatic. I always wanted that house, right? Well, now I have a house—a *big* house. But I didn't just buy a house. I really bought a way of life. A 12-acre farm—that's a way of life. We have a well, right? If a pipe on the well isn't corroded, then the electricity isn't right, or the pond has to be dredged, or you have to feed the apple trees—or this has to be done, or that. You know, it's never ending! Forget about financially. It is just a responsibility.

And then the office was extremely busy. In addition to that, my partner had an operation and was out for a couple of months during this whole period. That put *another* burden on me, because I had to cover for him and do his work, so it was a combination of a huge amount of pressures all coming at the same time. And then you have the responsibilities to your children. To your wife. *Forget it!* You really get to the point where you just want to blow your mind—get out, right? It's terrible.

These sentiments underscore the fact that part of the mid-life crisis hinges on a man's being squeezed in a viselike grip by two generations, while other demands upon him are also multiplying.

As a group, men in their middle years shoulder more personal and social responsibilities than anyone else. They feel threatened not only because they sense the tensions from both ends of the life cycle, reminders of their own waning youth, but also because they must support both ends financially. Typically they are responsible for parents whose incomes have been cut in half while their medical needs have increased; and for children who are attending college, where costs are mounting alarmingly.

In our society there is only a "fairly narrow band" of productive people who must provide for the unproductive ones, says Dr. Robert N. Butler, the director of the National Institute on Aging, who believes that much of the resentment felt by mid-life men is due to this heavy burden: Their responsibility, both individually and collectively, for the rest of the society. "They are angry at both the young and the old, and with other groups as well," says Butler, "because they see these groups getting 'all the benefits' while they, hard-pressed, pay all the bills."[1]

But the issue is not simply economic. This anger is especially intense among this generation of men because they feel as if they have *always* been in the middle, always been burdened by obligations. Taught to respect and please their parents, they were pushed prematurely toward work and duty, and thus deprived of a carefree youth of their own. Ironically, they then became the first generation of child-centered parents indoctrinated to indulge their youngsters' every wish, sacrificing their own needs and desires along the way.[2]

No wonder the handicapped generation feel cheated. Just when they expect to reap rewards for their sacrificial efforts, they find instead that their obligations are mounting, their sense of being pressured and put-upon increasing.

II *Changing Dependencies*

Like it or not, new responsibilities are often thrust upon a man during the mid-life period because of a milestone event: The death of his father. This searing experience has been described as "a scab that in no man ever heals" by author William Gibson, who wrote *A Mass for the Dead* to make peace with his own father, himself, and his sons.[3]

Freud regarded a father's death as both the most important event, and most poignant loss, in a man's life. He himself was forty when his own father died. Like many men, Freud suffered guilt for the hostility he had long felt for his father, and also began to appreciate him more. From that time forward, however, Freud surged ahead on a new path toward independence. Within the next few years his self-analysis, including dream interpretation, became increasingly systematic. And he is reported to have emerged from this period of his life "with a deep-reaching interior transformation."[4]

Not all men undergo such a radical metamorphosis. But in many instances a man's development does not really begin until he is freed from the shadow of a strong father, a release that may occur only through death.

A clothing manufacturer from Boston, Richard S., did not begin to establish any true direction until he was almost forty. Before then, although he had done traditional things like marry and raise children, his aimlessness was clearly related to the influence of his father, a dominating patriarch. After his father's death, Richard took over the family business and put his own stamp on it, separated from his wife of eighteen years, and made plans to marry the woman he had fallen in love with. He had just begun to have some sense of his own strength, as he explains:

> I had my own turf in sports, but it was a real hassle through school. I screwed around in college for three years, and then sort of drifted out of school and went into my father's business—which he wanted me to do. I

was sort of on the rebound from a really hot romance when I met my wife. She cared for me and I wanted to get out of my house, so I really drifted into getting married, too.

My whole frame of mind was drifting. I had nothing planned, no thought of where I wanted to be or what I wanted to do.

During my marriage I traveled a lot and sometimes I'd be away 100 nights a year. Every once in a while I had casual affairs, but nothing of deep involvement. At home we never had any hostility, but the marriage was unclose—an unbelievable lack of communication. I found it difficult to talk about things that were really bothering me, and Marge also ducked it. So we just never talked about a lot of things.

I met Ellen three years ago when I hired her as a designer. My father and I had a lousy relationship in the business. We really had some conflicts, which were all personality and power things. As I became more sure of myself I guess I became more threatening to him. I was trying to make some changes in the business, give it some organization. To him it was a one-man business—him, and me, and zilch. Then just about that time we found out he was sick. He had cancer.

Within the next month I got very involved with Ellen and spent a few nights every week in New York with her. I had never been involved with anybody I had really been close to before on a working basis. From that point on, all I wanted to do was be in New York and be around Ellen. And my father was dying, and I really had a torn kind of thing.

Then my father died—and it was a *relief*. The king is dead! Long live the king! I've got it all, baby!

During this period I was really riding high. I could have Ellen, and I could have Marge and my family—and they *both* really had to do what I wanted them to do. I didn't really think about the future, because I could have the best of both worlds. And I could be the image of my father. I had this uncle working for me, and my grandmother leaned on me, and I took over some of my father's charity jobs. It was really a wild scene. And I wasn't really thinking about all of this. It was just happening to me.

When my father was alive I guess I felt I couldn't compete with him. He held all the power strings. I know I was trying to live in his world, because after he died I tried to be everything he was. And then gradually I *stopped* trying to do everything he did. You know, being nice to all the people he was always nice to. It was a difficult period for me—strengthening and confusing.

I began to change from a person drifting to knowing where I wanted to be and what I wanted to be. I had a business I wanted to get together, and a personal life I wanted to get together. I've been building up the business with plans to sell it, and then move into some foreign investments. The deals are already negotiated and I've got a partnership formed. And then in the next year I'll be moving towards the divorce. It all happened, I think, because Ellen was there when something dramatic—some great change—was happening in my life.

Regardless whether a man's father is already dead or only now approaching death, the developmental challenge remains the same: If a man is to mature at mid-life he must give up his dependency on his father and assume the psychological burden of replacing him.

The difficulty in assuming full fatherhood is, of course, that it requires abandoning some very comforting fantasies. "In a way, this final taking-on of responsibility is like the last bite of the Biblical apple," says Dr. Edward Klein, a psychologist with the Yale group. "You're no longer the 'son,' the one who can't do certain forbidden things without full awareness of the consequences; you're the guy who's in charge of the whole show, the one who's entrusted to *take care* of others. The trouble is—who wants to let go of the apple."[5]

What is actually occurring at this stage of life, say the Yale group, is that a man is being forced to redefine his own role as a father, which means assuming more authority and learning how to be genuinely paternal. But this task is complicated by the fact that a man is being challenged to relinquish his own dependency at the same time that he is being confronted by new problems from his own children and from other younger people.

It takes special courage to assume this new paternal role when a man is being assaulted by reminders of his diminishing powers. To his maturing children he is no longer the omnipotent parent who can heal every hurt, conquer every care. The small child who used to gaze adoringly at a beloved father trundling him to the zoo or ball park has suddenly been transformed into a towering, terrible adolescent who glowers at him with disdain. Being caught in this generational crossfire, this double bind, is painful indeed when a man feels as if he is being undercut by his own children just when his father's death, or decline, requires him to be stronger than ever.

During adolescence the most highly charged issue for many parents, fathers especially, is that of sexual experimentation. Because sex is more open today than ever before, and more openly discussed, the repercussions are often disturbing for men who had a less permissive upbringing.

"It's a tremendous challenge," said one beleaguered father. "There's a fierce desire to say to your kid, 'No, you can't do that.' But inside there's really the agonized feeling, '*I* could never do that!' "

Suddenly many sexual matters which a man may never have questioned, nor even though about, now become topics for conversation in his household. When, for example, his teen-age daughter wants to discuss the latest magazine article on oral sex, he is likely to begin asking himself some questions about his own experience: Whether his own sexual life has been satisfying; how responsive his wife has been; and whether he himself is really a good lover. If he has in fact been unadventurous, this may be the moment that sparks a lot of internal conflicts about missing out on something.

"I knew my son was sleeping with his girlfriend," said the father of one seventeen-year-old boy, "but it didn't hit home until I discovered they'd been making love in *our* double bed when we went out. I exploded at the kid, really went berserk. It wasn't just the bed, of course. My wife was always lukewarm about sex, but I've been afraid to play around much. That incident sure changed my thinking. Now I'm wondering, Well, if my own kid is getting his rocks off, why not me?"

There is no doubt that this generation of mid-life men have trouble understanding and coping with the free-wheeling options now open to the young: sexual freedom, extensive travel, drug experimentation, prolonged schooling, exercises in self-exploration, and leisurely attempts to define work goals.

Some of the viable alternatives pursued by today's youth reflect the fact that they obviously hear the call of a different drummer. When it comes to going to college or choosing a career, many young people are making it clear that they are scornful of success and achievement as primary goals. They see work as a means rather than as an end. They want to earn money to buy land, or travel, or support some creative effort. Some want a personal sabbatical from college or graduate school to explore the world, an effort that often leads them to do manual labor—to work as truckdrivers, bartenders, carpenters, house painters, or moving men—while they make up their minds about the future.

Others, unperturbed by a pressing need to fix on career decisions, simply want to concentrate on self-awareness and enjoyment for a while. They say they are in pursuit of happiness, or personal growth, or a better understanding of other human beings. Such amorphous ambitions are not easily tolerated by fathers forced, for most of their lives, to tread a straight and narrow path bound by duty, discipline, and obligation. Thus, even though their children may not be rebelling in either an antagonistic or a self-destructive way, their simply following a nonconventional path goes deeply against the grain of an older generation's implicit faith in the work ethic.

III *Screaming for Daddy*

Generally the generation gap grows even larger when an adolescent rebels in a more radical manner than merely choosing a disapproved lifestyle. Given the many rapid changes in American society, the issues that parents must confront are more complex today than ever before. And since there is no longer a consensus on values, nor any clear-cut guidelines on how to socialize a child toward adulthood, parents often feel inadequate and confused.

These feelings increase at mid-life, when a man discovers

that it is far more traumatic to be the father of teen-agers than toddlers. Adolescents no longer rebel simply by drinking too much beer, flunking math, abusing curfews, or taking the family car for a joyride. They smoke and deal dope, get strung out on speed or heroin, shoplift and steal, or run away from home. Some disappear entirely, swallowed up by the underground drug culture or seduced by a religious cult like that of the Reverend Sun Myung Moon.

Steering a teen-ager through such treacherous waters is not easy, especially for this generation of success-oriented men who have often been too busy to pay much attention to their kids even during more placid periods. "These guys know a man doesn't make the cover of *Time* magazine because he's a good father," said one management consultant bluntly. "They may give lip-service to the sanctity of their family, but the corporate man who is really concerned with his children's development is rare indeed." Sometimes men who have been so preoccupied with work that they have largely ignored their children are dynamited out of their indifference only when a tragedy occurs.

"This is a perfect example of a mid-life crisis," said a New England psychiatrist, pointing to a telephone message marked "Urgent" from a man he described as a highly successful business executive. "My son was hurt in an accident and is dying now. Another child is very upset. Please advise," the message read. "This kind of man buys advisers when he needs them," commented the psychiatrist. "He had just recently woken up to the fact that he barely had any contact with his children. And now this."

Such heart-shattering incidents are not unique. "It's only when there is a total breakdown in the child and it destroys the family that we do something," declared entertainer Alan King not long ago, speaking from personal experience. "I saw it all . . . the glue-sniffing . . . the marijuana . . . and I excused it, any excuse,"[6] he said about his oldest son, Bob, who had gone from being a school troublemaker to using alcohol, barbiturates, amphetamines, and then to becoming a heroin addict at seventeen.

"I'm more aware now," claimed King at forty-four, acknowledging his failure as a father several years after his son had completed a rehabilitation program and gotten off drugs. "I thought because I was a success at any early age, I knew it all. I knew nothing." An active philanthropist who had "played a million benefits" and spent many years on the road, he recalls not wanting to discipline his child after returning from his travels. "When I did things with him, it was token, there was no continuity," he admits. "They are aware when you are playing at being a father. They can smell it, just as they can smell true affection, concern and parental guidance."[7]

King discovered that more discipline, consistency, and demonstrative affection are needed at home. "Now everyone kisses," he says. He also discovered that even though the demands of his career are atypical, many other men fail their children in a similar way:

The average father doesn't lead my life, but it's the same thing. He goes to work, comes home, says he doesn't want to hear about the little problems because he's had a tough day at the office, puts on the television and then goes to bed. He's on the road, too!

I see successful men running companies with hundreds of men; they know how to deal with every situation, how to discipline and reward in the business world. But the biggest business they are running is their family and they fail at it. When you've been through this, you find out how many other parents are going through it.[8]

King remembers the futility of reminding his son that he had given him "everything," including luxuries his own immigrant father could never afford. "What he wanted was not the material things but my affection and love," he now says with painful candor. "What my kid was screaming for was Daddy."

King heard the scream just in time. Two years later, when he realized that his younger son was heading in the same direction, smoking marijuana and sneaking out late at night, he had his son arrested for drug possession. "I had to stop him, and the only way—it was the last resort—was to call the police,"[9] said King, a man who is just beginning to realize at mid-life how difficult it is to be a daddy. "The greatest danger," he warns, "is that we see what is happening but we don't want to see it, we don't want to believe it."

Alan King is right. Many men in their middle years refuse to see what is happening to their children, refuse to hear them even when they scream. When a youngster gets in serious trouble with himself or with the law, they react, instead, by becoming immovably irate. Rather then face reality or confront the fact that their child, their own flesh and blood, has given birth to an illegitimate baby, stolen a car, become a political activist, or been convicted on a narcotics rap, they often deny the whole event, deny any responsibility for their child's behavior, by cutting off all communication.

Here is another instance where men of this generation reach an impasse because of impacted feelings. Not only are they inept at handling openly antagonistic confrontations with their own children, but also they frequently cannot accept the fact that their child has in some way failed, or that they themselves have failed as a father. Turning their back, they refuse to acknowledge that here is a situation they cannot solve, a person they cannot control.

"Such critical encounters with rebelling youngsters are enormously humbling experiences" for driving, ambitious men, says sociologist Norma Haan, who has interviewed many mid-life men participating in studies at the University of California's Institute of Human Development at Berkeley. One man whose daughter had become involved with drugs confessed this was the only problem he had ever tackled that he couldn't lick.

"He found out he couldn't order her, he couldn't bully her, he couldn't persuade her," says Haan. "And for the first time he felt really helpless about something that mattered terribly to him." Frequently such fathers want to cut their children off, in contrast to mothers, who are much less inclined to break the tie, despite their anger. The man's attitude is that he will refuse to support a child who is doing things he doesn't approve of.

"Some of them absolutely reject the kid," says Haan of the men in her study. "They don't know where the kid is, and they don't care to know."

IV Double Trouble: Interlocking Crises

It is not just a clash of values or changing social mores that account for the difficulties which arise at this stage of life between fathers and their children, leading eventually to dramatic fights, a breakdown in communication, or even a complete rupture. Much of the antagonism is due to the fact that both the father and the adolescent are going through turbulent life crises simultaneously. Both are in transition, both are struggling to cope with mysterious changes and monumental new challenges.

In a study of the generation gap between high school students and their parents, Marjorie Fiske, director of the Human Development Program at the University of California in San Francisco, found that more men then women felt threatened by "youth's deviation and challenge."[10] When questioned about their youngsters' goals, these fathers often responded with defensive and highly emotional rationales for their own lives.

"Doesn't he realize that he should be thinking about a house and all these other dull, routine, ordinary things?" said one father who, while fiercely denouncing his son's aspirations, was really admitting how unfulfilled his own life had been.

The real problem was not related to opposing values, since the young held long-term goals similar to their parents', but to the fact that those teen-agers were at the stage of struggling for self-identity, while their parents were at the stage of reviewing what they had achieved. This caused more conflict for the men than for the women, says Fiske, because although many men had been idealistic in their youth they were forced by the Depression to concentrate on survival and security, thereby compromising their own youthful goals. Thus they were often uneasy about their youngster's vague work ambitions because they felt that the worth of their own life strivings was being undercut by their children's rejection of practical concerns.

From this perspective we can see more clearly why the freedom of movement enjoyed by youngsters today so frequently stirs up resentment among men in their middle years. On one level a man may claim to be proud of his ability to give his child advantages he himself never had, but on a deeper level he often feels enraged that his children take for granted privileges that he had to earn by the sweat of his brow. To the older generation it is a deep affront that young people act as if they are entitled to pleasure as a human bu..right, whereas they themselves were taught it was something you had to work for and deserve.

Moreover, it is not simply a matter of a man's having been denied such tantalizing choices in his own youth. His rage may also stem from dissatisfaction with his present situation. If he feels impotent at work or in bed, or if he feels generally stuck and overburdened, deprived of meaningful options, the freedom and independence that his maturing children are enjoying will only accentuate his own sense of being imprisoned.

This simultaneous meshing of two turbulent life stages—adolescence and mid-life—has been called a time of "interlocking crises" by researchers at the National Institute for Mental Health who claim that it is almost impossible for a man to handle the problems that now arise, or expect his child to achieve a healthy independence, unless the man can successfully come to terms with himself and develop a sense of his own self-worth.

This conclusion comes from a five-year study of troubled adolescents, conducted by psychiatrist Helm Stierlin and his associates, which revealed that the fathers of teen-agers in serious trouble had all failed to resolve their own crisis, and that this failure was clearly related to the child's difficulty.[11] Disappointed in their own lives, these men either neglected or brutalized their children to such an extent that a bitter breach often ensued, accompanied by disturbed behavior on the part of the adolescent.

Ordinarily, say these therapists, with the increasing awareness of declining physical and sexual powers, a man in his forties goes through a crisis where he doubts the value of his work efforts and his marriage. If the resolution of this crisis is to be successful, he must grieve long-time aspirations now out of reach and reassess the meaning of his achievements; or he must strike out on a new course in either work or marriage.

In this study of troubled adolescents, however, the men were unable either to grieve successfully or to find a satisfactory new course of action. Instead, they suffered from depression, which showed up most clearly in a loss of energy and distorted relationships with their adolescent sons and daughters. (By and large these findings apply to fathers and sons, but the general theory also applies to daughters, say these researchers. With sons, a pattern of resignation and withdrawal was most common. With daughters, such fathers tended to seek self-confirmation by becoming intrusive and seductive.)

Most of these fathers were found to be frustrated, unhappy men who were either dealing with a substantial gap between their goals and the realities of their life, or else devaluing what success they had achieved. Seeing themselves as weak or impotent, they tended to be jealous of their son's sexual vitality and freedom from tedious work. In turn, such envy produced two destructive patterns. Sometimes the father overidentified with his son, even admiring the youngster's "potency" in defying authority, and tried to live out through him what he himself had missed. This usually led to a pattern of resignation, with almost complete abdication of the fathering role; or else to a kind of detached and hand-wringing and nagging, with no effective limit-setting.

The other alternative, even worse, was for a father to reject and devalue his son by being harshly punitive and by engaging in an "annihilating fight." Instead of a conflict over content, how to live best, with implicit acknowledgment of the adolescent's right to choose, this kind of fight is a personal assault. Rather than focusing on what the child *does* (smoke pot, for example), the father attacks *who he is* by defining him as an incorrigible criminal. The terms of this brutal attack are such that the son cannot survive with his self-respect intact unless he completely erases the image of his father as a worthwhile person, or breaks with him entirely, or both.

In this group of troubled adolescents what followed were abrupt and bitter separations, failures of differentiation between father and son, and long-standing alienation between them. At the root of these difficulties, say these researchers, was the fact that these men were unable to confront their sons openly because he men had failed to establish a strong sense of their own worth, failed to resolve their own "integrity" crisis. But, the researchers insist, this resolution is essential for the healthy development of both father and child.

V *Learning to Be Genuinely Paternal*

For this generation of mid-life men, learning to become genuinely paternal is made more difficult by the fact that they have never been encouraged, or trained, to take fatherhood seriously to begin with. On the contrary, *machismo* demands as a point of masculine pride that a male be clumsy in the domestic sphere, even emotionally insensitive. This Dagwood Bumstead syndrome, which portrays a man as bumbling and childish, is reflected throughout the media, but nowhere more relentlessly than on TV. Program after program insists on the incompetence of the American male to the point where, as critic John Leonard has observed, Father *never* knows best.[12]

In accord with the dictates of the masculine mystique, men of this generation have been not only prepared but also indoctrinated to fail their children. Thus it is not surprising that a major trauma is often required to shake a man out of the safely detached paternal perch to which he has retreated. Sometimes this occurs only when the marriage, rather than the child, has gone wrong. Then divorce jolts men into confronting themselves as fathers for the first time.

Divorced after twenty years of marriage, William Fine, the president of Frances Denney Cosmetics, prefaces his own reaction by describing a movie scene that affected him deeply. It shows the end of a big Saturday outing where a father has taken his son hiking, bowling, and picnicking—everything the child has always wanted them to do together. About to be dropped off at home, the boy says, "You know, it's really much better having you and Mom separated." When the father asks him why, the boy replies, "Well, you know how you're always so busy, and worried about work, and making up lists of everything you have to do. And now I finally made your list!"

"It was kind of devastating," says Fine, admitting that his own experience after leaving his three children was strikingly similar:

> I took my kids for granted when I was living with them—and stopped taking them for granted when I moved away. You know, your wife-rudder is gone and all you have, in terms of family, is your children-rudder.

In an almost unnatural way I probably clung to a couple of my children more than I should have.

When kids are born I think a lot of men don't have anything to do with them as babies. I never liked babies. I couldn't talk to them. So you wait two or three years until they are talking and they get a little bit interesting. Then you try to play football and they can't catch—so you ignore them another two years.

Finally at about five they sort of become people. Before that they were sort of things that the mother ought to take care of. Now you start to feel the magic of growth, and you say, "Gee, that's my kid!"—and you get feelings of pride. Then you kind of lose it for awhile. They go to school and have little problems, and you tell your wife, "You take care of that." And then at about twelve I think you really *begin* to get interested in them. But you want the pleasures and not the problems.

In my case divorce made me very proud to have the problems. I was a little jealous of their habit of taking their problems to their mother. Hell, they had had a *lifetime* of having done that. Now there I was on the outside and they're the family unit—and I'm wondering why they don't come after their wise and successful father to ask how to solve some of their problems.

I hadn't *earned* any of that. But wanting their love—and all of a sudden feeling a little lonely—I made more of an effort. And now I guess I've pretty well succeeded with two of them. One still doesn't trust my judgment, because our record together is not very good.

Among the younger generation, attitudes are changing. A new concept of fatherhood is gradually emerging, due in part to the breakdown of stereotyped sex roles but also due to an increasing understanding that in an impersonal society men have an emotional need for their family.

"The new father," says psychologist Edwin Nichols of the National Institute for Mental Health, "no longer considers child care to be strictly women's work. He is much more aware of his child's emotional needs and he actively, intimately nurtures them."[13]

Such sentiments still seem alien to most American men. That the emotional link between father and child is mutual, that a father needs the close, confirming tie as much as the child, is a discovery that this generation of men often make only in their middle years, if at all. Again, divorce is frequently the impetus, awakening in the man who was previously cool and detached a new awareness of his own emotional vulnerability. As the following words illustrate, the need for love is sometimes expressed not only by a rebellious child, but by an anguished father who also screams when he feels lonely:

Leaving the kids really hurt me a lot. I used to have nightmares for months after that. Waking-up-screaming kinds of nightmares. There was a dream that in one form or another kept coming back to me. The children were visiting me in some house I was living in, and I take them down to see the river—and then there is this gigantic flood. Just the tops of telephone poles are sticking out, houses are floating away, and it's very frightening.

We just stand there watching this flood, and then this flimsy little boat floats past and one of the boys pulls it ashore, and says, "Can we all go in it?" And I say, "Sure—but be careful." So they go out in the boat and get caught in a whirlpool, and they're spinning round and round and screaming, "Daddy, Daddy, save us!" And I'm saying "Let me see. I know there's a life-preserver here someplace. It's probably on a tree." And so I'm wandering around looking at trees . . . and I just wander away.

And I always wake up screaming. Sometimes there are different dangers, but it's always that kind of dream. Which is partly them drowning and partly me drowning. I don't think it's too mysterious what all that means.

More than just a statement of one man's feelings, this moving testimony underscores the mutual dependency that connects all fathers with their children. Whether they realize it or not, many other men, married as well as divorced, are also drowning at mid-life. Not simply because they are heavily burdened by responsibilities, but also because they have ignored, abandoned, or rejected a child. When these ties are severed it is not just the child who sinks, but the father as well.

The emotional interdependence between the generations is what Erikson meant when he talked about a man's "need to be needed," and about generativity. And it is what the Yale group mean when they talk about the new developmental challenge at mid-life for a man to become genuinely paternal and to assume more authority and guidance as a father.

It is important for a man to cultivate this side of himself without waiting for a divorce or other trauma to occur. It is important not simply for the sake of his child, but also for his own enrichment and growth. Forging a deeper, closer connection to the younger generation is a way of validating who he is, what he has learned and experienced. It is a way of retaining his humanity.

When such enrichment fails altogether, when a man fails to develop his capacity for generativity, Erikson warns that there will be a pervading sense of stagnation and personal impoverishment. What is the alternative? In terms of the interlocking crises, Stierlin and his associates make a strong case for a man's engaging his adolescent child in a "loving fight," an action that, they suggest, will strengthen both father and child at this stage of life.

A man's defining his own values and what his life means is crucial, first, because it is only when a man has a strong sense of his own worth that he can allow his son to differ with him and thus "lose the battle" partially, without feeling threatened. Rather than abdicating the role of a strong father or waging an annihilating fight, he will then be able to oppose his son's different choices directly and openly—that is, engage him in a "loving fight" about principles and values.

"The father's willingness to engage the son in man-to-man battle conveys the father's respect for his son's emerging manhood, his feeling that his son is a worthy opponent," says Stierlin. "From his father's respect the son internalizes his own manhood."[14]

Despite disagreement about specific values, this "loving fight" is vital for the son's self-definition because it enables him to identify with his father's sense of commitment. But it is equally important for a man's sense of self. His integrity will be enhanced because although the son will now emerge as a man different from his father, he will also carry on his father's tradition in many important respects. It is through this "loving fight," then, that the attachment of child to parent is transformed into respect and love between two adults.

At mid-life a man's becoming whole, developing the feeling side of his personality, is essential not only for revitalizing his marriage, or sustaining a love relationship, but also for managing the heavy responsibilities that come with being the generation in the middle. It is no longer enough to be the breadwinner. At mid-life a man must provide emotional as well as economic support for both the young and the old. He must assume more authority and guidance, dispense more care and concern.

It is difficult being caught in this double bind. Nonetheless, becoming a father in the fullest sense, learning to be genuinely paternal, can yield enormous dividends. When a man adopts a more loving, nurturing stance toward the younger generation, he also validates himself. Because of his guidance, his generosity, the young will carry on his tradition and thus confirm him in ways he cannot do alone.

Chapter 10   Making It: The Urge for Independence

I *No More Mountains to Climb*

When an important goal has been reached, a long-standing ambition realized, many mid-life men suffer from what poets have called "the melancholy of all things completed," a malady psychiatrists sometimes describe as "success depression." The crucial issue is not what a man has achieved in fact, but how he *feels* about his achievements.

Consider this portrait of a contemporary man in anguish. Now forty-four, Fred is a renowned newscaster who is in turmoil about both his personal and his professional life. Dedicated and energetic, he had made a name for himself—and a great deal of money—by his late thirties. He had acquired political clout, met many fascinating people, and was traveling constantly. In fact, he traveled so much that he rarely saw his second child until she was about five. But he had obtained everything the American dream promised.

Soon after he had bought an expensive home, complete with swimming pool and tennis court, in the best section of Washington, D.C., he looked out the window one day and wondered, with a sense of numbing despair, "Am I really going to live on *this* street for the rest of my life?" He had just turned forty.

Suddenly that hard-earned, deeply desired home seemed like a prison. And so did his marriage. Before long he became romantically involved with a movie star. He had power and fame and money. This woman represented glamour and excitement. Eventually he decided to leave his wife, although he didn't ask for a divorce. "I was riding high and beginning to believe my own press clippings," he recalls.

For the next three years he traveled far and wide with the

actress, intrigued by her dazzling lifestyle and intense vitality—so different from the predictable routine and placid wife he had left. During this period he virtually abandoned his own career to assist his mistress in hers. Gradually, however, he began to tire of the nomadic life and to resent the way this strong-willed woman manipulated him. After increasingly bitter fights, his fantasy-fulfilling affair came to a final, angry ending.

Fred then settled in New York, alone, to resurrect his reputation. Although he felt compelled to resume his badly neglected career, his work bored him, just as it had already begun to bore him when he'd left home—primarily because he had reached the top of his field. And so in going back to the same old thing, he was riddled with conflict and knew, in his heart, that the time had come to establish new directions and new goals.

"I have to find out what I really want to do with my life," he insisted when he consulted a psychotherapist. Several months later he concluded that he needed his home, needed the soothing structure of the family circle. Also, he confessed, he needed his adolescent children—perhaps more than they needed him. And so he returned to his wife, who agreed tentatively to accept him on his own terms. "I can't promise to be faithful," he had said.

Their relationship is still a tenuous one, fulfilling only partial needs. He spends long weekends in Washington and works in New York. Leading a split life disturbs him, but as yet he has found no better answers. Plagued by both a patchy personal life and an unresolved career crisis, he cannot make a total commitment in either sphere.

Of his present work he says, "It's not something for a grown man to do." He has been toying with the notion of writing a book, or going to law school, or even entering politics. Yet he is reluctant to leave a job that provides substantial economic security.

In the meantime he relies on tranquilizers or sleeping pills. An old prostate condition has been kicking up, and he is bothered by his receding hairline. He also jokes about drinking too much. The hell of it, he says, is that no one ever told him he would feel so despondent when there were no more mountains to climb.

This sentiment is shared by many successful men in their middle years, including those who react less dramatically than Fred. When a man has accomplished everything he set out to do and doesn't know where to turn next, or when despite the public recognition and rewards bestowed upon him he still feels unfulfilled, success becomes a macabre joke. Or, as writer Larry L. King put it, "little to call on when nights grew dry and long and empty."[1]

Contemplating the ignominious fate of the "success-haunted" men of Watergate who paraded across his TV screen several years ago, King was prodded to go back in time, recalling the intensity of his own youthful drive, recalling how he had boasted to a high-school classmate, "One day, ole buddy . . . I'm gonna have boatloads of money, and people gonna *hear* about me."

In his mid-forties, King concluded: "If I had not made boatloads of money I had, by boyhood standards, got near to a small canoeful. I had published books, been nominated for prizes and—yes!—had even been mentioned in the New York *Times*. I lived well: dined with U. S. Senators in Georgetown, occasionally accompanied rich ladies. It wasn't exactly *bad*, you understand—hell, sometimes it was real good. I never once thought of trading it back for my youthful oil-field or cotton-field sweat—but, somehow, it had failed to set me free or ring my bells."[2]

Modestly, King describes what he achieved as a certain "tinny, minor fame," but a similar disappointment is also felt by men who make it on a major scale, men who do succeed in accumulating "boatloads" of money.

"It was Christmas week and I had gone skiing with my wife and my children in Aspen, Colorado, and one afternoon it suddenly dawned on me that I had accomplished every objective I had set out for myself," said Peter J. "I had a senior partnership in a large accounting firm and a thriving practice. I had written two novels, and, by God, they had both become best sellers. And I had just made a couple of million dollars in the stock market.

"I was thirty-seven years old and I was dead! I had nowhere to go. I think at that moment I decided, not consciously and not deliberately, that I was going to put everything in the ashcan and start over. I had lived out the first half of my life, and wouldn't it be fun to smash everything and start again? That was my insight of the afternoon."

Within the next year Peter J. resigned from his accounting firm, sold all his investments in the stock market, and also got divorced. Now happily remarried, he continues to write and is contemplating starting a business of his own. But he has not yet attained the inner peace he craves or figured out the meaning of success:

> Anytime I take on anything new I seem to have a marvelous time while I'm working, and then when I've *got* it I don't want it anymore. The real happiness is in the process of getting to it, but I haven't yet found out what you do when you get there.
>
> It's ludicrous to spend the rest of my years continually getting there and throwing it away, which is essentially what I spent the first half of my life doing. That's not a sensible way to live your life! There must be a proper way to view it when you achieve a goal and get what you want, and I haven't worked that one out yet.
>
> I have a lifestyle now where I don't have to work, and yet I *have* to work. I mean inside I have to work. I do a number of things which I really do enjoy and savor. A great deal of success or accomplishment is not one of them, however. I can't cope with that.
>
> You see, as soon as I hear the word "success," something sort of rebels. I don't consider that I've ever *had* success, really. I've managed to achieve certain limited goals, and get the rewards in terms of money, or in some situations, acclaim. And in that way I exceeded what I set out to get. But to me success has to be measured in terms of some sort of *internal* contentment. And that I have never had, and never will.

II *The Fate of the Dream*

In America success has always meant making money and translating it into status or fame, but we have at the same time always felt a deep moral need to justify money-making. Thus the stewardship of wealth doctrine, which prevailed until the nineteenth century, scrupulously distinguished material success from "true" success by tying the latter to the character ethic, to giving, and to service.

Since the 1930s, however, the personality ethic has been dominant, aided by an outpouring of advice by everyone from Dale Carnegie to Norman Vincent Peale on how to manipulate other people in order to get ahead. Though this shift upset the precarious balance between material success and true success, a peculiar ambivalence remains: Americans still feel that success *ought* to be something else, something ennobling that has nothing to do with money.[3]

Our novelists and playwrights, reflecting this ambivalence, have long been intrigued by the irony of the failure of success. Writers like Theodore Dreiser, Sinclair Lewis, John P. Marquand, and Arthur Miller have said repeatedly that there are only two tragedies: not getting what you want, and getting it. Success is not a destination but a journey, they suggest. The mountain has no top—only plateaus from which to start another ascent.

At mid-life "making it" has two aspects. The first involves the judgment society issues on whether a man is a success or a failure. It relates to continuing pay raises and promotions, to climbing the ladder, and to the Horatio Alger myth, issues already discussed. But there is a second aspect, more elusive and complex, which is internal. It relates to the dream, a man's personal vision of his own future, a vision that contains a deeply felt sense of his own unique possibilities and promise.

In our society every young man is encouraged to weave and embroider his own interpretation of the American Dream. Indeed, such fantasies of greatness often serve as spurs to achievement and as crucial sustaining forces during periods of misfortune. They do so, at least, until a man approaches forty. Then the situation changes, for this is the time when the fate of the dream becomes known, the time when a man either achieves his dream or else realizes that he never will.

Either way, there will be new dilemmas to contend with. Contrary to popular belief, the man who realizes his dream does not necessarily have smooth sailing ahead. Though attained, the youthful dream may seem meaningless, or unrewarding, in the context of his changed values and matured judgment. Or it may have cost him more than he thinks it was worth. At best, a man must still reconcile the gap between reality and fantasy, and accept the inevitable disillusionment that ensues. Furthermore, there is the problem of what to do next, besides mechanically repeating his previous accomplishments, and where to find a new source of inspiration and energy—for that is what a dream provides.

Until recently only men had dreams in America. Women had hopes—hopes of snaring a good man and getting married, hopes of settling down and being provided for. But that is changing slowly, and women are daring to dream and plan for their own future achievements, confident that they too have a contribution to make. Today, in fact, more women than men have a dream for the second half of their life, and with society's approval they are acting on it. Having completed the task of raising their kids, many woman are heading in an entirely new direction at mid-life, intent on making their mark on the world.

To date American men in their middle years are not as fortunate. Our society has not yet sanctioned, nor even recognized the need for, a new and different dream that men over forty might pursue with joy and purpose. The standard male dream still focuses solely on success, to be measured by money and power, and it must be achieved before this watershed age, or not at all.

Those men who have already made it by mid-life must find the courage to construct another meaningful vision for their future without society's help, a challenge that we will consider shortly. But what about the men who *don't* make it, the ones who must now face the fact that their private dream, long cherished, will never be attained?

Little is known about how men reconcile themselves to this devastating knowledge, or about how they revise unattainable aspirations to fit their actual achievements. In a classic study entitled *Automobile Workers and the American Dream*, Ely Chinoy has shown that by the age of thirty-five, the watershed age for blue-collar workers, most of these men had either transferred their dreams outside the company, dreams of small businesses or farming, or else had abandoned all efforts to realize them. After that, although many workers contemplate leaving the factory, few do. The majority try to maintain their self-esteem by redefining success to mean the accumulation of material possessions and the attainment of security, or by projecting their hopes on their children.[4]

Judging by what scanty evidence exists, including personal testimonies, middle- and upper-class men make equally painful compromises at this juncture. To survive with his sense of worth intact, a man must be able to come to terms honestly with what he *has* accomplished and what he will never accomplish. Too, he must be able to grieve for the loss of his now unattainable dream and do so with genuine feeling—with regret, not rancor. He will then be free to revise his priorities, formulate a new dream, or make other changes in his life that have nothing to do with work.

The most dangerous casualties occur when a man blindly pursues a goal that he can no longer realistically attain. We all know such men who, against all odds, stubbornly refuse to relinquish a dream of becoming president of the company, or making a million dollars, or achieving fame. Approaching fifty, or sixty, their obsessive drive to make it big has locked them into a self-defeating compulsion to compete, or chained them to a suicidal round of frenzied work activities. Determined to appear successful, even when they are not, they cling desperately to the symbols of wealth and power—the Cadillac, the co-op apartment, and the country club. Their lifestyle has become more important than their life.

In time the man who refuses to give up an unrealizable dream not only destroys all his chances to make realistic, meaningful changes, but also destroys himself. His senseless, driven pursuit of impossible goals produces nothing but specious victories, and his self-deception leads to a life tissue of lies too thick to puncture or escape. Unable to achieve his dream, unable to let it go, he ends in despair—embittered and defeated.

By contrast, Dr. Daniel Levinson tells about a man in their group, a forty-three-year-old biologist, who had the courage to abandon an unrealizable dream at the right time. "I can tell you exactly where I am in biology," the man said. "I'm right at the top of the second level, and there are not many guys ahead of me. But I'm not at the top level, and that ruins everything."

He thought it over. He knew what he had achieved and what he hadn't. He had tenure at his university and an enviable reputation among his colleagues. But his dream of doing great laboratory work that would ultimately lead to some world-heralded scientific discovery was gone, and it therefore would be pointless to continue doing the same kind of research. Despite the conflict and the pain, he is shifting his direction and moving out of the laboratory to find another arena where his talents can be better used.

"He is facing the problem," says Levinson. "He won't go on doing the same thing with the illusion that he might still accomplish something he won't. He no longer has the illusion he will win the Nobel prize, and he has managed to achieve a new kind of honesty and realism. And one can see he's not just going to stagnate."

Concern about the fate of the dream usually subsides after a while. The little voice asking, "But what do you *really* want?"—so loud at around forty—gets quieter by about forty-five, when a period of restabilization begins, according to the Yale group. By then a man will probably have made some changes in his life, for better or for worse. If not, he will be inclined to reduce the turmoil, make his peace, and settle for what he can be comfortable with.

III But What if the Dream Comes True?

In our innocence, we Americans have long cherished the illusion that success and happiness are the same, while simultaneously ignoring the fact that the American Dream, once attained, often fails to bring contentment and peace of mind. But the social upheavals of recent years, the Vietnam War and Watergate, have sobered us all, forcing us to embark on a national orgy of self-scrutiny and criticism. We celebrated our two hundredth birthday painfully aware of our own limitations, willing to admit our failings along with our accomplishments, willing even to examine our simplistic devotion to the ethic of achievement and competition.

It was in this spirit of self-reflection that a CBS television documentary entitled *But What if the Dream Comes True?* dramatized our national malaise several years ago. An engrossing portrayal of the paradoxes of success, this documentary featured Sam Greenawalt, age forty-one, a white Anglo-Saxon Protestant whose dedication to hard work and getting ahead had won him the senior vice presidency of a Detroit bank.

A former football player and an ex-Marine, Greenawalt commutes to work from the affluent suburb of Birmingham, Michigan. Most of the men who live there, we are told, have climbed the corporate ladder and are fighting to stay there. Automobile and advertising executives, engineers and bankers, they are all American success stories.

Greenawalt also started at the bottom of the ladder, trusted in the system, and climbed to the top. "But when you listen to him you detect the first faint shudder of discontent," says the documentary's narrator. Shown racing through the door to his office, where he works ten to twelve hours a day, Greenawalt says: "I was trained to be extremely competitive. . . . You want to get the best you can out of yourself, and you have to push in order to get it and you have to hurt yourself to get it."[5]

His sumptuous lifestyle bristles with contradiction. Greenawalt moved to Birmingham seeking safety for his family, but the problems of the outside world—crime, drugs, and dropouts—are pushing into the suburb, increasing the possibility that his children will reject what he worked so hard to achieve. And his wife, having discovered that "she cannot share her husband's world," is trying to make her own by attending sensitivity sessions.

The family rushes to escape the "hassle" of their regular routine by driving four hours every weekend to their second home, an isolated retreat called "the cottage." And we learn at the documentary's end that the Greenawalts are moving to the still more opulent suburb of Bloomfield Hills, where all the executives are at the very top. "It's like the camel driver going to the next oasis," says Sam.[6]

The documentary concludes by suggesting that the dream is destructive: "The American dream grants you your wishes, and then cuts you into pieces. You struggle to reach Birmingham, but once there, you find life fragmented, family life threatened, the pressures as high as the taxes. So you look for something better, and that, in the American tradition, means an even bigger house in an even better neighborhood. . . . The new house is the new dream."[7]

This judgment is too harsh. Though this documentary quite rightly questions our middle-class values, it fails to acknowledge the ability of middle-class, middle-aged men to re-evaluate or change them.

Interviewed five months later, Sam Greenawalt insisted, "There is a large measure of discontent, but they didn't show the balance." They didn't show the things in his life that he found stimulating and satisfying. Even more important, they didn't show that he himself was asking the same questions that the documentary raised. Sam Greenawalt is too smart to confuse something better with a new house. Asked to describe his feelings about what he has achieved, and what he still wants, he said:

> When the film was being made I was still struggling—still scratching. Frightened every minute. Just putting out as hard as I could every day. You have to do that. This is a real, real competitive existence. Everybody depends on you. You *have* to produce. Every minute!
>
> All I wanted then was to be a darned good banker. And I wanted to produce for the good of the organization. But I didn't want the organization to have that pervading influence on everything I do in my life. And I fight that all the time.
>
> I was raised in a quite structured family. My father was very much the boss of the family, and he wanted things done just so. And he expected a great deal from us as youngsters, and thank God we produced for him. He was a stockbroker, and I worked with him for three years. I didn't like the brokerage business, and I saw what his life was like. Rigid and boring. He's always been the corporate man, but he doesn't know any different. Because of him I'm more sensitive, probably more introspective—more desirous of breaking a pattern.
>
> I feel *trapped* right at the moment, you know? I can't go anywhere. Shoot . . . I get phone calls on my vacation. I went off to Sun Valley and I had three or four phone calls out there before I even hit there. And as it goes on, I can see the trap getting bigger and bigger and bigger—and all the more consuming. You see, what I am now is a paid gun. And I'd better shoot straight, and fast, and often.
>
> I think to myself that now I'm doing this for a reason.

I'm doing it because I want to give substance to my children's existence. I want them to be proud of the fact that I am producing, and I would like to see them get at their goals in life. At the moment I'm a banker, but in eight or nine years I might not be.

I know where I am now, and I know that I'm looking for something other than what I'm doning. I've made a good deal of money in the last two years, and damnit, if I want to retire now, I could. But I *know* that's not right for me. I don't want to continue on being the corporate man forever, and then they release me at sixty-Ove and I'm all burned out. *Then* what do I do? You sit down and wonder what happened to your life.

Okay. So where do I want to be? I want to be in a position where I'm the owner of a company, where I can skim off if I want to, or take a salary out of it. And I figure if I can inject the money with some of the skills that I have, and put it together with a group of guys, we might be successful.

I'll tell you, the second half of my life might be entirely different from the first half. I want to have more time to myself when I want it. To have more time to enjoy my wife, you know, and my family. But I have to do it for myself.

Contrary to the documentary's suggestion that the new house is the "new dream," Sam Greenawalt is concerned with more complex issues. Struggling to redefine success, he is trying to disentangle himself from the corporate web. And, having lived out the American Dream in a conventional sense, he is now trying to structure a personal, more mature, dream for himself—one that will enable him to work on his own terms. And become his own man.

IV *Boom: Becoming One's Own Man*

At mid-life this feeling of being constrained within the corporate structure, which Sam Greenawalt complains about, is normal and natural. Having outgrown certain dependency needs that they once had for the security of a paternal organization, many men begin to yearn or a new kind of independence.

Such yearnings are so common that the Yale group call this the BOOM period, a time of Becoming One's Own Man. Not a separate life stage, it is actually a peaking of the "settling down" period and generally occurs in the middle to late thirties. A key element in this period is a man's feeling that no matter how successful he has been thus far, he is not sufficiently his own man.

This new urge for independence usually comes as a surprise. One of the myths of our culture is that people are finished with the business of growing up in their twenties. However, this expectation ignores the fact that the life structure created in early adulthood cannot possibly reflect all parts of the self—and must therefore be enlarged later.

Another reason why this life structure must change is that it is based, to some degree, on illusions. One common illusion in the early thirties, for example, is for a man to regard himself as highly autonomous because he is now making his own way and his parents are no longer telling him what to do. In fact, however, his ambitions and goals are very much tied to what the Yale group call "tribal influences"—the institutions and groups that are important to him. And, despite being free from parental influence, he is likely to have found other authority figures to guide and protect him.

During the BOOM period a man finally begins to realize that he is not really as independent as he once imagined. He now craves more authority and wants to speak with his own voice. He also feels uncomfortably dependent on those with power over him. The writer feels unduly intimidated by his critics or publisher; the middle manager thinks his superiors control too much, and delegate too little; and the professional man chafes under senior colleagues.

This is the time when many men feel compelled to leave the corporate organization and strike out on their own, a desire that, as we shall see later, often leads to a second career. This same sense of being constrained can spread to other areas as well, however. And the man who now begins to resent his boss may also start complaining that his wife treats him like a little boy.

Breaking with a mentor is an extremely significant event during this period, the Yale group discovered. The person who was formerly so loved and admired, and seen as giving so much, is now felt to be heavily controlling. The mentor begins to appear to the younger man like a tyrannical and egocentric father, rather than as someone who fosters independence and individuality. Because the relationship has served its purpose, however, it can now be terminated—sometimes slowly and peacefully, sometimes abruptly and bitterly. After the separation a process of internalization occurs, whereby the younger man's personality is enriched as he makes the valued qualities of the mentor more fully a part of himself.

Having dispensed with this tie, a man is ready to BOOM: He is ready to give up being a son in the little-boy sense, and a young man in the apprentice sense. He is ready to assume more fully himself the responsibility of being a mentor, father, and friend to other adults. This sort of developmental achievement is the *essence* of adulthood, say the Yale group.

Relationships of this kind are also necessary to work through Erikson's stage of generativity vs. stagnation. The issue now is caring for future generations. A man cannot get very far with this task before forty, say the Yale group, but his breaking off with former mentors is the beginning. (They caution, however, that it is probably impossible to *become* a mentor without first having *had* one. The presence or absence of mentors was found to be of great importance during the twenties and thirties; and the absence of a mentor is often associated with developmental impairments at mid-life.)

This BOOM time marks the end of a man's battle to conquer his external environment, and sets the stage for the internal struggle of the mid-life crisis.

V *The Paradoxes of Success*

In our society the great paradox of success is that, on the one hand, whether a man succeeds or fails at mid-life matters greatly. On the other hand, it doesn't matter at all—because he will go through a crisis regardless.

During this period, say the Yale group, most men fix on a key event in their career that will symbolize their affirmation by society. Given an almost magical quality, this event can be a promotion, a new job, or some other form of recognition. The pressure of waiting for the outcome usually stimulates a man to make "the special bet" on himself, increasing his efforts to capitalize on this last big chance. If the outcome is favorable, the assumption is that the future is assured, and that he is all set. But this is not true. Whether affirmed or not, a man will have a crisis. Only the form varies.

The key issue is not whether he succeeds or fails in realizing his goal, or achieving his dream—but the sense of disparity he feels between what he has gained, in an inner sense, and what he still wants. It is not a matter of how many rewards a man has gotten—money, status, power, or fame—but of the goodness of fit between his life structure and his evolving self. A man may do very well in terms of reaching his goals, but find success hollow or bittersweet. The severity of his crisis depends on the extent to which he questions his life structure and feels a strong need to modify or change it.

Ironically, failure can yield unexpected advantages. When a man fails he may be in for a rough time, and have to deal with a narcissistic wound, but he will also be freed to ask what he really wants. For example, Bruce D. discovered that his being fired, at forty-two, from an advertising company was the best thing that ever happened to him:

> As soon as I got fired I felt this great weight off me. Then a headhunter called about another job and I thought, well, I'm a responsible father and all that shit so I'd better go for the interview. But when they offered me the job I felt so depressed again I said, "No!" I saw myself killing time for 20 years and getting $100,000 in the profit-sharing plan and then retiring. Just thinking about it was *horrifying*.
>
> So I made up my mind to freelance and I got some book assignments lined up. Now I won't have to sit in on client meetings and act as if I'm thinking seriously about whether toilet paper should be sold on the basis of softness or absorbency! I can write and live in the country and do what *I* want to do—and life will have some meaning. I feel I have a future now!

By contrast, success can sometimes be dangerously inhibiting in terms of future growth. If a man succeeds, his sense of inner turmoil may be reduced and he may be more inclined to stay locked into the same situation, thinking he can go on that way idefinitely. But men who deny the mid-life crisis are likely to lose the vitality they need to continue developing.

Equally ominous, many men who fail to resolve the issues presented around forty will experience a more severe crisis at fifty. This belated reaction can lead to a suffocating feeling of futility, or trigger bizarre, impulsive changes. The Yale group describe this as an instance where "the chickens come home to roost."

"It's a very simple notion," says Dr. Edward Klein, "which means that if you don't look at these issues in your gut when you are younger, and you just keep masking them over with Scotch tape, they are going to break out. They mount up in some critical mass—God knows, I don't know how to quantify that—and they build up over time. Then a man breaks out in some sort of inflated act."

Another paradox of "making it," says Levinson, is that "just at the time when a man seems to have accomplished all he set out to accomplish in his twenties, the meaning of it changes somehow." The reason for this is that he himself has changed and so have his values. In young adulthood a man was trying to make it in society's terms. By mid-life, however, after these contests have either been won or lost, he begins trying to make it in personal terms. Having arrived at the place where he was so intently heading, he begins to ask himself: Is this what I really wanted? Was it worth all I had to give up? And do I want to continue doing this for the rest of my life?

As an example of the dissonance likely to develop, Dr. Braxton McKee explains that somewhere along the career ladder, most often in his late thirties, a man usually takes an important step toward "making it" that involves deciding he must do things in his own way—and act with more authority. The minute he does that, however, he starts becoming more aware of what he wants for himself, and possibly more aware of how this differs from what the organization wants from him.

The result: "Just as becoming more responsible and autonomous helps him to reach his goals and to 'make it' within the original structure," says McKee, "it also puts him in touch with parts of himself that lead him away from it."

And that is the ultimate paradox of success: "Making it" leads to breaking it—and then breaking out. When a man gets there, when the dream comes true, he suddenly becomes conscious of all the ways in which reality differs from fantasy. This, in turn, causes him to search for new and different challenges that will satisfy a more mature, discriminating, and diversified self.

Chapter 11   A New Frontier: The Inner Self

I *The Mid-life Lust for Change*

Somewhere in their forties many American men yearn to transform totally a life that now seems sterile, stale, or senseless. They feel an urgent need to make dramatic changes, start fresh, embark on a radically different course—to be born again, in short.

Moreover, there is a feeling of desperation which insists that drastic steps be taken immediately—or else it will be too late. "I've always had this dream about owning a ranch, and for years I've been talking about quitting my job and moving out West," said one man. "But suddenly there's the feeling that if I don't get the hell out of here and do something *now* I'll be in the soup for as long as I live."

"Not another day dying alive!"—that is the battle cry of all men over forty who feel that life has passed them by. And very often those who have suffered the deepest disappointments, or cowered behind the greatest compromises, or stuck to all the sternest rules now lunge most eagerly toward radical change. No mere tinkering with a stagnant marriage nor toying with a stale career will do. They lust instead for a shiny new slate and stunning alteration. A total sweep. A grand slam.

But fear and trepidation often go hand in hand with this urgent desire for change, creating a powerful pull between opposing forces. A man may want desperately to change, but at the same time feel paralyzed by anxiety and uncertainty. What if he makes the wrong choice? What if he fails? How, in his position, can he afford to take monumental risks? Give up old roles? Forfeit responsibilities? How will his wife, his children, and his colleagues react? What will his boss say?

Dare he gamble so recklessly at this stage of life? Dare he try to realize the dream that has been burning inside him for years? Or is it already too late? Is the pursuit of lofty visions solely the prerogative of the young?

Unfortunately, such doubts and fears are, to some extent, legitimate. They spring from repressive sources that are deeply rooted in our society, sources that not only discourage but also fiercely disapprove of people—especially men in their middle years—making major life changes. It is a strange irony of American life that while we applaud novelty and progress in many areas, we prefer stability in human beings. Those who dare to make radical shifts threaten us profoundly, evoking suspicion and scorn.

"Most lives have been wasteful in comparison to what they could be,"[1] says Dr. Robert N. Butler, Director of the National Institute of Aging, who feels that we do not encourage people to be sufficiently resilient and flexible, open to new possibilities throughout their entire life. In favor of a radically revised concept of the human potential, Butler deplores our culture's overemphasis on the importance of a firmly fixed, established identity as a sign of mental health. Forcing us to continually consolidate our past choices, rather than review and renew them periodically, this static definition of health causes people to become frozen into set roles that limit self-development, he says. In turn, our society then defines as "sick" those who in their middle years switch careers, break up marriages, or adopt new lifestyles.

Despite this prevailing cultural prejudice, which claims that consistency is a basic human virtue, change a sin, some members of the helping professions are slowly beginning to recognize that people have a natural need to grow and expand, to continually evolve. Accordingly, some psychiatrists, psychologists, and counselors are now responding in a new way to mid-life men who feel stuck or stagnant. Contrary to the orthodox therapeutic approach, which urges adjusting to the status quo and accepting things as they are, this new breed of counselors is beginning to encourage change, sometimes even prodding their clients to risk more adventures with themselves.

Thus when industrial psychologist Lawrence Zeitlin counsels men over forty who are dissatisfied or in distress, he often challenges an overly cautious man by asking, "What the hell are you doing it all for? If you want to quit your job or leave your wife, why don't you do it?" Or he might take over a man's guilt by giving him permission to play out a particular fantasy. "Look," he would say, "you don't need psychiatric treatment and you don't need vocational guidance. You want to run off to Mexico? Go ahead and run off!"

His approach has had dramatic results. Sometimes a man's doing what he really wanted to do, even indulging in a brief escapade, resulted in his returning to his job or marriage reinvigorated. More important, this approach helps a man understand that his need for change is normal, not neurotic, and that he has underestimated his own ability to transform his life. "These men suddenly realized the trap they were in was of their own making," says Zeitlin. "They realized there was nothing in their lives—except their children, obviously—which was irreversible."

The greatest barrier to change is a man's refusal to face his problems realistically, says Zeitlin. Many men resist change by acting as if the problem is not quite "real," or as if it can be reversed by some simple gesture. In turn, they often seek counseling in the hope of getting a "magical" solution.

"What they don't want to hear," he claims, "is that what's happening is inevitable because of the type of person you are or the situation you're in. And there's just no way to change things other than drastically changing the situation—or drastically changing themselves."

II *The Magical Appeal of the Gauguin Myth*

More oriented toward action than introspection, accustomed to dealing with facts and forces outside the self, most American men in their middle years would rather change their situation than themselves. Among such men the Gauguin myth has a powerful appeal. It seems to promise that a man can achieve spiritual renewal by traveling to a distant land. The perfect magical solution, it implies that a change of situation will automatically change the self.

Glorified as a man of courage and daring, Gauguin is generally thought of as a hero so dedicated to his artistic calling that he was inspired, in his forties, to alter his whole way of life. According to myth, he abruptly renounced a bourgeois existence to devote himself to his painting, discarding the trappings of a corrupt civilization for a pure, primitive, and sensual life in the South Seas.

In fact, there was nothing noble about Gauguin's life—and very little that was even pleasurable. He was actually a driven, self-destructive man who failed tragically in his flight into fantasy. And though he set sail for his tropical paradise with a wish to be "reborn," and redeemed, he actually spent his last years as an embittered exile who never gave up his desperate desire to be acclaimed by the society he supposedly despised.

Contrary to myth, too, Gauguin's career switch was not a sudden revolt—nor was the break with his family. Though born and raised in France, he spent his early childhood in the exotic tropical atmosphere of Peru, an experience that continued to tantalize him. Married at twenty-four to a Danish girl, he worked as a Parisian stockbroker while devoting all spare time to his painting until he decided at thirty-four, after much debate, to concentrate solely on his art.

In the hope of finding patronage, Gauguin uprooted his family to Rouen; then, with none forthcoming, to Copenhagen, where his in-laws lived. Cut off from an art center, he failed to obtain artistic recognition in Denmark and eventually parted bitterly from his wife to return alone to France, where he lived and painted for several years in poverty.

Though he was now acquiring a reputation, Gauguin was so disturbed by his continuing commercial failure that he began dreaming about moving to tropical paradise. To him this migration meant freeing himself from money worries and recapturing his Peruvian childhood. But it also meant magical rebirth. Thus, after paying a last visit to his wife and five children, Gauguin finally decided at the age of forty-two on Tahiti as his salvation.

Once transplanted, however, he remained a constricted European who, according to art historian Wayne Anderson, was "unable to mine the gold of natural resources that Tahiti offered."[2] His search for a savage renewal miscarried in part because he approached his exodus to Paradise like a scientist on a field trip. Most ironic, given the sensual overtones of the legend, Gauguin was so alarmed by the sexual openness of the Tahitian girls, and by his obsessive fear of venereal infection, that he became temporarily impotent. Finally he compromised on whores, with whom he could feel safe.

Having fabricated a romantic image of himself primarily to enhance his artistic reputation, Gauguin remained motivated by a wish to return to France triumphant and vindicated. But this wish was shattered when he did go back two years later: An exhibition of his Tahitian paintings received a viciously critical reception. Devastated by this failure, he then returned to Tahiti to stay. "He knew now that he was no hero," says Anderson, "but only an old dog, injured beyond repair, going off to a quiet place to lick its wounds and die."[3]

The last chapter of his life was tragic. Consumed by poverty, disease, and loneliness, he deteriorated steadily and worked rarely. The death of his favorite daughter plunged him into a deep depression, followed by a series of violent heart attacks. He then began to contemplate suicide. In a final heroic effort, he rallied his remaining energies to paint a "spiritual testament" called "Where Do We Come From? What Are We? Where Are We Going?"

This work completed, Gauguin trudged off into the mountains, swallowed a box of arsenic, and lay back to die. Instead, however, he vomited up most of the poison, and in agony, finally dragged himself home. During the next few years he moved to a still more savage atmosphere, the Marquesas Islands, where his hut became the scene of raucous all-night orgies. Though crippled, he tottered around on canes carved with copulating figures on one handle and a phallus on the other, and he frantically consumed young girls. After a long and tortured decline, he died of heart failure at fifty-four.

The fantasy had fizzled. Gauguin's flight was motivated less by artistic dedication or daring than by self-loathing and irrational expectations. His journey to Shangri-la was actually a desperate attempt to flee from himself. Gauguin had "searched for a Paradise which would succor his dreamed self," says Anderson, "but in the end his green oasis consumed the dream, leaving him, like Adam, bereft of his Eden and forced to bear the consequences of his original self."[4]

That the Gauguin myth still lingers on today testifies to the awesome power of the fantasy that seduced him, and its continuing appeal for the contemporary male. It is a fantasy that is still being played out on similar terms. A perfect example is the case of John Koffend, a former *Time* editor who left his job and family to go to Pago Pago in 1970, and then wrote *A Letter to My Wife* to justify his actions. Ironically, this book describes many of the same destructive demons that gripped Gauguin.

Impaled on the hook of a belated mid-life crisis, Koffend wallows in self-pity and grasps at every excuse to avoid facing reality. His memoir opens with his living alone in a one-room apartment, sunk in a depression that remains unalleviated by a steady diet of liquor and pills. Not only is he impotent, but he is also convinced his sexual affliction is permanent. How did he arrive at such a frightful impasse? Well, his wife had recently divorced him after he told her he wanted to marry another woman. Then the "other woman" had deserted him too. Impotence, isolation, and withdrawal—these are the recurrent themes of the months he spent living in a befogged bachelor state, still plugging away at work, before deciding on Samoa.

Slowly he rebels. "It has occurred to me that I've lived all my life for other people," says Koffend. "Be nice to your mother. Don't slap your wife. Responsible fatherhood. Succeed at the job. Pick up your socks. . . . I'm tired of all that."[5] Scanning the landscape of his life, he sees nothing but ruin and feels exploited by everyone. Searching for scapegoats, he blames his misery on society—and his wife. Blotting out the fact that he requested a divorce, he blames her for getting it. "Why were you so willing to give me up?" he whines, accusing her of causing his impotence ("You are a castrator like my mother.").

This sense of impotence pervades all areas of Koffend's life. Because he feels helpless to change or improve anything from his past, he is ultimately driven to obliterate it. Looking back, he insists that remaining married would have trapped him in a sterile life—a passive victim of fate. Staying married "would have condemned me to a life sentence at *Time*, on the eastern seaboard, and in Westchester County,"[6] he claims.

In desperation he finally resolves to run. Dropping out becomes the only answer to his life. He clings tenaciously to his illusions, because they are all that remain. "I am sustained by the Pago Pago fantasy and doubt that I could live without it,"[7] he says. And what does he expect from pursuing his fantasy? Like Gauguin, nothing less than to be reborn. "As an act of resurrection or salvation, I've got to take a leap from the known into the unknown," he insists. "I've got to do it or go on living in the most pointless, unrewarding and dreary way imaginable to me."[8]

Driven by this existential terror, Koffend makes the final break. After spending several months in Samoa, however, he still resents facing the mirror and feels dubious about what he has gained. "I haven't changed," he acknowledges. "I've just changed locale."[9] Two years later he returned to New York, on his way to Hong Kong, and announced that life in paradise was boring. "I probably would have stayed if I had found somebody to hook up with," he complained. "Mostly, I was living alone and didn't like it one bit."[10]

Like Gauguin, Koffend found it a crushing burden to bear the consequences of his original self. "I'm just a very unhappy middle-aged man with emotional problems too big for him,"[11] he had confessed in his book. "I can't stand my thoughts in the dark. . . . I hate myself. . . . What in the hell was it that arrested my maturation? There's something obscene about being a fifty-three-year-old boy. . . ."[12]

This confession is the key to why the mid-life male's journey into outer space so often fails. No matter how spectacular the setting, the man who transplants himself with the hope of shedding a loathsome self will ultimately discover that there is no utopia so magical it will release him from his own skin. Or his own psyche.

III *Dropping Out: Flight or Fulfillment?*

Like John Koffend, many men in their middle years feel cheated when they discover that the ideals drilled into them—obedience, self-denial, and diligent work—have failed to deliver substantial rewards. Those who are unable to transcend their feeling of having been exploited tend to view themselves as victims, undercutting their own ability to make new choices. Anxious to flee, they grab at anything that promises release from their despair. Some drown their sorrows with traditional pain-killers like alcohol or drugs. Some deny their sorrows by plunging into promiscuous sex or compulsive overwork. Others are seduced by the siren song of youth.

Although our culture's neurotic obsession with youth is not

new, keeping people young has now become big business: Men are being wooed, along with women, to tint or transplant their hair, consume cosmetics, and banish sags with surgical uplifts.¹³ But the American male is no longer satisfied simply to look young. Today he yearns to copy the young as well—their values, attitudes, and lifestyle.

This topsy-turvy trend reached its peak in the late 1960s, a time of collusion between youthful trend-setters and a generation of older men who had never played. Thus the counterculture at its height—with the flower children and the Monterey Pop Festival—charmed many middle-aged Americans with its messianic idealism, sensual freedom, and gentle cry of love. Enchanted by the chance to enjoy an adolescence they had been denied, adults across the country fell in line behind these pubescent pipers. Grown-up men grew sideburns, switched to bell-bottoms and mod ties, tuned in to the rock beat—and turned on with marijuana.¹⁴

By 1970 much of the mystique of the youth movement had been destroyed. Heads had been busted in Chicago and bullets fired at Kent State. Woodstock had disintegrated into Altamont, heroin had taken its toll, and the Manson murders had brought the show to a bloody climax. The rock culture had turned into the dope culture, and the nation knew that the young were not the saviors they once seemed to be.

Despite this collapse, however, the beguiling ways of the young continue to entice aging males who feel overburdened and underappreciated. Some, having watched their own adolescent children sidestep responsibilities, become irresistibly attracted by the promises of carefree sexuality and hedonistic revolt that a youthful lifestyle seems to offer. This attraction is particularly strong among men who feel that their own life has been too work-oriented and constricted. Their disillusionment often leads to the relentless pursuit of pleasure and a desperate attempt to identify with the youth cult.

Some men straddle the fence by becoming weekend dropouts—dressing in jeans, smoking pot, and frolicking with young swingers. Others attempt a modern-day version of Gauguin's flight, rejecting establishment standards in favor of a radically different way of life. Rather than sail to the South Seas, however, these men can join the younger generation by taking off for less-distant retreats like New Mexico, Oregon, Colorado, and Southern California—a choice that usually includes experimenting with communal living, drugs, and new forms of sexual freedom.[15]

Men who drop out do so for many different reasons, some of which have nothing to do with recapturing their youth. In some cases their flight is motivated by fear and despair. In other cases it is inspired by a genuine search for a better, more human way of life.

Recently, for example, numerous magazine and newspaper articles have documented the fact that a growing number of affluent Americans are quitting the corporate world not for the sake of a new job, but for an entirely different lifestyle. Successful business executives and skilled professionals, they have all changed their minds about what they want and how to get it. At mid-life they have decided that their careers were actually of little consequence. "I discovered I had been chasing a phantasmagorical carrot all those years,"[16] said one executive.

In most cases these men have given up city living or suburban commuting for a simpler, more independent existence closer to nature. Typically the discontent accumulated slowly before the final decision was made. And very often their new choice—a farm, a ski lodge, or a boat—was the realization of an old dream. Some felt a strong desire to work with their hands, like the man who grows cranberries in Wisconsin; or the one who works as a toolmaker on a hundred-acre farm in Colorado, where he also raises animals, and hunts and fishes in his spare time.

Occasionally a profoundly moving experience that triggers a total re-examination of values inspires a man to turn his back on society. John Koehne, for example, is a former CIA official whose life was transformed at the age of forty-six by an experience in an encounter group. Until then he had led a conventional life: private schools, Yale, the Army, steady promotions at the CIA, and a fifty-thousand-dollar suburban home with his wife and three children. But when his agency sent him to a four-day encounter group, he returned "so damned different" that his wife wondered if they could continue living together. Suddenly he began opening up to himself and others, a complete reversal of his old ways. "This was just the opposite of the way I had been living for forty years," he says. "There was no possibility of ever going back."[17]

The following summer, Koehne persuaded his wife to participate in some encounter groups with him, and she too began to change. His transformation was further accelerated by rebelling teen-agers, who each, in turn, dropped out of boarding school. "I had to stop and look and begin to understand what was happening," says Koehne. "I wasn't the sort of parent who said, 'You're going to have my values or get out.' And as soon as I tried to understand the kids, questions began to come up about myself."[18] As a result of these new forces brewing, Koehne finally quit his job at the CIA a year and a half later.

"It wasn't right for me," he decided. "I just couldn't put my needs first there, not in the selfish sense but in the human one. I was putting the institution and the job first. It was a conflict of values—between the new set emerging for me and the existing set that society wants to impose."[19]

After leaving his job, Koehne and his wife spent ten months traveling in a camper truck, their new way of life as yet undefined. With no demands on his time, he found at first that he missed a "sense of obligation and compulsion." Gradually, however, he evolved a plan to establish a "growth center" based on the principles of yoga. After starting such a center in northern California, and living there for five years, John and his wife, Ana, have recently founded the Dharma Center in Virginia.

How well such middle-aged dropouts fare when they reverse gears and try to acclimate themselves to a totally new way of life varies greatly. In some cases the experiment fails, and a man eventually returns to his old patterns, dejected and disappointed. In other cases the man who makes radical alterations achieves genuine satisfaction and happiness.

Why the difference? Why do some men sink when they make multiple life changes, while others triumph? Most social scientists agree that a man's capacity for coping with dramatic change depends in part on factors related to his past history, ego strength, and flexibility. It also depends on how realistically he has chosen, in terms of expectations as well as self-awareness.

"When a man in his middle years starts asking, 'Can I really be that other person I always thought I could?' " says Dr. Lawrence J. Hatterer, a Manhattan psychiatrist, "some men just grab life by the balls and say, 'Of course! Why not?' They are the ones who have the vigor and confidence and aggressivity to start entirely new lives for themselves. But as a rule, if a man tries to change his love life and his work life and his home life and his money life—if he zonks himself with all those at once—let's face it, he's got to go under. Often it's the less mature or less aware person who thinks he's capable of altering all these things suddenly."

Dr. Harry Levinson warns that it is naïve for a man to think he can change himself into anything he wants, or literally start over from scratch at mid-life. "We cannot disregard our life history as if it didn't exist," he cautions. "Mid-life changes are outgrowths of what a man has always been. They are new directions." An excessively optimistic view of how much a man can change his life reflects an element of irrationality, which in turn usually veils excessive discontent with himself, says Levinson. A man will then seek to change his circumstances compulsively as part of a frantic effort to like himself better.

Thus when a man in his middle years decides to burst constraining bonds for the sake of a dream, the decisive issue is self-awareness: Whether or not he dares confront himself honestly and discard illusions about who he is. The man who runs away to avoid this self-confrontation will discover that his geographical move is but a mirage.

IV Pioneers: Exploring the Uncharted Self

"Sometimes I fantasize about hopping on a jet to South America and starting a whole new life," admitted one recently divorced man. "But the trouble is, I know I'll be there waiting for me when I get off the plane."

This wry comment contains a profound truth about the mid-life lust for change: It is futile for a man to change his situation dramatically without also changing himself. Movement per se—a move from place to place, or person to person—is not enough. Changing locales cannot heal a man's wounds, eradicate his worries, or transform his life. To be successful, the journey must have an internal dimension too.

Not long ago, Dr. John R. Coleman caused a stir when, at the age of fifty-one, he took a two-month sabbatical from his job as president of Haverford College to work as a laborer.[20] Traveling from Georgia to Maryland, Coleman worked as a ditchdigger, a garbage collector, and a sandwich-and-salad man in a Boston restaurant.

In *Blue-collar Journal*, a book he later wrote about his adventures, Coleman explains why he kept his intentions secret. "I did not tell anyone what I planned to do with my sabbatical," he confessed, "because I was afraid the response would be what part of me also said, 'Jack, that's crazy.' "[21]

But the move was in keeping with his convictions and desires. Although Coleman had often urged students to break the "lockstep," to take time out to vary the rhythms of their life, he knew that the advice he was giving to others was really meant for himself. Despite the real rewards of his presidential post, he felt keenly the peculiar loneliness that so often accompanies being in the top office. Describing the frustrations of always being regarded as "the president" but never simply as a man named Jack Coleman, he said: "I also knew I needed some other experiences. I wanted another me to come out from time to time."[22]

This is exactly what happened during his travels: Not just a flight of fancy, Coleman's sabbatical was actually a journey of spiritual renewal and self-discovery. He put himself in situations where he was not defined or limited by his usual identity—the job—but could experiment with new ways of behaving and responding, bringing to life parts of himself that were ordinarily forced underground. The result? He reclaimed a disowned part of himself, thus enlarging his own sense of self and his inner resources.

"Once, I thought I was leaving my identity behind when I set out on this leave," Coleman reveals at the end of his journal. "Now I think I may even have found some part of it along the way."[23]

Though Coleman's sabbatical was only a brief adventure in dropping out, it illuminates what the mid-life journey is really about: personal growth. A voyage of self-exploration, this journey—if it is to be fruitful—should be inspired by the myth of Odysseus rather than Gauguin.[24]

In the *Odyssey* the hero withdraws temporarily from a life situation that is no longer nourishing, in order to return refreshed, with his perspectives enlarged and a new sense of life's possibilities and his own potentials. The voyage is essential because it permits a man to withdraw from conventional roles and explore concealed aspects of a self that has shriveled within the boundaries of a repetitive, repressive situation. During this journey awareness expands and consciousness is transformed. In turn, this new awareness provides new ways to see one's future.

This metaphor of the Odyssean cycle as a means for self-renewal has important implications for all men in their middle years who want to infuse with new vitality a life that has lost meaning or become monotonous. Whether they embark on a voyage literally, or only symbolically—by disengaging from accustomed roles and retreating into the self—the process of separation is essential. It provides some solitary space, some silence, in which a man can listen to his inner voices.

The purpose of this temporary withdrawal is for a man to liberate himself from the clutch of the past and augment his sense of self, so he can create a better, more fully human future for the second part of his life. Instead, this enlargement is what makes meaningful new choices possible, because if they spring from the desires of the authentic self, these choices will not be arbitrary or random.

When a man disengages from familiar patterns and roles to embark on a mid-life journey, attitudes count as much as actions—especially how he views himself. If he is dissatisfied with himself and inclined to blame others for his discontent, or if he sees himself as a passive victim of fate with no control over his own life, any changes he attempts will be contaminated by this sense of futility. And therefore will be likely to fail.

By contrast, positive attitudes generally lead to positive actions. As we shall see in the following chapters, many men in their middle years are rapidly invalidating F. Scott Fitzgerald's contention "There are no second acts in American lives."[25] They are creating brave new possibilities for the second half of life—not by running away, but by reinventing themselves. Despite society's disapproval, they are renewing their options, revitalizing their lives, and designing new directions.

Courageous pioneers, these men are seekers, not dropouts. They have discovered that the new frontier is inner space:

the self. Exploring this boundless territory requires risking adventures within the depths of one's being. It is a lonely and often hazardous voyage, but essential nonetheless, because in this day and age there are no more magical solutions. "In the eclipse of God," writes cultural critic Theodore Roszak, "we have no place to begin but with ourselves. *Within* ourselves. All we have lost in the course of becoming this torn and tormented creatures called modern man . . . we discover again in the depths of our identity. There or not at all."[62]

In order to transform his life after forty, a man must start by transforming himself.

Chapter 12   New Directions: Work

I *Starting Over: A Solitary Venture*

Last on the freedom line, American men in their middle years are finally beginning to claim the right to redefine their lives. Young people, blacks, and women have been on the march for a much longer time, and now even groups like the Gay Liberationists and Gray Panthers are demanding room to grow. As oppressive stereotypes shatter with increasing frequency, it is not surprising that the need for change, first felt on the fringes, has now penetrated the Estabishment's core.

In search of new challenges at this stage of life, men recharge their batteries and expand their horizons in many different ways. Some take on a teaching post, become involved in politics, or dedicate themselves to a charitable cause. Some travel to new and distant places, learn another language, take academic courses for fun, or devote more spare time to interests like gardening, photography, boating, tennis, or painting. Others work for the improvement of the physical, social, or cultural environment. Provided there is commitment and enthusiasm, such shifts in leisure-time activities can give a man a new lease on life.

Still, such sideline shifts are not enough for many achievement-oriented men who have become disenchanted with their work and want something that will engage them more fully. Launching a second career in the forties, or beyond, may well be the wave of the future, according to some experts. Even now a rapidly increasing number of men are starting over in their middle years. Moreover, there is much evidence which indicates that countless others would like to do the same, even though they have not yet summoned the courage, or figured out the way, to make a meaningful change.[1]

Peter F. Drucker, professor of management at New York University's Graduate School of Business, believes that this desire to change direction at mid-life is more widespread than we generally acknowledge. A fervent spokesman for second careers, he reports that a magazine article he wrote several years ago on this subject elicited an incredible response. Despite the article's appearing in a magazine of only limited circulation, over seven hundred letters and hundreds of phone calls poured in from all over the United States—from ministers, professors, military officers, school principals, accountants, engineers, middle managers, civil servants, and others.

"Almost all recited a life story of substantial success," says Drucker. "Yet all asked: 'Now that I am forty-seven, how can I start doing something new and challenging?' "[2]

This restless yearning was no surprise to him. Drucker claims that an urgent need exists in our society to create "wholesale opportunities" for the middle-aged worker to launch a new career. "A second career at this age is a great deal more satisfying—and fun—than the bottle, a torrid affair with a chit of a girl, the psychoanalyst's couch, or any of the other customary attempts to mask one's frustration and boredom with work,"[3] he insists.

Important changes in our society have caused this increasing on-the-job slump, says Drucker. First, the notion that jobs ought to be personally satisfying—a brand-new idea, historically speaking—causes more discontent than in the past. Second, America has changed from an economy of goods to a knowledge economy. This means that a large group of people—"knowledge workers," or what the census calls "professional, managerial, and technical people"—must remain within a specific function or discipline, which invariably becomes tedious. Consequently, today's working life span, having increased sharply since 1900, is too long for all but a few who reach the top and preserve their zest. Still in his "mental prime," the typical knowledge worker is bound to become dispirited as he approaches middle age, says Drucker, "because he has reached his limit of contribution and growth in his first career—and he knows it."[4]

Despite the many valid reasons that prompt men to change careers at mid-life, however, one major problem confronts them: Sanctions and guidelines are not readily available. Starting over is difficult and inevitably fraught with stresses, uncertainties, and questions. But the services that now exist to help a man thinking about, preparing for, or already launched on such a venture are scant indeed. Moreover, our society frowns on such mid-life shifts: Men who job-hop, switch careers, or return to school this late in life are still suspected of being neurotic or confused.[5]

Here, ironically, educated women are ahead of the game. They can enter, leave, and re-enter the job market and be considered "interesting," or train for a new profession in their forties and be considered brave. In addition, more resources and available for women. Besides being able to air their fears and feelings more openly among themselves, they can generally find counseling services nearby. Partly because of the women's movement, our society has in recent years focused increasingly on the problem of women who want to work after their children have grown, or gone off to school. Thus many agencies that are designed to help the older women set new goals have sprung up throughout the country.

Men who wish to reshape their lives at a time when major change is considered inappropriate are not as fortunate. Talking frankly to a colleague might jeopardize their present job. Talking to the company psychologist or personnel counselor is more dangerous still. Most corporations have yet to recognize the existence of a mid-life career problem, much less set up facilities for a man to vent his frustrations or make changes. Outside help does exist, primarily in large metropolitan areas. But there are still far too few university psychologists, management consultants, and career counselors to meet the demand.

What all this means is that the man who changes direction at mid-life cannot count on much help. He must gather information and search out existing resources on his own, and then, with ingenuity and persistence, bend them to his purposes. Too, he must rally his own sources of support among friends and intimates. Those men who have made a shift insist that the satisfactions outnumber the sacrifices. But, as we shall see, starting over is still a solitary venture for most American men, a venture that requires both courage and determination.

II *Pain And Boredom: Impetuses for Change*

Despite an immobilizing fear of the unknown that makes tolerating the familiar preferable to risking something new, a man's work situation sometimes becomes so tiresome or grinding that he feels compelled to think about quitting. His distress becomes a vital force, pushing him to risk more than he might ordinarily dare. Thus long before new goals are formulated, discomfort can serve as an impetus for change.

"I looked around at my colleagues, and nobody was happy, nobody was enjoying himself," said one forty-four-year-old man whose own desperate boredom finally drove him to quit his job with a large shoe company, and then go on to study architecture. "There was always the low-grade discontent and bitching," he explained. "You know, 'Jesus, I have to do this,' and 'I have to do that.' All those unhappy people trudging along to their offices, trudging their lives away! It's sad but it's true. You can see it in the way they walk—stooped shoulders, dragging feet. Beaten people. I used to be part of it. And then when I couldn't stand it anymore I stopped being part of it. Now I feel reborn!"

To be reborn this way, propelled toward a revitalizing new commitment, a man must first permit himself to feel the anguish that invariably accompanies working at a job that he no longer likes. Because this message is often telegraphed in tricky ways, however, he must learn to interpret the signals, from his mind and body, that insistently urge him to restructure his life.

Painful physical symptoms are often the first clues. Not long ago, for example, a magazine article portrayed five midlife men who had quit their jobs for something radically different because work that was once enjoyable had now become intolerable.[6] Each man's switch was unusual: A salesman from Ohio became a teacher in Alaska; a Chicago stockbroker, fascinated by ecology, earned his doctorate in marine sciences; a Wall Street insurance broker opted for managing an inn in Maine; a Dallas veterinarian chose physical labor on a department store receiving dock; and a New Orleans policeman became a painter.

The most striking note in these stories was that all these men were plagued by disturbing symptoms before deciding to make their move. The salesman found that earning thirty thousand dollars a year had given him a nervous stomach, and kept him on the road four nights a week "going like the hammers of hell." The veterinarian became so jangled by people tracking him down on the telephone at all hours that he chose simple manual labor to avoid such tensions. The insurance broker said the commuter's grind not only caused him to drink and smoke and eat too much, but also fanned his anger to the point where he began saying "awful things" in sales meetings—and then ripped an office phone from the wall and even punched someone before deciding to quit.

As for the policeman, his work in the homicide division was so demanding that he rarely saw his family and hadn't had a real vacation in years. Exhausted from overwork, he finally slammed his fist into a wall, breaking two fingers, because "everything became too much." One month later he quit and turned to painting.

Such stories illustrate that an awareness of the appalling toll taken by doing unsatisfying work is a crucial first step toward new alternatives. Whether psychic or physical, pain is generally a signal that something is wrong, that change is needed. Thus a man should pay attention to the messages of distress that his body sends. If he is consistently impatient and irritable, if his anger level has escalated dramatically, if he is eating or drinking or smoking too much, if he develops high blood pressure or an ulcer—these may be signs that his work situation has become destructive.

Sometimes the signs are even more subtle. No obvious aches or ailments, no violent outbursts or dramatic mood changes. Instead, a man may be dispirited but not realize that something is wrong because he has trouble even admitting that he feels down.

"That's part of the male narcissism," says psychiatrist Bernard Hall. "We live with an idealization of what we should be as men more than women do, and we expect there isn't anything we can't handle. It's a foul blow to pride, especially for the All-American guy who's had a successful life, to be so depressed at forty-five he's close to tears."

In his experience, says Hall, the key problem is usually boredom at work, although most men who consult him with the mid-life blues are often out of touch with their own feelings of boredom and unhappiness. Instead they are usually drinking too much and inclined to blame something out-side themselves, like company policy or the new president. A great believer in career diversity, Hall says he is struck by the fact that many men of this generation are so security-bound that they cling to a job even when it's driving them crazy. By challenging a man on whether he really *must* stay in the same situation, Hall makes him consider more stimulating opportu-nities—a tack that often leads to productive changes.

Hall's convictions come from personal experience. After twenty-five years of working with patients at the Menninger Clinic in Kansas, he grew restless and then became "deeply depressed." Determined to improve matters, he explored other job possibilities for several years before shifting gears, at age fifty, to become head of the Community Mental Health Center at New York's Roosevelt Hospital.

"It takes an awful lot of guts to pull yourself out of some-place where you've won your spurs, and cut out to a new sit-uation where you're unknown," he acknowledges. "So I use this experience in a personal, anecdotal way with patients to let them know other guys have done it—and they can too."

After many years of doing the same kind of work, almost all men suffer from a sense of stagnation. Not even cler-gymen are immune to mid-life depression, and the confusion that usually accompanies it, as Rev. Clarke Kimberly Oler, parish priest of Manhattan's Church of the Holy Trinity, tes-tifies:

This is the third church I've served, and I'm forty-six now. I've enjoyed my parish work very much, but in the last two or three years I have increasingly questioned where I go from here. I'm not thinking so much of leav-ing the ministry, but I don't feel too turned on by the idea of just going to another parish and doing the same thing.

I've changed places but never changed direction. Now I'm beginning to ask questions about changing direction. I don't know exactly where these feelings of dissatisfac-tion came from, but I think the fact that I've been here ten years now precipitated some of the questioning.

I've also come to the conclusion that it has something to do with my time in life. My age. I keep feeling in my head that forty-five is the big crucial time, kind of a watershed age. I have the feeling that the number of options open to me have suddenly narrowed very dramatically. Earlier in my life I felt that I could do anything I wanted, and that if after being a parish minister for a while I didn't like it, or wasn't good at it, or was unhappy, than I could just go into something else. But now I don't have that sense of having all those doors open and available to me.

Anyway, about a year ago I began to feel quite depressed. Actually I didn't even realize it at first. I just felt kind of anxious and very hyperactive, I guess. And then one of my good friends who is a psychiatrist was having dinner with us one night, and he said, "You know, you seem really depressed." He picked up little signs. He picked up the hyperactive thing and the heaviness in my manner—like I didn't seem to be enjoying myself and wasn't laughing as much. And irritability—things like that.

He suggested I come in and talk to him, and we had a few sessions together, and he recommended therapy for me on the basis that I was exhibiting symptoms of clinical depression and should work it through. So I did go into therapy for six months, and I began to realize that some of my feelings and some of the depression had nothing to do with the vocational pressure, but rather with other conflicts. So I began to work on some things which were long overdue—which was really very helpful to me.

The psychiatrist pointed out that when you get depressed and you don't have any way of dealing with your depression, one way of reacting is to get busier. And all you experience is the busyness—the sense that you've got to keep all these appointments, got to keep moving. The therapy allowed me to experience the depression, too. And then to be able to move with it, and live with it, and explore how to work out of it.

After working through his depression, Rev. Oler made another constructive move by seeking career counseling. This helped him take a good, hard look at himself and begin to sort out his priorities for the future, as he explains:

When you've been in a situation as long as I've been in the ministry you lose a lot of perspective on yourself—and you even begin to wonder if you've been a misfit all those years. And that was the kind of thing that was disturbing me at one level of my life. So another thing I did was to go to the Northeast Career Counseling Center in New Jersey—which is an organization set up by churches primarily to help people think through whether they are in the right vocational spot. And if they want to make a move they get a kind of profile on their own interests and abilities as a guide. The process includes some searching questionnaires and a battery of tests.

Going through that, I felt it was really the first time in my life I had any objective data on myself. And what I learned about myself was that parish work is very close to being the thing that I do best and find most satisfying. At least I knew I wasn't in the wrong slot—and that eliminated a lot of anxiety! So I felt very much reaffirmed, and I got a lot of strength back from that. It didn't alter the fact that I would still be facing some kind of change in the next few years, but it gave me the feeling that I could take my time a little bit more about working on it. And so I picked up a lot.

One of the ways in which I've changed is that I'm less interested and less patient with the administrative side of parish work—which I used to get a big kick out of. Now I want to focus down more and develop some skills more deeply. The sense of being constantly stretched out all over the map in sixteen different things is no longer attractive to me.

The big key question for me right now is to find out where to focus—and *how*. I think that the area I really want to concentrate on is counseling and group work. I've done a lot of this, but I've never had time to develop the skills necessary for being a better and more effective counselor. And I'm increasingly resentful of things that block me from doing this. I also enjoy teaching very much, although I have very little chance to do it here.

So I think my next move will be in the direction of counseling—maybe working part-time as a counselor and part-time as a parish minister, with somebody else running the business end. Or maybe into a city agency, or into a school where I can do teaching as well. Right now I'm exploring the kind of training I would need to make this sort of move.

While investigating this matter of schooling, Rev. Oler ran into two problems that often confront men who want to change direction. The first is that the rigid requirements of many colleges and universities make it hard for an older student to enroll.[7] And the second is that men frequently sabotage themselves by imagining they need more formal training than they actually do.

Rev. Oler discovered that one institution he visited, where part-time enrollment had been permitted previously, now demanded three years of full-time work to obtain certification as a pastoral counselor, a change that obviously favored younger men. But he also discovered that he was inventing some difficulties. When he told several colleagues that he couldn't make a move until he had the proper certification, they said his "need" for a piece of paper reflected his own insecurity about being qualified—but was not realistic. Given his years of experience, they advised, he should simply take a few additional courses and credits. That dialogue was a revelation, says Rev. Oler. It convinced him he didn't need elaborate credentials, freeing him to explore more flexible alternatives.

III *Evolving Needs, Evolving Values*

Like Rev. Oler, many men in their middle years are discovering that their desire for a new challenge can best be met by shifting the direction of their work, rather than making a total career change. Thus a man might transfer his special skills from the business world to government; or turn from research to teaching; or switch his focus from products to people; or move from administrative tasks to training and counseling; or broaden his influence by writing and lecturing. Though less dramatic than second careers, such shifts may be a more realistic option for the man who wants more stimulation but doesn't want to discard his expertise.

The man who makes a mid-life shift is often motivated by

a desire for more independence and autonomy. He wants the freedom to express his own evolving beliefs, the freedom to do things his way—a need that may require his breaking away from a particular person, or from an organization. Once again, however, as the following two case histories show, he may feel forced to leave a confining situation even before he has fully clarified where he is heading, or why.

Sometimes the pain prodding a man to make this break is an abrasive relationship with a colleague, partner, or boss. Leo W. was forty-three when he quit his job as the manager of a music and entertainment agency, and then set up his own shop. He did so primarily because the animosity between him and his boss had become insufferable. Leo W.'s decision evolved slowly, as he explains:

I worked for a medium-sized agency that specialized in club-date entertainment. We booked and assembled the orchestras, set the shows, and engaged the entertainers. Before I resigned I had been there about thirteen years, and I was really running the place. The guy who owned it had given me more and more responsibility, and I knew all the ins and outs of the business.

It's very difficult to explain what happened with this man. I guess it was a combination of the two of us growing older and changing, and gradually becoming more incompatible. A close business relationship is sort of like a marriage, and we were together constantly. You do the business in the day, and then at night you go out and play.

Also he was having family problems, and part of that rubbed off on me. It was a case of constant harassment and constant intimidation. He would castigate me in front of people for real or imagined affronts. Things sort of built up for a couple of years until there was a really terrible personality clash.

And I began to feel that gradually I was losing some part of myself. I began to feel I was losing part of my manhood and my human dignity—the phrase I lit on at the time which, whether I'll admit it or not, is very important.

It began to seep over into my home life, and I became periodically morose and upset. Usually when I'm upset it's inside, and I'm able to cover it, for good or for worse. By nature I'm a very placid person and I rarely become angry. But I suddenly realized I had cracked twice under the pressure of the situation. I blew up at him. I lost my temper. I was irrational. I cried, literally. We had a screaming match—and when I tell you it was the first time since 1945 when I was in the Army that this had happened to me, consider the magnitude of it in my own mind!

As it became harder and harder to come home and change into what I was ordinarily, I finally realized it couldn't go anywhere but further down. I felt I *had* to do something. And the final decision was made in total disregard of security and money and status. It was based purely on what was happening to me personally and emotionally.

I fooled around with the possibility of buying a small club, but I didn't feel I knew enough to get into that. And I didn't want to go back to teaching, which I had once done. So setting up my own shop seemed the logical step. I was pretty well established in the trade. I had some financial backing, and I got some key people to make the move with me. I really wanted to continue in the same business because that's where all my contacts and friends were, and I had worked at it for many years and gotten all my degrees in music.

Despite making his change primarily to get out of a destructive situation, Leo W. soon found that the joy of working independently was intoxicating. Though going it alone has been tough, he is determined not to give up:

When I quit the itch for independence wasn't strong, but now I realize how much it means to me. When you are in business for yourself there is nothing like it. Nothing can match it. Even when you do it wrong the whole thing is your baby! It's a very important thing for a man and I feel it very strongly.

And that's one of the reasons I haven't given this up, even though it's not in good shape financially. Somebody else would take a quick look at the books and say, "Throw that out!" But you have this tremendous satisfaction, and you are loath to give it up. I'm still optimistic it will go ahead, and I really don't want to work for anyone else. One of the things I've thought about often is that I never worked for anyone I either admired or respected—and that's a tough realization to come to in your forties.

It may sound cornball, but you're talking about the same independence the farmers have when they till the soil. It's your mad thing, it's your baby, and you don't want to see it die!

Often the conflict that causes men to change direction relates to a fundamental shift in values. In the process of maturing, a man finds that his beliefs have changed so dramatically they no longer mesh with the work commitment he made long ago. He will then experience discord between his evolving "self" and his old "structure"—which can prompt him to move on. The more self-awareness he has, and the more consciously he recognizes new forces stirring within him, the easier his decision will be. But since this recognition often comes slowly, some men may have to act out their discontent in disruptive ways before truly understanding what caused it.

A forty-two-year-old lawyer, Bob S. only recently acquired a strong sense of what he stands for. Barely conscious of the internal changes that were influencing his actions, he actually provoked a senior partner into firing him before he recognized the depth of his own opposition to his law firm's values. With the wisdom of hindsight, he describes his evolution:

I first went to work for a large law firm that hand-fed very wealthy corporations. Some of the causes we fought for were not particularly noble and I didn't really believe in them. But I was making a good living and working in a reputable field, and I let myself be persuaded I had a chance to be a partner. By 1962, however, the place had become overcrowded with candidates. So I found myself looking for a job.

We had two kids then and were in a financial vise, so I moved to a smaller firm of the same kind—without any serious reconsideration of the milieu in which I would be working.

Several years later my wife decided to go to social work school, and I followed her career with great interest. This was also a period of increased social unrest in the country, and I became more and more attuned to that—and at the same time more unhappy with my partners, with whom I had *nothing* in common politically. I also went with my wife to a sensitivity training group, which was quite an eye-opening experience. It made the normal commercial world look pretty tough, and seemed to be quite a contrast to the way our firm was being run.

I began to realize I had been working contrary to my basic political beliefs ever since I came to Wall Street. I was brought up by a father who began as a dirt farmer and never had any sympathies for business. And I suppose I came to Wall Street to spite him, but I really don't know. I just gradually grew more conscious that what I was doing *wasn't* what I believed in.

Without really understanding why at the time, I began to find the firm absolutely intolerable—and it showed. I was handling my interpersonal relations with those guys very badly. Several times I got so angry I went up in flames, and even told one partner what I really thought of him right to his face. Finally they threw me out—"invited" me to resign—and I had to stand on my own feet.

That's when I decided to take a personal sabbatical, which led eventually to my changing directions.

Forced to re-evaluate his situation, Bob S. gradually clarified the values he endorses and wants to represent. Now he no longer labors for the nation's largest financial and industrial interests, but works instead for the city government in the field of low-income housing. He feels his transformation is just beginning:

My wife had been working with tenant groups, and doing volunteer work for them. I had always been interested in housing anyway because we had renovated two homes—so that's how I decided to specialize in low-income housing. I did some reading and studying for a while, and then I decided to take this job with the city government—at about half of what I was making. I'm not deluding myself I'll accomplish very much, but I will learn the trade. And then after a few years I would like to do something that means working for social change, although I don't know what yet.

My social beliefs are such that I honestly could not in good conscience continue to work for the commercial interests of this country. I just couldn't. But I also have the feeling I got sick and tired of bringing in forty thousand dollars a year and having everybody standing around waiting for it. I recognized the extent to which the average male in this society is *expected* to bring home the bacon. My wife and I had been talking about sharing the load, and about both of us enjoying our home and our kids—and so now we've put some sanity into things and we're doing it!

There was no one I really talked to about making any of these decisions except my wife. And I think I made a mistake in not going into therapy. I talked about it, but I didn't do it. I wish I had, and I may yet. I've always had difficulty in exposing myself—either by expressing my emotions, or else by exposing myself to criticism.

Now I'm very conscious of being calmer and stronger, but I feel I have quite a way to go to mature. Maybe I've started to mature. I'm being very candid with you about what happened to me. It was very clear to me that I had to grow up, grab the bull by the horns, and *do* something—push a little bit to set my own direction. I still have a long way to go to develop a gyroscope inside me. But I view what I've done as just taking the first step in a new direction.

IV *Risks and Rewards*

Some men change the direction of their life because pain pushed them out of a situation that had become unbearable. They may not discover a better alternative until after making this break, as we have seen. Other men change because they feel pulled toward something more meaningful: a deeper commitment, a different intellectual interest; more creative freedom; or a calmer way of life. Even so, they too will experience pain. They are giving up something familiar for something unknown. They are taking a risk.

Men who have made such moves say the rewards ultimately outweigh the risks. But, they insist, uncertainty and sacrifice are part of the package. If a man who makes a major change ignores either, he will be sadly disillusioned.

"Society has you pigeonholed, and if you want to get out it's very hard," says Dr. Harold Lear who, at age forty-seven, scrapped his lucrative medical practice as a urologist to enroll at the University of Pennsylvania for postgraduate training in psychiatry and sexual therapy.

In retrospect, his decision to give up a steady income astonishes even him. "I was always concerned with money," he says. "I always had to be. And then to decide the hell with it was just incredible!" He actually entered school before being sure the funding he had applied for would come through. For six months he and his wife lived on a very stringent budget, and even borrowed money, until he finally did receive a NIMH grant. Finding an organization to fund him in the first place was difficult, says Lear, who is convinced he got the grant partly because one of the NIMH agencies was fascinated by the fact that "this character had actually quit his practice and was studying without any income whatsoever."

Before leaving the hospital in Connecticut where he had worked, Lear encountered some dramatic reactions from his colleagues. "Some people were very supportive," he says, "but others resented me and became very hostile."

Lear emphasizes that his move into a new field was made only after he had seriously re-evaluated his own talents and interests, and had gotten advice from people whose opinions he respected. His move was prompted partly by the realization that "I was working hard to make money to *get away* from working hard to make money. And that cycle seemed crazy!" Enthusiastic about his new life, he adds: "I also found that if you're doing the same thing constantly there is a deterioration. Change is a renewal, and this whole experience has been fantastic. A sheer joy. It's been the most rejuvenating thing I've done since I've been in practice!"

Some men who make a mid-life shift turn an avocation or creative talent into a second career. Though previously trained in or dedicated to painting, music, acting, or writing, they generally have had to abandon their creative calling and find other work to support their family. Later, when they feel financially secure, or their children are launched, they may turn again to their art. Often, however, this decision means trimming the budget and simplifying the family's lifestyle.

When Harding Lemay left his job, at forty-five, as vice president of Knopf publishing house to devote himself to his own writing, he did so in part, he says, because "nothing at work nourished my self-respect or held my attention." He also found himself becoming increasingly irritable ("I would come home a snarling beast") after spending his days being nice to people he didn't like. Describing what finally led him to resign, he says:

> There is something every man feels uses the best in him. And I think we become very mean people, men do, if we're not living up to what we think we are. If you don't like what you do then you don't like what you *are*. I'm absolutely certain of that. And if you don't like who you are, your poor wife and kids pay for it.
>
> That's what really forced me into examining it, and then saying, "If this is really what I want then I'm not the kind of guy I want to be." And once a man reaches that point, then I think the next step is almost automatic.

The summer after he quit, Lemay went with his family to their summer home on Fire Island to begin writing his autobiography, *Inside, Looking Out*. The envy he aroused startled him. "The curious thing was the number of men who came up to me," he says. "Surgeons, lawyers, advertising men— men who were making much more money than I was, averaging $50,000 to $150,000 a year, and who had magnificent oceanfront houses. Out of about 200 families there, I must know 100 men well enough to talk to. And that summer I don't think there was a man under 50 who didn't stop me. The conversation usually centered on, 'How did you have enough guts to do it?' "

Sensitive to the fear of taking such a risk that provoked these queries, Lemay stresses that he left his job primarily because he had something "tugging" him away—something more important to pursue. And before making his move he had already written five full-length plays. "I don't think I would have had enough guts to jump into a new life without having explored it," he insists. "I don't think you do it unless you've had years of hoping or wanting to. It's not an easy decision. It really isn't."

Although changing careers at mid-life is generally thought to be a choice that only the affluent can afford, or would even desire, there is evidence that many blue-collar workers feel a similar need for renewal and more freedom of movement at this stage of life.[9] In fact, their wish for change is often so strong that they are willing to undergo considerable hardship in order to make the switch. That, at least, is the case with a group of two hundred policemen and firemen in New York City who are training for second careers as professional nurses.

Designed to reduce the personnel shortage in nursing and attract more men to the field, this unique experimental program at Hunter College-Bellevue School of Nursing is federally funded, which means the men do not have to pay for their training. Still, the sacrifices they made to prepare for their mid-life switch are most impressive. Their rigorous schedule requires attending classes 3 nights a week for 2½ years, in addition to working full-time. Keeping abreast of their reading and studying cuts into their weekends and sharply curtails time spent with their families. And, most humiliating, these men have had to adjust to moving from a supermasculine career into one considered feminine.

"The first group that came to us were very brave," says Professor Louise Jennings, the project's director. "They were laughed at and called 'Nancy Nurse' by their colleagues. But now that they've broken the ice, more men in their departments are interested." (Because the younger men rejected this course initially, the average age of the first class was forty-five; in the second it was thirty-five.)

Generally these men were attracted to the program because they knew employment would be guaranteed when they finished, and because they found the prospect of traveling to different parts of the country appealing. Planning to supplement their retirement pension with income from their new career, they see themselves working in different capacities: in emergency or operating rooms; in industry or schools; or even becoming owners of nursing homes.

Their reasons for enduring this grueling study routine vary, but most say that staying on the job for more than twenty years is much less feasible today than in the past. Policemen stress violence and social change, and firemen underscore health hazards and the physical toll. Wanting to find another work direction for the future, some of these men had already tried various business ventures, without much luck. Others were even willing to spend their own money for training—to become an X-ray technician, for example—but found that full-time study was required. Thus for men without a college education, this opportunity to become a professional nurse was welcome indeed.

"When I heard about this course it was like somebody opened a window in a closed-up room!" said one policeman. "I could *breathe*. I could see a way out for myself." In his view the sacrifices that he is making now are well worth the satisfactions he envisages for the future:

> It took a lot to sign up for this course, knowing the reaction we had to face back at the stationhouse. You have to have some guts to go ahead and say I'm going to change my whole conception of what I want to do, how I want to fulfill myself. At one stage of my life, money was the big thing, but I'm not interested in the cash value of life anymore.
>
> Like me, some of the guys are going around the clock. There are days you go to work, go to school, go home to sleep—and start again at 5 A.M. It's tough, and you're putting in a lot of time and effort. If a guy wants to change his job he has to have moxie. And if he doesn't, he's never going to do it!
>
> I've spent seventeen years of my life missing everything. If there was a picnic or a wedding or a christening I always had to say, "No." I was working. Now I'll have a job where I can say, *"Yes!"* And maybe I'll just work three or four days a week, and home will be wherever me and my wife want it to be. We'll be free!

V *Running Toward Life: A Mutual Decision*

"I could never have made this change or taken the cut in salary if my wife hadn't been working," said lawyer Bob S. about his mid-life shift. "So in my case women's lib has turned into men's lib—in spades!"

Most men who change direction in their middle years, are equally emphatic about the importance of having whole-hearted support from their wives. Emotional support is essential, of course. But, in addition, some men could not possibly embark on new ventures that require returning to school or reducing their salary unless their wives contributed financially as well.

When Leo W. quit his managerial job in the music and entertainment business to set up his own shop, his wife not only agreed to their digging into savings but also went to work. Without her co-operation he wouldn't have had a prayer of succeeding, says Leo W. "If your woman doesn't understand, God help you!" he warns. "You can't even get into something like this otherwise. Without Lynn's backing this would have folded two or three years ago. We're both very much concerned with each other's rights and desires and aims and hopes—and always have been for the twenty years of our marriage. My wife is a rather special girl, and she was with me 1,000 per cent."

Whether or not a wife goes to work, however, her willingness to accept a reshuffling of priorities and tolerate financial uncertainty is crucial. Harding Lemay and his wife, Dorothy, now live comfortably because he supplements his income by writing a television soap opera, and by teaching. But when he first left his publishing job, things were not so rosy.

"There were times we were down to three dollars," says Dorothy, "but then something always rescued us." Despite such moments of anxiety, she is delighted with the change and feels the family is much closer now that her husband has more time for them. When he first quit, she recalls, "A couple of my friends said, 'I don't see how you dared to let him do it.' As if I could have stopped him! But even if I could, I didn't want to. It's not fun to live with a man who is miserable. Now he sings in the morning, and life is much better!"

From a woman's point of view, the pressures become even greater when her husband leaves the business world for an entirely different way of life, renouncing his former standards of success and security for a more independent existence in the great outdoors. Such dramatic departures from city or suburban life do not necessarily lead to divorce. They may even strengthen a couple's relationship in time. But initially the marriage often hangs in the balance while a man grapples to define his dream, and his wife ponders whether she is willing to join him.

Such was the case with Jack and Lisa Hobbs, who each scrapped promising careers in San Francisco for life in the wilderness of British Columbia. That was in 1968, when they were both forty. Jack headed the science department of a private high school, and Lisa was a newspaper columnist. Several years later she wrote a deeply moving account of their experience, which describes her husband's fiercely felt dream and her own struggle to accept it.

Prior to their move, Jack had become disillusioned with teaching and fed up with the "rat-race pressures to be successful." At first he had been looking only for a summer escape for the family. But after he found isolated property on the west coast of Vancouver Island, and they spent some time there, his desire to make the move permanent became a compelling force. Ready to go it alone, he told his wife that "it mattered so much to me that I didn't care whether she followed me or not. I had a real deep-seated need—like a bomb pushing me from the inside."[10]

Lisa claims that this tremendous upheaval was their last chance for survival as a couple. After eighteen years together they were each, for different reasons, feeling a need for change. While her husband was becoming consumed by his dream, she was developing a new feminist consciousness that made her unwilling to endure guilt feelings caused by work assignments far from home. Their marriage was already troubled when Jack's search for a remote retreat began, Lisa recalls. At the end of their first summer in the wilderness, she was horrified when he said wistfully, "Wouldn't it be nice not to go back? To jump out of bed with joy in the morning and not give a damn about how we looked or acting smart or getting ahead?"[11] Knowing that part of herself still clung to the city, and aware of her still-unresolved struggle to establish her full identity, Lisa protested. "You'd be running away from life!" she proclaimed.

No, said Jack: "Quite the opposite, we'd be running towards life."[12]

When they returned to San Francisco, the subject was dropped. "It would take Jack and me one full year of ambivalence, probing, introspection and, at times, fearful tension and conflict before both of us arrived at the point where we had the courage to do what had to be done,"[13] says Lisa. Gradually, however, her own feelings began to change as she discussed with friends Jack's desire to make a permanent move. "Millions of other men" wanted to do the same thing, she discovered:

> As I began to speak about these things to friends, cautiously at first and then more and more openly, I was surprised to find an instant response.
>
> Many women told of their husbands being obsessed by this dream—the dream of freedom in the land of the free and brave, the dream of being their own boss, of starting a task and being allowed to see it through to its end, of not having to dress, look and speak for twelve hours a day like actors playing before a critical audience.
>
> In confidence they spoke of their husbands' recurrent depressions, irritability, moodiness and melancholy that sometimes bordered on madness. I glimpsed a nation of men caught in the wheels of the vast American dream machine that consumed body and soul for $200 a week.[14]

Listening to these confidences with an open heart and an open mind, Lisa began to shift her position. She and Jack began to talk more honestly about changing their life—and finally made a mutual decision to move.

Certainly their move to the wilderness presented enormous challenges. Jack was undaunted, however, by the run-down condition of their acre-and-a-half sanctuary, which was purchased for $10,000 along with a dock and a small cottage. Though the building projects engrossed the whole family, he did most of the work almost single-handedly. Besides renovating the cottage and building a dam to produce electric power, he also slowly constructed a new hillside home. When not laboring physically, Jack now spends his time reading and working on a fictional biography.

Lisa describes how their confrontation with the whims of nature, and with isolation, led to continually unfolding discoveries. As each month passed, they exercised more freedom: in sleeping and waking, dress, play, and physical activity. Finally, she says, they graduated "to the greatest freedom two beings who live together can experience—the freedom to say what you are really thinking and feeling rather than what you should be thinking and feeling. This is the fountain of youth."[15]

Two years after their move they took another big step by reversing traditional sex roles. When their money ran short, and the children's boarding school tuition had to be paid, they agreed that Lisa would be the one to live and work in the city during the week—writing for the Vancouver *Sun*— and return home on weekends. The switch was made naturally and simply, with respect for each other's deepest needs.

As a result of their courageous decisions, Jack and Lisa Hobbs have transformed themselves and their relationship. Says Lisa: "The freedom we have found has loosened us forever from all traditional concepts and has freed us to move and flow with ease as life demands. . . . On the brink of middle age we are finding growth, excitement and fascination in a twenty-year marriage."[16]

Chapter 13   New Directions: Marriage

I *A Second Chance: Changing Partners*

Today we no longer assume, as we did in the past, that marriage is forever. We know that in our complex, rapidly changing society a lifelong marital commitment has become increasingly difficult to sustain. After fifteen or twenty years of togetherness, the contemporary martital relationship is almost invariably corroded by dullness or differences, as many couples in their forties are discovering for themselves. Husband and wife may each be pulling in opposite directions, or simply feel suffocated by sameness or realize that they have grown apart and become hostile strangers who share little.

Faced with an impasse of this sort, many men in their middle years choose to divorce—not because they are seeking to escape marriage, but rather because they want to exchange a boring or unhappy marriage for a more satisfying one. Intent on revitalizing their life by shifting course, they hope that changing partners will give them a second chance at happiness.

Through the years the development of men and women frequently proceeds in mismatched steps, as we have seen. At mid-life a sexual reversal occurs, which means that many women are becoming more assertive and seeking an active role in the outer world, while men are becoming more emotional and turning inward. Whereas this disparity can often be the basis for mutual support, providing the foundation for renewing a relationship, it can also be the basis for mutual resentment.

For the man who is beginning to become aware of emotional needs he never knew he had, one solution—if he cannot achieve the intimacy he craves within his marriage—is to divorce and remarry. "Serial marriages" are the wave of the future, predicts Alvin Toffler, and that is the style many Americans have already adopted. Now such splits and rematches are occurring increasingly during the middle years, and the evidence is overwhelming that these second marriages are usually better than the first ones. The explanation is quite simple, say the experts: People who remarry are more mature, experienced, and confident. They know themselves better, and are less likely to need excessive support or confirmation from a mate. They also tend to work harder at making the marriage successful.

Today it is becoming increasingly common for a man in his forties to leave his wife for a woman half his age. More popular now than ever before, such marriages seem to rejuvenate men who worry about declining energies and diminishing powers. Moreover, in contrast to the scornful judgments passed by a stranded wife, the choice of a younger mate does not necessarily mean that a man is emotionally immature.

In such matters appearances are often deceptive. What is condemned at first glance as regressive behavior may actually be a more complex case of late development. For example, Herb C. is a reporter in his early forties who had been married fourteen years when he fell in love with a much younger woman. Now planning to divorce and remarry, he does sound suspiciously like an infatuated teen-ager when he describes his romance:

> When Laura walked into my office two years ago it was no more than ten minutes into that first conversation when it was quite clear to both of us that something very extraordinary was happening. There was a chemistry that was almost literally crackling in the air. We are fond of telling each other now that we were made for each other, and I genuinely believe there is something in her head and psyche that very much mates with my own, and I think both of us recognized that from the outset.
>
> We really are very much alike. And there is very little to remind us that there are twenty-three years between us, because *she* is young and enthusiastic and terribly bright, and *I* am young and enthusiastic and terribly

bright. We even share the same prejudices and the same view of the world, and we're tickled by the same kinds of things.

I'm going to sound like a sophomore if I tell you what it's been like. It's been falling in love for the first time. It's been finding a woman who is *my* woman, who is everything I always wanted. It has been a hopelessly fairy-tale romance, quite lollipop, you know. We really feel that way about each other. It is a classic love affair which, to us at least, far surpasses anything we know in history. Like the Brownings were beginners, compared to us!

On closer examination, however, it becomes apparent that Herb is not replaying the joys of adolescence, but is developing his capacity for emotional intimacy for the first time. His choice of a younger woman relates both to his earlier lack of direction in some areas, and to his recent growth in others.

Herb's work efforts had been sporadic, and his employment record spotty until he was about thirty-five. Thus he had always depended on his wife, who held a well-paying job, for economic security. Because of sexual inhibitions on both sides, their marriage had settled into a sterile living arrangement—one that Herb found quite comfortable for years. In his late thirties, however, he finally began to experience some success in his career. This increased his self-confidence and sense of personal worth. In turn, as he grew less dependent on his wife and more discontent with his marriage, he became eager to form a loving relationship.

Given this history, it is understandable why Herb was attracted to a younger woman like Laura, who was relatively inexperienced with men. Whereas an older woman might have overwhelmed him at a time when he was just asserting his independence, Laura bolstered his new-found sense of strength. Nourished by her unqualified admiration, he was able to let down his guard and learn from her. Here, too, Laura's age was vital: Like many other contemporary young women, she was extremely open and expressive emotionally. This allowed her to act as Herb's emancipator in the realm of feelings, freeing him to establish the kind of intimacy that many American men cannot manage until around forty any-

way, despite their business success. Delighted by his transformation, Herb describes the pleasures of a give-and-take
relationship:

An interesting thing going on here is that there is a
great deal of role interchangeability. Sometimes I will be
the teacher and Laura will be the disciple, and sometimes she will be the teacher and I will be the disciple.

She is a totally free kind of person, quite uninhibited.
What I mean is we had an occasion to take a drive together on one of the major thruways recently, and it was
the first time I ever had fellatio performed on me during
a 90-mile drive! She expresses herself in every way. She
hollrs when she wants to holler, and she performs fellatio when she wants to perform fellatio. Just whatever
occurs to her to do, when there's no significant reason
not to do it, she does—and I find that very good. I am
somewhat more circumspect in my life.

One of the ways in which she's *my* teacher is giving
greater expression to one's feelings. We verbalize everything, which is something she has helped me to do and
that I never did as freely as I do now. I've come to understand that a feeling of tenderness, a feeling of love, is
of only half value if it's not shared—and that's something I have learned from Laura. Because she does it,
and she requires it. And if I don't pat her bottom often
enough, or tell her that she's gorgeous, I hear about it.
And I'm glad to hear about it. It's very important to me
to give her what she wants and needs.

It was almost a little intimidating at the beginning because I really had never been exposed to a woman who
demanded so much, and was so open in her demands.
Laura wanted it all and she said so. She's an extraordinary person, and an enormously giving person. But I
was aware at the outset that she wanted more than I had
ever been called on to give before, and it worried me a
little bit because I didn't know if I was prepared to accept that kind of relationship.

Because of course it means two things. It means that I
have double the pleasure and double the fun. But it also
means that I have double the anguish. If she stubs her
toe *I* hurt—which means my toe hurts twice as often as

it would otherwise! I didn't know whether I could handle that, so it was something of a conscious decision on my part to try.

Now Laura is my best friend and I am hers, and we respond to each other and nurture each other and comfort each other. I have gotten tremendous feedback from her about myself as a male and as a sexual person and as an intellectual person. And it has been common for my friends to say, "You seem like a different person now—much warmer and more open."

The way I feel about what's happening is that I am taking the final step toward being a grown-up, and I hope that will be expressed in every aspect of my work life and my private life.

The younger woman aside, it is apparent at this stage of life that many men are discovering a new need for closeness. Suddenly aware of the lack of intimacy in a marriage that has become emotionally distant, or discordant, a man is likely to become more critical of an unsatisfactory home situation that, in earlier years, he tolerated with forbearance.

This was the case with Michael B. who, as we saw in a previous chapter, divorced his wife after fifteen years because he began to resent the absence of communication between them. Theirs had been the typical marriage of the 1950s, based on traditional sex roles. He had gone out into the world, and changed in the process of becoming successful. She had stayed at home, limiting her life to the household and kids. Approaching forty, Michael complained that Shirley had become a "nonperson." But, he confessed, his devoting himself exclusively to his business had been costly too: It had left him "less than a whole person."

Since then, Michael has made up for lost time. He has now been married for a year to his second wife, a divorcee in her thirties who was an accomplished workingwoman when he met her. For him, this second marriage is like a second life. Based on deep love and honesty, it has transformed him as a person and caused him to revise his priorities. Newly aware of himself as a profoundly caring human being, Michael describes how this metamorphosis happened, and what it means to him:

I had met Eve briefly at a party while I was still married—and I was attracted to her. So right after I left home I pursued it, and we started seeing each other. Something special was there from the beginning, but there were layers of each other we had to peel off to get to the bottom. For about six months we went through some very, very difficult times together, and we finally found there were no more layers left. We were simply able to talk about anything—anything on our mind—to each other.

We've been married a year now, and we can do it to this day. It's incredible. Whatever comes up gets discussed out in the open so nothing ever lies there to fester and be upset by.

Eve and I have both changed enormously. The experience was unique for both of us. It was the first time either of us really had a relationship with somebody. And whatever gave us the courage to see the problems we faced also gave us the strength, somehow, to survive them. When you take two people with 3½ decades of layers of experience, and suddenly say, "Now open up," because you see something happening to you—that's very traumatic.

I now have an entirely new set of values about what's important in my life—how you lead your life, how you have relationships. I don't run away from them now. My business is still important to me, but it doesn't take precedence anymore. Before I had superficial social relationships. Now it's a much smaller group. I feel it when people feel close to Eve, respond to her—and I realize the absence of that before. Because we're not one; it's not "me and a wife." We're two. It's Eve and me.

One thing I've found with this opening up of emotions which I've never talked about is that there is a possibility for violence in me that never existed before. If I had been walking down the street with Shirley and someone had attacked her, I assume I would have done the right thing—but it wasn't anything I thought about. Now I'm very protective, and if I feel a threat of any kind to Eve I immediately prepare to do violence! To defend. To attack. If I see some guy trying to make a pass at her, I'm ready to go.

Before nothing bothered me—maybe because I didn't care. I wasn't in touch with my feelings. Or they were so submerged they would only come to the surface in an extraordinary moment. Now I'm more aware, my senses are more aware. All the time.

I really don't know what more you could have in a relationship. I consider myself very lucky. Most of the people I know are unhappily married. Because of what's happened to me, guys in this company have come in to talk to me—and what they wanted was to find the guts to look at themselves. I detected that painfully, and it was a shock to me. I've become sensitive to this kind of unhappiness, which I didn't see before, because I was one of them. You never open up any of the feelings. When I did I looked at myself and everybody else from a new perspective, and I suddenly realized the extent to which most men cut off their emotions. They work out compromises, and even when they are unlivable they usually don't do anything about them.

The decision I made to divorce changed my life. It changed everything in my life—including what my future holds and the way I want to handle it. Taking the chance that Eve and I did, I took a chance with my life. Now I find myself more willing to take a chance on other things within that life. It's a terrific way to live—to do what we really want to do, and not worry what other people think, and not feel tied to being president of this company forever. My success has been earned, and I've enjoyed it—but it's not enough anymore. There will be a point in the not-too-distant future when I want to cut down my obligations to everything except Eve and myself so we can, as she says, "smell the flowers all over the world."

II *Revitalizing the Long-term Marriage*

In the future, long-term marriages may become as obsolete as dinosaurs. No one will worry about how to preserve them, because it will be automatically assumed that you dissolve a marriage when it no longer works. Divorce is a common solution to marital woes today, of course, and many men have already gone that route once, or twice, before they reach their forties. But others are still struggling to hold together a relationship of fifteen or twenty years' duration.

This is not an easy task, especially for a generation of men and women who were taught that you grew up, got married, and lived happily (more or less) ever after. When dissatisfactions mount, as they do almost invariably at this stage of life, there is a tendency to blame the institution of marriage itself, as if the marital relationship were something fixed and immutable.

But the fact is that marriage is a process, a fluid relationship that assumes many different forms throughout the years, a relationship that is always either growing or deteriorating. Moreover, the marital bargain that each couple makes is unique because it is based on a psychological contract incorporating their individual needs, desires, fantasies, and expectations. Frequently, however, the terms of this contract have never been openly discussed. Despite the fact that it is much more difficult to renegotiate an old marital contract than make a new one with someone else, this is the challenge facing mid-life couples who want to revitalize their relationship: To the extent that either of them has grown and changed, they will have to hammer out a new contract that accommodates these changes—a new bargain, based on old roots but purged of old rules.

Unless such an effort is made, many members of the helping professions do not hold out much hope for long-term marriages. "I'm really not convinced that our pattern of marriage is a very good one for more than twenty years," said one marital counselor off-the-record. "Many people I see are really just dead on the vine. They live a pointless, meaningless kind of life." Other experts claim that a muted accommodation may be the best some couples can manage. In time they settle for a static union, by detaching and disengaging from each other, because they cannot bear the conflict continually required to achieve something more creative.

When mid-life couples do decide to renew their marriage, rather than merely continue it, they generally do so only after considerable struggle and effort. Because rates of growth differ, and circumstances and interests change, two people have to face these changes and confront each other with their feelings if they are going to enliven their relationship—a painful process, indeed. Some few couples manage to do this continuously, and their partnership evolves steadily throughout the years. More often, however, resentments accumulate silently until an explosive crisis shatters the deadlock. Couples who refuse to deal with this mess either settle for a hostile truce or run to get a divorce. Others open up the hornet's nest and work through their difficulties.

It can get very messy, but the revelation of an affair sometimes precipitates a thorough restructuring of a stagnant marriage. Consider the case of Martin V., a Detroit executive who began feeling restless and dissastisfied at thirty-eight, despite having just begun an exciting new job. Married twelve years, he and his wife, Carol, had no major problems. But he was tyrannical at home, and the tensions had built up. A taste of success made Martin feel that he deserved a more spectacular woman, a wish that led to his falling in love. Devastated when his brief affair ended, he impulsively told his wife about his romance. His confession blew open their relationship, involved months of talking, and finally resulted in their building a new way of life—together. Martin tells what happened:

I was really very immature when I married Carol, and I would yell at her a lot and try to make her into something else. She was very shy and for quite some time she just suffered quietly. I was trying to make her change, but I was also undercutting her—being critical, telling her she couldn't do things well. Really being mean. Slowly she began to consolidate strength and get angry, and let me know she wasn't going to take that stuff. But I hadn't changed a great deal. So just before things blew up we weren't arguing much and there wasn't any open hostility, but she was sad and disappointed and confused by me. And I was impatient and uncharitable and greatly self-pitying.

I had come into the company at a much higher salary than very experienced people, and I really felt quite alone there. Sometimes panicked and scared shitless, really. So I was aggravated by the pressure, and my wife was getting more unhappy about the hours I was keeping, and things were getting tenser and tenser.

With the new work pressures I began to realize that having this suburban family life was really a terrific business handicap. And I began to think Carol wasn't enough for me—that I needed a jazzier, more socially competent person, someone who would attract people to me and be a great hostess. I had this terrible Faustean feeling that I wanted something better, and I would trade an awful lot for it. I wanted to dress a different way, lead a different kind of life, have a different kind of wife—all that "fresh start" stuff was terribly appealing.

Then I met this woman at a party. She was a journalist—a marvelous brunette with terrific legs and a nice big chest—and she was smiling at me in the most interested way. I went right back to where I was when I was 17 years old! I really couldn't believe anyone that nice could be interested in me!

Anyway, we talked and she was just delightful, and I asked her to dinner the next night. We went to a French restaurant, drank quite a bit and began to be very drunk and very much in love. Just tumbling into each other. Sucking each other's fingers and exchanging wine between our lips and stroking each other—totally ignoring our meal and outraging the chef. That night she was the most beautiful woman I had ever been with!

We went back to her apartment and she said, "I'm not going to sleep with you tonight because I'm awfully tired—but we will soon." So we kissed a lot and held each other, and then I went to my hotel room and I stayed up all night, just thinking. I had really fallen deep! And she had even worked me into a whole marriage thing during dinner, which even at the time I knew was slightly absurd. But I kept thinking over and over, "I'm going to have to *kill* myself!" Not really with conviction, but the words kept springing to my lips.

I couldn't resist calling her two days later, which was Saturday. But when I did she said she had thought about it more, and she just couldn't risk falling in love again and losing. I went catatonic. I had to hang up after barely croaking out, "I understand"—but I was *devastated*. When Carol and I sat down to dinner my eyes were brimming and I just couldn't talk. She kept asking me what was wrong, and finally I lost all control of myself and told her I was in love with another woman, but

It was over. She started to shriek and got hysterical, and then we both burst into tears and I confessed the whole thing.

At first she was bitterly unhappy and kept saying it was all over for us. But we talked, we talked endlessly for two months. We'd sit up in the bedroom and talk and fall asleep, and then wake up and talk some more. We were getting it all out—all my feelings about her, and all her disappointments in me. And sometimes we had great tearful embracings and we'd make love. And sometimes I would come home at night and she would have written me beautiful long letters telling me how she felt about things. Angry letters, loving letters. There were times when I thought I had wounded her too deeply and she would never forgive me. But we went on, day by day, working it through.

There was great suffering, but we finally began to put it back together. Carol had said that if we were going to stay married she had to be part of my world—and that we would have to move into the city. That our lives had been too separate. Having a dream house and managing a demanding job—it had all soured. I loved the house but it had become a menace. So that's what we did several months later. We moved into the city.

It has worked out beautifully. My wife isn't isolated anymore, and she is blossoming and having a marvelous time. And now I'm with her and the kids much more and there's more fun, more to do. Marvelous entertaining, with people pouring through our house. And Carol can dash out and join me at any old thing. These are very rudimentary things. But you alter the circumstances and you alter the essence.

We've had great companionship since the move, and in a funny way I feel this is sort of a second marriage. My life has changed enormously for the better—largely because of the way that whole experience was grappled with.

Though Martin's romance may seem too brief to have threatened his marriage, the fantasy elements exerted tremendous power over him, making this affair much more significant than others he deemed "merely sexual." His experience is by no means unique. At this stage of life, when a man is ripe for love, even a fleeting affair can stir up deep feelings.

As we have already seen, the tendency for a man to become more emotionally expressive in his forties has varying consequences. Martin's story contains an important message for the wife who feels threatened by her husband's mid-life changes, because it illustrates that the "other woman" is often the catalyst who releases the parts of a man's self that had lain dormant—the tender, impulsive, caring parts. Thus despite a man's announcing that he has simply "fallen in love" with another woman, the wife who understands that something more profound is happening will realize that her husband's new capacity for feeling can frequently be turned back toward the marriage.

Couples who cannot cope alone with a highly charged marital crisis are turning with increasing frequency to marital counselors or psychotherapists for guidance. Such authorities generally help couples understand that an affair does not necessarily mean the end of a marriage, that they can live through it and sometimes even learn to build a better relationship than they had before.

Underlying most attempts to revitalize marriages is the notion that people grow and change, and that their relationship must too. Couples in treatment of almost any sort soon learn that they have expectations of each other that have never been discussed. They discover how to clarify, and alter, these expectations as they fashion a new foundation for the future. They also discover how to avoid rigid role-playing, express their feelings openly, and give each other more freedom to grow by becoming less dependent and possessive.

"What most people are experiencing at this stage of life is that they are not close," says Donald Smith, the former director of New York's American Foundation of Religion and Psychiatry, who has counseled many mid-life couples. "They are kind of bored with one another, and they just don't feel close. It doesn't always work, but the most effective thing we can do is help them learn to talk to one another honestly about what's going on with them. How they are feeling about themselves, their life with one another, and their fears and anxieties. That's the key thing.

"If they really work hard in a counseling relationship, most people learn some new things about how to communicate on a feeling level with one another. And life, therefore, gets a little bit more open and free, and a little bit more exciting—because their emotions are what's important to them. They learn to enjoy new things, things they were unwilling to get into before. And they learn, I think, a higher level of being together."

III *The Male Crisis: A Shared Plight*

How will a woman react when her husband starts grappling with the turbulent changes of the mid-life crisis? Usually, she will feel confused and threatened and angry. Only dimly aware, at first, that real changes are taking place, she often complains that she has lost contact with him. He may still be doing all the "right" things—coming home at the same hours, observing the same family rituals—but he doesn't really seem to be there. Moody, irritable, or detached, he may seem strangely reticent to talk. Or he may be excessively impatient with the children and no longer willing to bother with their problems. Or he may suddenly evaporate behind a cloud of supposedly urgent business matters.

The woman who instantly concludes that this puzzling behavior is a personal rejection of her will be in trouble. Her first response will be to become clinging and demanding, a real nag. If, however, she is able to stand back a bit and see this as something *he* is going through—and probably having difficulty coping with—she will be in a much stronger position, not only to survive herself, but also to help her husband maneuver through a painful transitional period.

When, as often happens, a man is absolutely unable to voice any of his feelings of unsettlement, the challenge facing his wife will be compounded. For her own sake she must recognize that even her best efforts to persuade him to communicate with her may fail. If she can avoid taking the signs of his discontent personally, that will help, and so will her having outside activities to occupy herself with. During this difficult period her husband will have to work through some of his problems alone, and the more she can be absorbed elsewhere, the better.

To appreciate still further how a woman can deal constructively with her husband's mid-life changes, and how it feels for her to share his plight, let's consider a specific case. Donna and Fred M. were both thirty-nine, and had been married eighteen years, when new issues suddenly disrupted their placid existence.

A lawyer from Chicago, Fred began to do some serious stock-taking, which not only threatened his marriage but also led, eventually, to his altering his life in dramatic ways. Three years later, with the dust just settling, Donna tells how she reacted:

> All of a sudden this whole holocaust invades your household, and you feel a tremendous amount of insecurity.
>
> The most important change was Fred's indecisiveness. Before there weren't a lot of gray areas in his decision-making. Then all of a sudden he comes up with these *crazy* alternatives that I just wasn't used to. New choices about what he wanted to do, how he wanted to live—things that were sort of inconsistent with how he would normally have behaved.
>
> There were a lot of fantasy ideas that seemed far-fetched for a man who had been on a straight road to "success" and had a pretty clear vision of what that meant to him from age twenty on. Now, all the things he had never questioned, he began to question. It made me feel very insecure because I didn't know what was going to happen, and some of it was threatening to me, certainly. He was questioning the marriage, questioning his sense of responsibility.
>
> How did I handle it? *Ignored* it! That was my immediate reaction. What do you do when you're frightened by something? You sweep it under the carpet and hope it's going to go away! Then I began to take it very personally—which was how things erupted and we started talking about it. But that wasn't for six months. It took me six months to realize there were definite changes going on in Fred.

During the next year Fred made a major move: He gave up a high-salaried partnership in a law firm to strike out on his own. Having been through a similar struggle for independence six years earlier, when she became a free-lance photographer, Donna could be supportive. But things became more difficult for her when, soon after the job change, Fred announced that he now wanted to be "emotionally irresponsible" too. Though he didn't feel their marital separation would be a permanent break, he insisted that he needed some "thinking time"—and some freedom. Donna tells how she reacted:

The idea was totally unexpected. But for several months this horrible thing he was feeling about responsibility had been coming through to me—so I wasn't bowled over by it. What saved me was that because of my own awareness I didn't feel he was doing it *to* me. I felt he was doing it *for* him. And I think that's the whole big ballgame. That's really where it's at. Once you can see that, you can decide—if there's love and kindness and caring on both parts—how best to handle the situation so everybody's going to come out all right.

There was no question of loving, but there was a question for him of re-evaluating. We were sixteen when we fell in love, and twenty-one when we got married, and I think he was asking whether that sixteen-year-old boy had the right to determine where he would be for the rest of his life—without his ever really having investigated his feelings about it.

The sexual thing was a big issue, and we did talk about that. He wanted freedom to investigate his sexual needs *and* his involvement needs. Not just have a breezy affair, but could he be *involved* with another woman?—which he claims he had never really been. And he needed the freedom to explore that without feeling guilty.

I felt threatened—and I recognized the enormity of the risks. But I must admit I felt some excitement, and I wanted to take advantage of it myself. And this is where I think we succeeded better than most people, because we were able to honestly communicate our feelings, and also achieve a fairness in the arrangement. Some women who go through this become martyrs. They walk around saying, "Poor me!"—and then lock themselves in the house with their kids and lie prostrate on the floor!

They're not doing anything for themselves, and they become the injured party.

Fred was very giving and understanding in all this. He wanted something for himself, but not at my expense—and that was the very mature part of his personality that was great. He stayed at the house with the kids two nights a week, which allowed me to live on my own at my studio. And so we were both able to get an illusion of freedom.

When I really got chicken was the night he was leaving. I cracked up. I remember that. I had a big emotional scene, and we both cried, and did a whole number. Like we were parting forever. Because we were both mature enough to understand that if we were doing this—and it was so important to him that he had to work it out outside the marriage—then the risks were *real*.

But I certainly thought my risks in *not* allowing him to do this were far greater. To me, that meant the risk of having a very ordinary, dull, compromised marriage for the rest of our lives—which I was not willing to settle for.

Despite occasional waves of fear and loneliness, Donna created an active social life for herself that included men, and kept busy with her work. She expected the separation to last about six months, but it was only two months later when Fred decided he had "done his thing"—and that his emotional commitment was to his wife. Both forty-two now, Donna and Fred have reshaped almost every aspect of their existence together, including the values they endorse, the friends they see, and the way they spend their leisure time. Most important, they have established—for the first time in their lives—a genuinely loving relationship, which Donna describes:

What came out of it—our both passing through this holocaust—was the ability to really communicate on deep levels. Before, I communicated but Fred didn't hear. Now he hears. And there is certainly a great sense of security in our marriage that we never felt before, which makes it easier to live your everyday life!

Now there isn't anything we wouldn't express to each other. I used to feel that when I was emotionally down Fred was *gone*. I mean, go find him! He was busy in the office, and had fourteen appointments that night, and seventeen people coming into town the next day, and would I please go handle my emotional crisis by myself. Quietly. But now when I'm miserable and depressed, he does *not* run away. He's willing to sit down and talk about it, and we usually work out some solution.

Or I say I've got to get away by myself for a few days, and ask him to take care of the house and kids. And the answer is *Yes*, unquestionably Yes. Before it would have been one hassle after another. He was threatened. Where was I going? Why did I have to do that? And I was threatened because he was hiding in his busy work to get away from what I was feeling, because it was too oppressive for him. But we don't have that kind of hassle anymore. At all!

And because there's been so much communication we understand each other's weaknesses better—and we've stopped arguing about those niggling, horrible things that make marriages so stinking. Part of that, I think, is that he's now accepted me as the person I am because this is where he wants to be. And if I'm his *choice*—and he's chosen to recommit himself to the marriage then I've got to be superspecial! And so some of my little faults can be overlooked.

Five years ago we didn't have a marriage. We were two people who lived together because we had chosen to when we were sixteen. We liked each other a lot, and were maybe even best friends, and we lived together very well. But *around* each other—certainly not *with* each other the way we do now.

When a man changes gears at mid-life, suffering the pangs of dislocation that usually accompany this shift, his feelings of anguish are bound to affect his marriage—for better or for worse. How well the marriage survives these changes depends on many factors, obviously, but among these a woman's ability to tolerate her husband's depression is crucial. Equally important, as Fred and Donna's story shows, is how much caring and mutual respect existed between two people before.

If there is a basic bond of warm feelings, it is possible for a couple to come together on a deeper more honest basis when the crisis period ends.

By contrast, the fate of the marriage will probably be less happy when a man's discontent with himself includes resentment toward his wife; or when he feels terribly disappointed by what he has done with his life, and angered by the part he believes his wife has played in this scenario. In such instances, even though a woman may feel that their marriage is tolerable, if not ideal, she may still be unable to salvage the relationship. Her own feelings of betrayal and abandonment will probably undercut any attempts at reconciliation.

"To the extent that the wife is in the grip of feelings of moral outrage and victimization ₂ . . . there is probably nothing she can do to keep the marriage together," observes Maria Levinson of the Yale group. "And perhaps, if they have been moving apart over a period of years, the marriage isn't worth saving. It might be liberating for both, and a relief for the children, if they simply went their separate ways."[1] For a real reconciliation to occur, significant changes in their relationship have to be made. Rather than being merely sympathetic, she points out, a woman "would have to be prepared to grasp the magnitude of [her husband's] despair, to share it in whatever ways she could . . . and to see their joint plight as containing also the possibility for their further development."[2]

To be sure, such understanding is a great deal to expect from any woman, especially at a stage of life when she is probably making some changes of her own and suffering from doubts and insecurities too. In need of reassurance herself, she may feel that it is grossly unfair for her to have to bolster her husband while her own needs go unmet. And she may be right: It is unfair. But faced with the fact that her husband is in crisis and therefore unable, at least temporarily, to meet her emotional needs, a wife must try—if she believes her marriage is worth saving—to look at her situation objectively.

This does not mean that the woman who has decided to stand by her husband during this trying time should become a martyr or bear the burden alone. To the contrary, she should seek out nurturing friends with whom she can safely ventilate her anxieties and anger, enlarge her sphere of interests to whatever extent possible, and—this above all—never forget that her own survival is of primary importance. Describing what she learned from personal experience, Donna counsels as follows:

> What would I advise other women? Well, the big thing for me was that I had lots of people helping me recognize that Fred's changes weren't a personal affront to me. And I think any woman who's having trouble coping during this period should get as much support as she can from anyone she trusts—family, friends, or a therapist.
>
> I also think it's very important for a woman to care about something else. Nobody should be totally committed to one thing—marriage. You *must* have some sort of outside commitment. And if you don't have it before you start feeling some of these changes in your husband, quickly, quickly run out and find something! Start looking, start dabbling, start opening up. Because if you get desperately threatened nobody has a chance. But if you open yourself up to other things—to the world, people, anything—you will begin to feel your own security within yourself.
>
> At a certain point when this starts happening you must take yourself out of it. *Detach*—I guess that's the right word. You must sort of detach from it and put it in perspective.

IV Reinventing Marriage

In America today there are many signs of revolt against marriage, including high rates of divorce and infidelity, as well as a growing number of couples who are living together unwed. But this does not mean that marriage will become extinct, say the experts. To the contrary: Traditional patriarchal marriage may be dying, and along with it the notion that wedded harmony depends on a master-servant relationship, but meanwhile marriage is being reborn in new forms every day. Before our eyes it is changing its contours, shedding its standard but straitlaced shape to assume a wide variety of flexible forms that are better suited to the human needs of contemporary men and woman.

In the future, says author Morton Hunt, we will have an even greater need than we do now for love relationships that offer intimacy, warmth, and reliability. Thus he predicts that the marriage of the future will be a free and unconstrained union of a man and a woman who are companions, partners, and sexual lovers. It will exist only as long as it remains valid for both people, and it will rarely last a lifetime.[3]

Clearly we are already heading in this direction, as couples of all ages struggle to discover what suits them best. Embarked on a bold new experiment that our society has not yet fully sanctioned, such couples have discarded the approved script on how to play husband and wife in order to design marital bargains that mesh with their personal preferences. We read about these novel arrangements, gossip about them with relish, and occasionally even meet friends or neighbors who have broken the old marital mold. But despite our assumption that such daring innovators are rare, more Americans than we might suspect are experimenting today with the myriad new ways of being married. The fact that over one million people have enrolled in marital enrichment programs or marital encounter groups, which are usually sponsored under conservative religious auspices, is one indication of this revolutionary trend.

More flamboyant choices aimed at loosening the bonds of matrimony include those made by couples who decide on open marriage, or sexual "swinging" or communal living. Other, less radical innovations are being tried by the increasing number of husbands and wives who are commuting to work in separate cities during the week, while living together only on weekends. And then there are those couples who, having rejected the standard stereotypes, are choosing to reverse roles. According to their agreement, the woman goes off to the office each day while the man stays home to mind the kids. Or, in another version, both partners agree to divide the household chores, take turns with the children, and maybe even grant each other permission to enjoy separate vacations.

Different strokes for different folks, as the saying goes. These are but a few examples of the ways in which couples today are rewriting the marital contract to suit their own individual needs, ignoring traditional rules that hamper their relationship and hinder their growth. Which is not to say that revamping a marriage in mid-stream is easily accomplished.

The barriers to change, substantial enough when a single individual is concerned, are greater still when they involve two persons. Moreover, this generation of mid-life men and women, having been victimized by the masculine and feminine mystiques, are likely to experience some soul-shattering conflicts as they struggle to replace conventional roles with more fluid desires and demands.

But difficult does not mean impossible. Despite the obstacles that chain people to the past, couples now in their middle years who want to reinvent their own marriage have ample resources available to help them. In addition to the growing number of marital counselors and therapists now practicing nationwide, growth centers, couples groups, and weekend marathons are becoming more widespread. Such group experiences provide couples with a unique opportunity to explore new ways of getting in touch with themselves and their mate, new ways of communicating and relating. And in the process they help to open their imagination to other possibilities, other patterns of being married.

Even for couples who are not yet ready to risk exposing themselves, guidelines for change are available. Countless books on every aspect of married life, including the sexual, are now in print—and some of them are excellent.[4] Moreover, the existence of books that deal candidly with the most intimate aspects of personal relationships is but part of a larger trend in our society whereby issues that were once considered taboo—too embarrassing, too private—are now being openly discussed, not only in the media but at social gatherings as well. Influenced by consciousness-raising sessions, women today are leveling with one another about their personal lives, including sex and love and marriage, with a candor that would have been considered shocking not long ago.

From all these sources—couples groups, books and articles, and more open discussions—men and women in their middle years are learning that there is not just one way to be married, but many. By itself such knowledge is not a solution, of course. But it can be a start, a stimulant, a way to initiate a thought-provoking dialogue between a husband and a wife who have discovered, after many years together, that their marriage has become deadly dull. Or just plain deadly. The next step, for those who still care enough to struggle with the impasse, is for a couple to embark on a series of experiments until they evolve a new relationship that preserves parts of the old pattern that are still viable, but also includes some changes. By trial and error they can then originate, in terms uniquely tailored to the two of them, a way of living married that is more pleasurable than the pattern they adopted automatically in their youth.

Being able to make such a creative choice is one of the joys of becoming middle-aged. Popular wisdom notwithstanding, it is only those over forty who really know who they are, what they want, and how to get it. In contrast to the young and innocent, whose idealism is often impotent, men and women in their middle years have sufficient experience, sound judgment, and financial resources to translate their desires into deeds. Maturity, it turns out, does have special rewards: It means possessing the courage and confidence to redesign one's life, and one's marriage, to suit personal proclivities. Society be damned.

Section V SURMOUNTING THE CRISIS

Chapter 14   The Metamorphosis from Boy/Man to Man

I *Toward Self-renewal*

The mid-life crisis is a time of metamorphosis. It is a time when the American male crosses the boundary line that separates the boy/man from the man. But as we have seen, this critical turning point not only offers new opportunities, it also poses new dangers. To resolve the crisis a man must first appreciate what the crossing really signifies.

"Beyond question I found myself at mid-life in a radical crisis," writes Sam Keen, author, editor, and teacher, in an autobiographical memoir. "My emotional capital seemed exhausted. My past looked infinitely richer than any future I might create. Depression lurked and easily invaded any empty moment. I had either to surrender to despair or mourn the death of my old life and find some way to begin again.

"For many months I was a victim of bitter confusion. And then gradually my struggle to create or discover a new life began to take form. I came to the realization that I was living out a myth that gave my pain, conflict and dislocation a meaning. With a sense of relief I now understood the central message of the Christian myth: You must die in order to be reborn.

"I had been living the story of the hero who must descend through the dim winter light into the underworld of chaos and pain before he can spring up into the miraculous light of the ordinary. Through discovering that the myth which informs my life with meaning involves the belief that all life is a process of beginnings without end, I found the terrors of the mid-life identity crisis becoming transformed into an adventure."[1]

239

So too for other men in their middle years: Surmounting this crisis demands a transformation of beliefs and a change in attitudes. This in itself is a monumental undertaking that requires a man to revise his definitions of what it means to be a male, an adult, and a human being. There is a profound connection between what we expect and what we get in life; and our expectations include what we believe about human nature and about ourselves.

Mid-life is a time for transformation. It is the time for a man to change what he believes about himself from negative and self-denying to positive and self-affirming. It is the time for him to redefine the facts of life and enlarge his sense of possibilities.

One of the major challenges facing this generation of mid-life men is to break out of the masculine mystique. *Macho* values that require a man to be tough, competitive, and always in control turn out to be boyish virtues. After forty they fail to sustain.

It is hard work to be manly in the traditional way, and it is too confining. Men are as capable as women of a broad range of feelings, but the mystique will not allow a man to reveal the depth of his inner experience to himself or to others. Thus he is obliged to hide much of his real self, to repress his real feelings. Fearful of exposing weakness or vulnerability, he must be continually tense, guarded, and armored. Such emotional repression is dangerous and self-destructive. It causes a man to lose contact with his inner self and with reality.

Worse still, because the conventional male role carries with it a chronic burden of stress, it may be a factor related to the American male's shorter life span. Today it is becoming obvious that many apparently physical illnesses have a psychological and, ultimately, social root. Heart disease is an illness that belongs in this category, and it is time we recognize that fact. There is strong evidence, as we have seen, that Type A behavior—a composite of our society's most admired male traits—too often leads to premature death.

To surmount the mid-life crisis, then, a man not only needs a new definition of masculinity but a new definition of health and sickness as well. Masculinity in the old sense is predicated on too narrow a base: the work role. Defining a man primarily as a producer and an achiever leads to a sickening way of life. Ironically, though, being manly also makes it difficult for a man to recognize when he is sick. Trained to ignore his feelings in order to pursue his goals, he is less sensitive than women to inner signals that tell him that all is not well. Tuning out these inner distress signals until they can no longer be ignored, he is unlikely to heed the signs of his own sickness until the lethal aspects of his manly way of life have brought him to the point of total collapse.

At mid-life when a man is forced to confront his mortality and recognize that his years are limited, it is vital that he learn to take care of himself in wiser ways than the masculine mystique allows. It is time for him to recognize that he is neither a machine nor superhuman. It is time for him to let go of heroic imperatives in favor of more humane values. The life he saves may be his own.

The American male has been conditioned to experience himself in negative ways. He has been conditioned to accept a static view of what it means to be an adult—rigid, inflexible, and in decline. And in accord with most Western religious doctrines, he has been taught that human nature is essentially evil, that man is doomed from the start.

We are partly creatures of our own images, and these images have practical consequences in terms of how we live and the choices we make. At mid-life a man's beliefs about himself—and about what is still possible for him—tend to become self-fulfilling prophecies. Thus if he believes that he is devoid of free will and that nothing he does can alter or improve his life, the odds are that his actions will be futile. Similarly, if he believes that aging is a curse that congeals the self, that life is all downhill after forty, the odds are that for him it will be.

This matter of self-fulfilling prophecies relates not only to how a man views himself in particular, but also to how he views the human potential in the larger sense. To make significant changes at this stage of life he must first believe that change is possible. More fundamentally, he must believe that human beings are sufficiently creative to make meaningful choices throughout their entire life span.

Implicit in the new concept of adulthood proposed by developmental psychologists like the Yale group is a vision of human nature that differs radically from the one we have become accustomed to. This vision comes from many different sources: From Eastern religions, existential philosophers, humanist psychologists, and psychoanalytic thinkers. What is emerging from these combined sources is a more positive view of man's inner depths than that proposed by Freud. One basic difference is that whereas Freud conceived of the unconscious primarily as a storehouse for repressed memories from the past, theorists like Jung maintain that possibilities for the future—seeds of growth—are also contained in the unconscious. This change in emphasis has resulted in a more optimistic vision of human nature, whereby man is seen as possessing an inherent capacity for growth and change.

This view of man as an evolutionary creature with an instinctual need for purpose and meaning, a creature capable of assuming responsibility for his own life, became the basis for the human potential movement in the 1960s. Today that movement has expanded considerably, in scope and impact, to include a wide variety of disciplines and therapies, both Eastern and Western. Now known as the consciousness revolution, it is unified by the central belief that man can achieve self-transcendence through increased awareness of the physical, emotional, and spiritual dimensions of his existence.

Convinced that we have underestimated our capacity to lead open, evolving, and meaningful lives, a growing number of Americans are joining this revolution to explore new avenues for personal change and renewal. Like some of the men we have heard from in this book, they are proving that an affirmative view of the human potential is valid. They are proving that people can reshape their own future continually, regardless of age. They are proving that growth is a lifelong process, that a person's capacity for self-development does not diminish through the years. Accepting this vision of what it means to be human is a prerequisite for surmounting the mid-life crisis.

Adult growth is more complex than that of children, obviously, and more painful too. It is a normal process but not an automatic one. When Jung said that human beings strive for wholeness, he emphasized that this striving had two aspects: It is a natural process, on the one hand, but it is also work— a task to be accomplished. Similarly, Erikson stressed that each developmental crisis could be resolved for better or for worse. Growth is a risky business. More disturbing still, it is disturbing. The process of growth includes stages where a person feels despondent and in despair.

Here again we need to revise our definitions of sickness and health. In the adult, anxiety and depression often accompany inner growth. Those tormenting emotions are in fact inherent parts of the process. On the surface such symptoms may look deceptively like illness, but if they are treated like pathology the possibilities for growth will be undercut.

Psychic pain, like physical pain, is a sign that a person's way of life has lost its meaning or become sickening. At mid-life such pain usually means that it is time to move on, time to discard old beliefs, old habits, and old values that have been outgrown, in order to find new ways to restructure one's self and one's life. The challenge is stimulating but scary. It beckons a man into unknown territory, both within himself and without. Moving from the old to the new is not likely to be quickly or easily accomplished. There will be a time of not knowing, a time of conflict and confusion.

This will be agonizing to endure unless a man comprehends what is happening within him. More important than the particulars of this crisis period, the specific issues we have already examined, he must understand the growth process itself—especially its death-and-rebirth aspect. This is a difficult concept to grasp because it is alien to our industrial culture and our scientific way of thinking. By contrast, in many other societies where the metaphors for life and time are taken from the natural world, crossing from one life stage to another is ritualized by rites of passage that symbolize a death-and-rebirth process.

Traditionally the rites of passage had three phases: (1) social disengagement and psychological dying; (2) a time and a place of isolation outside familiar boundaries, which anthropologist Arnold van Gennep called "the neutral zone"; and (3) psychological rebirth and social reintegration.

What seems like sickness or personality disturbance during the mid-life crisis is comparable to the experience in archaic cultures of being in the neutral zone. This meant a vigil in the wilderness, usually a forest or desert, where the person was exposed—utterly alone—to the terrifying powers of the psyche and the universe. This was supposed to be a time of access to visions and voices, a time when life-turning discoveries could be made. But it was also a time of terror and chaos.

Recognizing the perils of this passage from the old to the new, archaic cultures understood that the pull of the unknown future can be frightening. They therefore prepared people for this experience of lostness and dread that is so often felt in the midst of profound change, and helped to ease them through it. In such societies, too, the initiate not only realized that his elders had survived but also that new opportunities awaited him on the other side of the passage.

In our culture no such preparation and no such promise are offered to those who experience a similar kind of psychological death and rebirth. Lacking such supports, the American male must maneuver the painful mid-life passage on his own. He must recognize that the terror and turmoil that he feels are not signs that he is going crazy. Rather the feeling that everything is falling apart, that the old ways are futile or meaningless, is a prelude to self-renewal—or rebirth. It means that the metamorphosis is under way. New beginnings and new adventures lie ahead.

II *Guidelines for Growth and Change*

Faced with the painful issues and perplexing options that arise during the mid-life period, a man can decide to spin his wheels and stagnate, or he can decide to move on, change, and grow. The choice is his to make.

Every man's crisis is unique. Although it generally occurs at around forty, it will vary both in severity and in timing. Neither a sickness to be cured nor a problem to be solved, it nonetheless involves distress. Here are some guidelines to ease the passage:

Take the Mid-life Crisis Seriously. Don't minimize the importance of this event. Face it and recognize it. Confusion at this stage of life is not a sign of immaturity or unmanliness or neurosis. It is not something to apologize for or be ashamed of. You should take this period seriously by coming to terms with yourself, facing reality, and recognizing that your time is limited. Make the remaining years count—every day, every moment.

Recognize the Need to Mourn. The mid-life period is a time of loss and change. It is primarily a mourning experience. Feelings of anger and sorrow and disappointment for the loss of youth, and with it the loss of an illusion of omnipotence and immortality, are common. You need to talk about these painful feelings with someone you trust. If they interfere with your work, or with your enjoyment of life, you might even consider talking to a good therapist. This mourning is a healing process that will free you to make new choices. "In the process of talking," says Harry Levinson, "the wise man reworks his life experiences and his feelings until he is all mourned out and no longer afraid of being mortal."[2]

Take Responsibility for Your Own Life. It is time to recognize that you, and you alone, are responsible for your life and the situations in which you find yourself. Once you become aware that the traps you complain of are largely of your own making, you will also see that you have alternatives. Think about how to change what you dislike. Ask yourself what prevents you from making changes. Every man has his own way of escaping life's pressures: drinking excessively, chasing women, working too hard, or sleeping or eating too much. Become aware of the ways you try to escape during this stressful period and make sure you aren't running away too much—rather than facing your problems and finding solutions for them.

Become responsible for who you are as well as for what you do. Evaluate your strengths and weaknesses. Find out what you like about yourself and what you don't. Consider how you might want to change. As part of this effort, listen to your wife, your children, and your friends. Those who are close to you may be trying to tell you things you need to hear. Don't dismiss their feelings or their observations.

Re-examine Your Values and Goals. Think about the different areas of your life. Which do you find satisfying? Which are meaningless to you? Think about what is really important to you. Are you living in accord with the values you claim to endorse? Are you working at something you believe in? If not, what could you do differently? What are your goals for the future? And are those goals in keeping with your values? If your life is too work-oriented, consider broadening your range of interests and opening yourself to new ideas. Your mind and your imagination, like your body, need exercise. Read more widely, go to lectures or museums, and make friends with people whose interests differ from yours. Try to make room in your life for activities that are neither productive nor purposeful, but simply pleasurable.

Learn to Substitute New Sources of Gratification for Old. Flexibility is the key to aging well. A cultural study of mental health among the elderly found that the mentally ill clung most rigidly to the predominant American values: achievement, success, autonomy, and control.[8] Ambitious and competitive, they still aspired to earlier goals and were unable to perceive satisfying alternatives. The mentally healthy, on the other hand, were able to adjust to changing circumstances with more flexibility and forbearance. Less compulsive and more relaxed, they seemed freed from earlier social imperatives. Most important, they were able to substitute new sources of gratification for old ones no longer available. This study found that those people who had a broader and more flexible spectrum of values in middle life were most likely to remain healthy later.

Get in Touch with Your Feelings. Become more aware of your feelings and learn how to express them. When you push your feelings aside to avoid losing control, they end up controlling you. Talking about them increases your self-awareness and contributes to your well-being. Experience your painful feelings, including those of vulnerability; they are part of your inner life, part of your humanity. Try to express your anger when you feel it, directly and appropriately. This is much healthier than letting angry feelings accumulate until an explosion ensues. Learn more about what makes you resentful, what triggers your rage, and consider ways to change those situations. Pay attention, too, to what delights and pleases you. Discovering what excites you will tell you more about what you really want. It will also give you some important clues about the direction in which you might like to move for the future.

Respect Your Body. Accept the fact that you *are* your body, that body and mind cannot easily be divided. Health has to do with both. Though mid-life is the time you should begin to take care of yourself by watching your diet, exercising, and avoiding excessive alcohol or pills, this kind of regime is not sufficient by itself. Enjoying your body—finding a pleasurable balance among work, relaxation, and play—is also an essential aspect of health.

As we have seen, too many American men die prematurely; and the stress imposed by the traditional male role is a factor in these early deaths. Stress is a normal part of living. Without some pressures and challenges, life would be boring indeed. But some forms of stress should be curtailed, especially the destructive tendencies of so-called masculine behavior: the effort to always control yourself and your environment; the need to compete in all areas of life; the inclination to dismiss all nonproductive activity as meaningless; and the inability to be open or expressive. The body pays a heavy price for such behavior.

Listen to the messages you send yourself. If you find yourself depressed or irritable, manic or bored; if you suddenly have sexual problems or little interest in sex; if you are always tired or cannot sleep; if your blood pressure goes up; or if you seem to be having more headaches, stomach aches, or hangovers, don't dismiss or ignore these symptoms. Find out what they mean, find out what your body is trying to tell you. Consider if your way of life has become sickening, if you need to change your habits or patterns, or even extricate yourself from a destructive situation. Body wisdom is often more profound than reason.

Break the Type A Pattern. As we have seen, heart attacks have been linked to a particular behavior pattern by cardiologists Friedman and Rosenman. The Type A striver is excessively time-conscious, highly competitive, and inclined to push himself to the limits. A victim of "hurry sickness," he must learn how to slow down. Emphatic about the need for a Type A man to change his pattern, Dr. Friedman suggests the following:

Discontinue polyphasic thinking. The habit of thinking about several things at one time produces a terrific mental struggle. Any man who catches himself doing this must cut it out at all cost, even though he thinks it is useful.

Listen without interrupting. Concentrate on listening to another person's conversation without ever interrupting, no matter how long it goes on. Patients are advised to practice with their wives by trying never to bring them to a point.

Read books that demand concentration. "I want my patients to have new friends—friends they can respect, whom they can't talk back to, or interrupt," says Dr. Friedman. "And that means books. I want them to find something as important to them as the numbers game." He suggests reading philosophy or a complex novel by Proust.

Have a retreat at home. Every man should have a place in his house—besides the bathroom—where he can be alone. He should have a place for privacy, a space of his own, where he can have the leisure to think and "to meet himself."

Restructure trips and vacations. Avoid jam-packed, hectic business trips and too much traveling in one day. For conventions and business meetings, arrive the night before and rest; then stay another day after it's over instead of rushing home immediately. Vacations, too, should be relaxed, unhurried, and noncompetitive.

Plan some idleness in every day. Each day should allow room for idle time. Get up half an hour earlier in the morning so that you can be more relaxed about dressing, breakfasting, and being with your family. Avoid scheduling too many things in any one day. Whenever feasible, take a long lunch break—preferably *not* with business associates. Keep a clean desk, free of debris, those accumulated reminders that usually trigger guilt. Enjoy the time saved by taking a new look at the world: Walk in the park, go into a church and listen to the organ, watch people stroll by, saunter through a museum.[4]

Underlying these directives, says Dr. Friedman, are three main points: (1) Things worth being are better than things worth having; (2) live by the calendar rather than the stopwatch; and (3) consider any day that does not contain something of memory value—something related to beauty, love, growth, or novelty—a lost day. Though designed for the Type A man, these prescriptions should be helpful for all men in their middle years. They offer a man a program for restructuring his life to allow more room and time to explore his thoughts and feelings—and this is certainly a necessary step in passing through a mid-life crisis.

To revitalize his life after forty, a man must acknowledge that change is possible and that new options exist. He must be willing not only to entertain new ideas, but also to open himself up to new aspects of experience. He must be daring enough to risk having some adventures with himself. Here are some general guidelines for making mid-life changes:

Be Realistic. Evaluate realistically what you can and cannot change about yourself, what opportunities for change are actually available, and what risks are involved. Remember that an attempt to change can backfire. Ask yourself how you would respond if it did. Beware of making any change that, if it failed, would shatter your self-esteem. And don't expect that changing your situation, or changing locations, will transform you as a person.

Harry Levinson suggests that a man start by getting "accurate feedback on who he is." This means carefully checking out how you see yourself compared to how you actually come across, by talking with a trusted friend, your wife, or a professional counselor. "Some guys will perceive themselves as big and mighty and aggressive," Levinson explains, "but usually they are much more passive and compliant in fact. And if a man deludes himself with that kind of thing there is bound to be disappointment." Increasing your self-awareness will enable you to make more rational decisions about what changes are possible for you. If you do not come away from such scrutiny feeling respectful of yourself, however, you should consider going into therapy to make internal changes before changing your situation or your job.

Take an Inventory of Your Life. Deciding what changes to make can be troublesome. Despite feeling restless and dissatisfied, many men are confused about which aspect of their life to alter. Just knowing you are miserable, but not knowing *why,* is bound to be paralyzing. To break this deadlock, industrial psychologist Lawrence Zeitlin advises, first, that you try "to get a reasonable leg" on the combination of factors causing your discontent. You should try to define the actual problems and objectify what you really want. To this end, Zeitlin suggests making a "cold-blooded inventory" of your life's assets and liabilities by writing every conceivable factor on a scale from 1 to 10. "Go someplace where you have nothing to do but sit and think for several hours," he says, "and be totally honest with yourself."

Next, he advises going through a "what if?" scheme to look at the consequences of every possible action that might change and improve matters: What if I quit my job? Go back to school? Move into the city? Stop paying the mortgage? Take a year off? What if I decide to get a divorce? Consult a therapist? Try a marriage counselor? Start having an affair? Or stop having one?

Test Your Ideas on Others. Having carefully evaluated your feelings about every possible move, and arrived at some tentative notions on what to change, you should then test your ideas by discussing them with other people. If the home situation is tolerable, a man might talk first to his wife. "He should really level with her," Zeitlin suggests. "Tell her about his frustrations and anxieties and fears, tell her he feels trapped in his life. And maybe she'll level with him, too, and talk about her problems. They might even arrive at some important decisions together." Talking honestly with a number of people will enable you to externalize and put limits on your problems. You can then begin to work toward some realistic solutions and make some meaningful changes.

Avoid Making Too Many Changes Too Suddenly. Don't make changes impulsively without thinking and talking about your plans first. Sudden extreme changes rarely pay off. It takes a lot of preparation, both internal and external, to change old habits and restructure your life. Moreover, all change is stressful and involves an element of loss. To cope with this stress you need some "stability zones" in your life, some areas of comfort and safety. You also need to consider carefully the consequences of your actions. Too many changes in too short a time can even lead to illness.

Try Small Changes First. Paradoxical as it sounds, you need not make a dramatic change in order to change your life dramatically. If you want to transform your life, the most effective way to begin may be to take one step in a new direction. Taking this first step, even if it is a small one—like changing a habit, signing up for a course, cultivating a new friend, learning another language, altering a daily routine, or pursuing a new leisure activity—can lead to bigger things. Especially if you have been feeling trapped, making one minor change can be a major breakthrough. There is a snowball effect. One change often precipitates another, then another, culminating eventually in a series of changes that amount to a genuine metamorphosis.

What is happening is that with each step you confirm your own ability to make choices and take responsibility for your own life. From this you gain strength and energy, facilitating additional changes of greater proportion and greater risk. Part of this process is internal change—a new feeling of self-assurance, a new attitude about what is possible.

It has even been shown that something as simple as adopting a regular exercise routine can produce definite personality change. When Professor A. H. Ismail of Purdue University put a group of men, aged thirty to sixty-five, through a four-month program of strenuous calisthenics and running, the least fit men were found at first to be much less emotionally stable and self-confident than the fittest. By the end of the program, however, this first group had improved sharply on both counts.

"We have established a fact that is more important than the value of exercise," says Ismail. "If something as tangible, direct, and accessible as a physical exercise program can cause such distinct and rapid changes in personalities of middle-aged men, there probably are other experiences that can change supposedly crystallized personalities. The adult personality may be much more plastic than we thought."[5]

The mid-life crisis is a stormy transitional period that is marked by internal changes, by conflicts and challenges. Like the turbulent period of adolescence, it leads to a new and calmer stage of life: middle age. But unlike the earlier crisis, that which occurs in the middle years still seems mysterious and is too often misunderstood. It is time we learn to recognize both the perils and the potentials of this crucial turning point.

In essence, the mid-life metamorphosis from boy/man to man means becoming more authentic, independent, and authoritative. It means getting in touch with parts of the self that had been dormant earlier. It means integrating head and heart, masculine and feminine, body and mind. Becoming a man in the fullest sense means becoming whole.

A moment comes when there is a shift
from destruction of the old
to borning of the new.
The crisis is over. . . .

The renewal of the self has always been described by
    metaphors.
The process is poetic.
It is like:
a butterfly emerging from a cocoon;
coming out of a dark cave into the sunlight . . .
shedding an old skin;
breathing deeply of fresh air;
being born again. . . .

For me the most helpful metaphors are political:
        liberation;
        a psychological Fourth of July;
        an end to tyranny—the tyranny of the oughts,
                        dissatisfaction, perfectionism,
                        moralism, intellect,
        the overthrow of psychological capitalism in
            which the head (capital) controls the body;
        the transfer of authority (power) from outside
            to inside. . . .

                                Sam Keen
                                Beginnings Without End[6]

Chapter 15   Coming of Age in America

The man who craves renewal at mid-life cannot count on much help from society. For the most part he will have to work through this crisis period alone, and to do so he will have to struggle to overcome in himself many of the beliefs he shares with the culture in which he lives.

This is a shame. It is imperative that we as a society not only recognize and acknowledge the existence of the mid-life crisis and other adult transitional periods, but that we also give full support to the development of the human potential. We should do so not only to enlarge our culture's view of the life cycle, but also to bring it more in accord with the actual rhythms of individual lives. As things stand now, our society is set up to maximize wealth and power rather than human fulfillment. It is time for a transformation of values, a change in vision.

Today it is becoming increasingly apparent that our materialistic, competitive way of life is causing human obsolescence. With our emphasis on commercial values we have adopted a mechanistic view of people. We prize them when they are productive, discard them when they are not. To be old in America is to be discounted and discredited. To be old is to be powerless and isolated. By denying the elderly an opportunity to participate in our society we strip them of their humanity, deprive them of their dignity, and in the process we amputate our own life span.

These inhuman values and attitudes are also hard on men in their middle years. Responsible for both the old and the young, they bear a heavy emotional and financial burden. Some try to escape these overwhelming responsibilities by drinking excessively or dropping out or simply disappearing.

Others drop dead from too much stress. Many men who would like to alter their style of life, shift directions, or change careers lack the financial resources to do so. Others, unable to find social sanction for such undertakings, are afraid of the risks that such a change might entail. So they plod on in the same stultifying routine with nothing to stimulate them, nothing to look forward to.

Burned out or bored or disillusioned by the time they reach their forties, these are the men who become alcoholics, who sabotage their corporations by absenteeism or shoddy work. Alienated and discontent, they are of little value to the organization, to society, or to themselves. They have become victims of psychological pollution, the industrial fallout that results when a society values profits more than people.

To prevent such disasters, to preserve our human resources, fundamental changes are needed. In this increasingly complex technological era, it is urgent that we find ways in which the separate needs of the individual and the organization can be combined into a common cause so that both can grow and change with purpose. We must reorganize our society and our institutions to make them more responsive to human needs. We must develop a society that is structured in such a way that people can continue to develop, to find hope and meaning, throughout their lives. This is an enormous undertaking but an essential one.[1]

To make the middle years more rewarding, we should begin by abolishing our rigid concept of the life cycle whereby a twenty-year block of intensive education is followed by a forty-year block of tedious work, which is then topped off by an empty time of retirement—the time when, as we know, many men disintegrate or die. As an alternative, Dr. Robert N. Butler, the head of the National Institute on Aging, has proposed that we reorder the adult life cycle into more flexible periods of education, work, and leisure, which continue throughout the entire life span. This would enable men in their forties to grow, to gain spiritual refreshment, and to change direction periodically without risking everything.[2]

Corporations should grant the mid-life man a sabbatical to rest or study or even pursue interests unrelated to his job. Portable pension plans would facilitate a man's moving from one company to another without losing what he had built up.

Private and public funds for education, unemployment insurance, and Social Security would all have to be reallocated to support such a basic change. The federal government might be the place to begin conducting experiments of this kind.

Similarly, continuing education should be part of life. We should make it easier for adults to weave periods of formal and informal study into the working years. Colleges and universities should expand their responsibility to the adult population, not only to offset obsolescence by offering retraining programs but also to make the learning experience a lifelong process. In addition, these new approaches to continuing education should be developed in partnership with business, industry, and labor. Higher education must be viewed not as a privilege for the young, but as a resource for everyone from eighteen to eighty-five.

To revitalize their lives, men in their forties also need more second-career opportunities. Both government and industry should address themselves to this problem. At the present time most institutions do everything possible to discourage occupational change. This is a mistake. The need for new work options, far from being an elitist concept, also extends to the working-class man. In a study of malaise among male union members over forty, industrial gerontologist Harold L. Sheppard found that 35 per cent, based on their own aspirations and goals, were good second-career candidates.[3] To facilitate such change we need mid-career clinics, an idea proposed some time ago by John W. Gardner, former Secretary of Health, Education, and Walfare. Such clinics would help men re-examine their goals and consider changes. It is apparent even now that there is a pressing need for such centers to provide information and guidance.

Our social systems are still too rigidly geared to the present rather than the future, to what people are instead of what they are becoming. We need more facilities to advise and support individuals who are undergoing major life changes. One new approach, suggested by Alvin Toffler in *Future Shock*, is "situational groupings."[4] Such groups would be for people who are passing through similar life transitions at the same time. They could join together temporarily to share their experiences, trade ideas and insights, and help each other cope. In addition to groups, says Toffler, there should be individual "crisis counseling" available. Today men who want advice must turn to psychiatrists or vocational specialists or physicians or marriage counselors. What is needed are crisis counselors who are experts, not in psychology or health, but in specific transitions such as job changes or relocation or divorce.

We also need counselors for the normal crises of adult life. The helping professions should pay more attention to these life-stage problems and develop programs for the healthy rather than the sick, programs that people could attend without being stigmatized. In addition, the business community should take the mid-life crisis more seriously in their planning and programming. To cope with mid-life stress, men need the opportunity to talk about it. Corporate physicians or medical centers should provide time for this; business groups and managerial training programs should have the topic on their agenda; and company educational programs should inform their employees about the pressures of this period.

Changes to improve the middle years, like those just mentioned, cannot be put into effect without a fundamental change in our attitudes and values. We need a new vision of aging, a new vision of the human potential. We need to discard destructive myths and obsolete beliefs.

Our society's single-minded emphasis on productivity and profits has been costly: It has alienated most of us from the experience of our own possibilities, including the possibility of re-inventing ourselves and reconstructing our lives continually. Socialized to believe that there is only one way to be, one role to play, most American men in their middle years have trouble imagining or inventing new purposes and new identities when the old ones have run their course or been outgrown.[5]

We might begin by changing our perspective on aging. Contrary to myth, growing old does not mean becoming senile, sick, or sexless. The elderly do not become less responsive to innovation and change, according to scientific studies. Nor do they suffer a loss of intelligence or creativity. But in our society the potentials for late life have been largely unexplored. We do not help the elderly age with dignity and purpose, nor do we support them in developing fully until the end.

But it doesn't have to be that way. By changing our vision

of aging we can give *ourselves* a gift: the gift of a more vibrant, vital life. To this end we might look for inspiration to a unique program called SAGE, which was designed to counter negative attitudes toward aging and revitalize the later years. Using a wide variety of Western therapies and Eastern disciplines, including yoga, meditation, body awareness, breathing therapy, and massage, SAGE was launched in 1974 by California therapist Gay Luce.[6] Having begun with a core group of twelve people aged sixty-five to ninety-five, it has since expanded in size and scope. Staff members are now conducting training workshops, as well as serving in convalescent homes and residential care facilities.

This innovative program has produced astonishing results among the elderly: Migraine headaches have disappeared; the deaf have recovered their hearing; and those who were considered senile have regained their mental agility. "I've seen people in this group change their physical and mental outlook," says Frances Burch, sixty-seven, one of the original dozen. "They're more open and responsive, their lives are more exciting, and they have more possibilities and choices. . . . I've seen things go on here that are amazing—self-healing."[7]

Another member of the core group, Worden MacDonald, comments: "I think the most important thing to me is that I'm sixty-eight years old, and probably for the first time in my life, I've experienced real joy in my association with people. My father was a Presbyterian minister and quite an old fogey, an old-timer. He was a fine man, but he was against dancing, playing cards, and having fun in general. So I truly was an old man most of my life.

"I wanted to look good. I was taught, 'What will the neighbors think?' so I didn't do what I wanted to do. I did what I thought people would want me to do, but I've gotten over that. I began having fun, enjoying myself, and feeling free to do what Mac would like to do instead of what the neighbors would like me to do. It's a real joy and I'm grateful."[8]

A pioneer project in developing a new image of aging, SAGE, is demonstrating that people over sixty can transcend the expectations of our culture. It is proving that old age can involve as much growth as early childhood. It is giving us a new perspective on the rich potential of our own humanity.

We need more programs like this. We need to study not

typical but optimal aging patterns in order to change our beliefs about our own future. We need as public policy to make
a major commitment to research in the behavioral sciences.
We need multi-disciplinary studies on the process of aging
that are aimed not just toward the extension of life but also
toward its enhancement. We need to know more about how
to live a healthy, vigorous, productive, and meaningful old
age.

We need similar studies of the middle years, studies of individuals who have lived full, creative, and evolving lives. We
need to raise the level of our expectations, to enlarge our
sense of possibilities. Since we are a society that until now
has not only disbelieved in adult growth and change but dis-
couraged it as well, we need to know more about what we
might become—rather than what we already are.

There is a crying need in this country for basic life-cycle
education. "No one tells the child that he is a unique person
and has a unique range of possibilities before him," observes
Dr. Robert N. Butler. "No one prepares him to be continually growing for a lifetime."[9] Learning about the life cycle
should begin at an early age in the public schools, says Butler. Children should be taught about our culture's rites of passage, and learn to anticipate their own personal future. They
should be given some sense of the stages of life: what it
means to make marital choices and embark on parenthood;
the problems of the middle years; what old age will be like;
dealing with death and supporting a grieving person; and why
we have such customs as funerals.

Many primitive socieites are more advanced in these matters than we are because this knowledge is passed on in symbolic ways. Having become civilized, or at least indus-
trialized, our society has some catching up to do in the
realm of human wisdom. Now that we know all about how to
make a good living, it is time we learned how to live.

Like the American male in his forties, we as a nation are
finally coming of age—not just because we celebrated our
two hundredth birthday, but also because we have lived
through two World Wars and the Great Depression. We have
even survived bloody civil-rights battles, political assassina-
tions, Vietnam, and Watergate.

America has lost its innocence. We are shedding our illusions, groping for new values, and trying to change. We are

struggling to mature. Perhaps then the time has also come for us to become less heroic and more humane. Instead of demanding that men serve our institutions in the interests of economic growth, we should transform our institutions to serve men—in the interests of human growth. This would be a bold beginning.

NOTES

Chapter 2: New Hope for an Old Problem

1. Anne Morrow Lindbergh, *Gift from the Sea* (New York: Pantheon, 1955), pp. 86-88.

Chapter 3: Machismo *Kills*

1. Bernice L. Neugarten, "The Awareness of Middle Age," *Middle Age and Aging,* Bernice L. Neugarten (ed.) (Chicago: University of Chicago Press, 1968), p. 97.
2. Elliot Jaques, "Death and the Mid-life Crisis," *The International Journal of Psycho-Analysis* (Oct. 1965).
3. Neugarten, op. cit., p. 97.
4. Ibid., p. 96.
5. Estelle Ramey, M.D., "Weaker Male Sex Needs Women's Help," *Modern Medicine* (Jan. 10, 1972).
6. Thomas H. Holmes and Minora Masuda, "Psychosomatic Syndrome," *Psychology Today* (Apr. 1972).
7. "Adolescent Suicide," *Time* (Jan. 3, 1972).
8. On Friedman and Rosenman, see: Meyer Friedman, M.D., and Ray H. Rosenman, M.D., *Type A Behavior and Your Heart* (New York: Alfred A. Knopf, 1974); Walter McQuade and Ann Aikman, *Stress* (New York: E. P. Dutton, 1974); Nancy Mayer, "Leisure—or a Coronary?" *Travel and Leisure* (Jan. 1972); Walter McQuade, "What Stress Can Do to You," *Fortune* (Jan. 1972); Friedman, Brown, and Rosenman, "Voice Analysis Test for Detection of Behavior Pattern," *JAMA* (May 5, 1969); Friedman and Rosenman, "Etiology and Pathogenesis of Coronary Arteriosclerosis," *Cardiovascular Disorders* (Philadelphia: F. A. Davis, 1968); Rosenman, "Prospective Epidemiological Recognition of the Candidate for Ischemic Heart Disease," *Psychotherapy and Psychosomatics* (1968), Vol. 16, No. 4–5; Rosenman, "Emotional Factors in Coronary Heart Disease," *Postgraduate Medicine* (Sept. 1967), 42:3; Meyer Friedman and Herman Uhley, "Management of Coronary Artery Disease," *Postgrad-*

uate Medicine (Sept. 1967), 42:3; and Rosenman, "Emotional Patterns in the Development of Cardiovascular Disease," *J. Am. College Health Assoc.* (Feb. 1967), Vol. 15, No. 3.

9. On support for the Type A theory: In recent years much supporting evidence for the Type A theory has come in from other scientific investigators. Dr. Friedman estimates that more than twenty studies have now confirmed his own findings. One stunning example: In 1975 the results of a ten-year study from the University of California at Berkeley, comparing the high rate of heart disease among American men to the low rate among Japanese men, proved that the difference was largely cultural—not culinary. Contrary to the usual argument that a low-fat diet of fish and rice was the reason, this study of four thousand Japanese men living in the United States found that those who plunged most fully into Western ways—adopting an aggressive, competitive style— were five times more likely to get heart attacks than those who clung to their traditional Japanese lifestyle, even if they switched to a high-fat diet. This Berkeley study clearly undermines the importance of diet, while condemning stress American-style as a major cause of coronaries. "Culture and Coronaries," *Time* (Aug. 18, 1975).

Chapter 4: Horatio Alger Lied

1. On study of job problems in the middle years: "The Middle Years" is a special issue of *Industrial Gerontology* (Sept. 1971), written by A. J. Jaffe, Bureau of Applied Social Research, Columbia University. While analyzing the educational backgrounds, occupational movements, and family structures of mid-life Americans in 1970, Jaffe concentrates on job problems. He presents his analysis in terms of the "younger" (35 to 44) and "older" (45 to 54) middle years, and views the mid-forties as the "watershed" of life. The number of persons aged 35 to 54 is expected to increase from 46.4 million in 1970 to 48 million in 1980—and to 78 million in the year 2000.

After about 40, says Jaffe, "upward occupational mobility and increased earnings largely come to a halt. And therein lies one of the main problems for men in the middle years, especially the older ones, for in our society the lack of continued 'progress' is tantamount to failure."

The middle years group contributes 4 out of 10 persons to the labor force. They have a median number of over 12 years of schooling, which makes them almost as well schooled as persons in their late twenties or early thirties. Among men, those with maximum education usually enter the occupational ladder nearer the top, and have a better chance of remaining there throughout their working lives, than do men with little education—who start nearer the bottom and at best climb only partway up. During the middle years some more highly educated men continue to move up; some of the less schooled start slipping down; and the majority tend to hold onto whatever rung they had already reached.

Earnings follow accordingly. The major increases—5 to 7 per cent per year—occur prior to and during the early middle years. After that, earnings tend to increase only as fast as the general economy grows—about 2 to 3 per cent per year. In 1969, middle years men had a median annual income of almost $9,000, compared to $6,400 for all men. During these years, however, family income rises faster than does the man's income alone, because more wives work. The largest proportion of women in the labor market, 55 per cent, is reached from ages 45 to 49. The fact that his family is not living "better" solely because of his efforts may also trouble a man at this time, says Jaffe, depending on the extent to which he is "imbued with the 'machismo' complex." This study stresses that lack of continued upward job mobility is a key factor in the "Middle Years problem." Those men who are not frustrated by this fact are already in top positions, or have gone as far as they originally aspired, or are content to be "braves" rather than "chiefs."

Although this chapter, *Horatio Alger Lied,* focuses primarily on the drive for achievement and success among middle-class and upper-middle class men, Harold L. Sheppard has suggested that blue-collar workers at mid-life may also suffer from the inability to advance farther or to change jobs, as well as from the psychological effect of having working wives. See Harold L. Sheppard, "Who Are the Workers with the 'Blues'?" (Washington, D.C.: W. E. Upjohn Institute for Employment Research, Sept. 1970).

2. On age discrimination: The quote from The National Institute of Industrial Gerontology is a statement printed in every issue of their journal, *Industrial Gerontology.*

3. On occupational obsolescence, see: Harrison M. Trice and Paul Michael Roman, "Occupational Risk Factors in Mental Health and the Impact of Role Change Experience," *Compensation in Psychiatric Disability and Rehabilitation,* Jack Leedy (ed.) (Springfield, Ill.: Charles C Thomas, 1971).

4. On Shumaker: After 10 years in industrial work, Dr. Benjamin Shumaker obtained his Ph.D. at 49 and switched to the academic world, still maintaining a selective private practice. His findings are based partially on his 1970 doctoral study of 261 "successful" men in career counseling, *Characteristics of*

Adult Males Who Voluntarily Seek Career Counseling Services (University of Michigan, unpublished).

5. On malaise among American workers see: *Work in America,* W. E. Upjohn Institute for Employment Research, Report of a Special Task Force to the Secretary of Health, Education, and Welfare. (Cambridge, Mass.: MIT Press, 1972).

6. Babbitt quote: from Sinclair Lewis, *Babbitt* (New York: Random House Modern Library, 1922), p. 401.

7. On recent survey of businessmen: This survey is based on questionnaires sent to 7,200 American businessmen enrolled in the General Management Division of the American Management Association. The survey was conducted during September and October of 1972, and generated 2,821 usable replies. It states: "Success writers who maintain that the personality ethic has dominated the American idea of success for the past 40 years or so will find support in the AMA survey. . . . Young people, according to Daniel Yankelovich, may disagree that respect and authority automatically accrue to those with title or position, but in American business today, according to their elders, the boss is still the boss!" Dale Tarnowieski, *The Changing Success Ethic: An AMA Survey Report* (1973).

8. The Trice quote is from: Jack Leedy (ed.), *Compensation in Psychiatric Disability and Rehabilitation,* pp. 162-64.

9. Ibid.

10. On the study of drinking pathology see: Harrison Trice and James A. Belasco, "The Aging Collegian," *The Domesticated Drugs: Drinking Among Collegians,* George Maddox (ed.) (New Haven: College and University Press, 1970), pp. 218-34.

Chapter 5: Prisoners of the Masculine Mystique

1. On the masculine mystique see: Karl Bednarik, *The Male in Crisis* (New York: Alfred A. Knopf, 1970); Warren Farrell, *The Liberated Man* (New York: Random House, 1975); Marc Feigen Fasteau, *The Male Machine* (New York: McGraw-Hill, 1974); Harvey E. Kaye, M.D., *Male Survival* (New York: Grosset and Dunlap, 1974); and Fred McMorrow, *Midolescence: The Dangerous Years* (New York: Quadrangle/The New York Times Book Co., 1974).

2. See Jack O. Balswick and Charles W. Peek, "The Inexpressive Male: A Tragedy of American Society," *The Family Coordinator* (Oct. 1971).

3. On the relation between emotions and disease, see: Walter B. Cannon, *The Wisdom of the Body* (New York: Norton, 1932); Flanders Dunbar, *Mind and Body: Psychosomatic Medicine* (New York: Random House, 1947); George L.

Engle, *Psychological Development in Health and Disease* (Philadelphia: W. B. Saunders, 1962); and Edward Weiss and O. Spurgeon English, *Psychosomatic Medicine* (Philadelphia: W. B. Saunders, 1957).

4. On the emotionally armored male, see: G. H. Barker-Benfield, *Male Attitudes Toward Women and Sexuality in Nineteenth-century America* (New York: Harper & Row, 1976); Peter Gabriel Filene, *Him/Her/Self: Sex Roles in Modern America* (New York: Harcourt Brace Jovanovich, 1974); Sidney M. Jourard, *The Transparent Self* (New York: D. Van Nostrand, 1971); Desmond Morris, *Intimate Behavior* (New York: Random House, 1971); and Ira Progoff, *The Symbolic and the Real* (New York: McGraw-Hill, 1963).

5. Jason Miller, *That Championship Season* (New York: Atheneum, 1972), pp. 96-97.

6. The "Communication Skills and Personal Growth Workshop for Men" was held at Oakland University's Continuum Center in Rochester, Michigan, in February 1972. The leader was Jon Greenawalt, personnel manager of Guardian Industries.

7. On mid-life as a period of mourning, see: Elliot Jacques, "Death and the Mid-life Crisis," *The International Journal of Psycho-Analysis* (Oct. 1965); Harry Levinson, *Executive Stress* (New York: Harper & Row, 1964), pp. 265-82; and Harry Levinson, "On Being a Middle-aged Manager," *Harvard Business Review* (July-Aug. 1969).

8. Harry Levinson, "Easing the Pain of Personal Loss," *Harvard Business Review* (Sept.-Oct. 1972), p. 84.

9. On the male's turning inward, see: Bernice Neugarten (ed.), *Personality in Middle and Late Life* (New York: Atherton, 1964), pp. 44-89; and M. Fiske Lowenthal and David Chiriboga, "Transition to the Empty Nest," *Arch. Gen. Psychiatry* (Jan. 1972), Vol. 26, pp. 8-14.

10. Maggie Scarf, "Husbands in Crisis," *McCall's* (June 1972).

Chapter 6: A Life-cycle Perspective

1. Erik H. Erikson, *Insight and Responsibility* (New York: W. W. Norton, 1964), p. 132.

2. Erik H. Erikson, *Young Man Luther* (New York: W. W. Norton, 1962), pp. 18-19.

3. Most researchers in the burgeoning field of developmental psychology admit that measuring adult change is difficult. Adults are less enthusiastic than children about participating in a research project, and less available as captive groups. Moreover, agreeing on criteria to measure their development is often an insurmountable obstacle. Assessing change in cross-sectional studies means relying in part on the subject's recollections of his past and on his subjective reporting,

which some researchers shun as inaccurate. On the other hand, longitudinal studies—which follow one group of subjects over many years—are costly, slow, and difficult to carry out. They also pose the problem of separating historical and social changes from individual, developmental ones. In addition, since no single comprehensive theory of adult development has yet been accepted, the problem of capturing the complexity of adult behavior through controlled empirical studies is compounded even further. This is why, in most studies of adults, researchers are more inclined to look for continuity through time, rather than change. It's simpler. "It is not the conviction that personality change occurs in adulthood, but the methods for measuring these changes, that psychologists are lacking," says Bernice Neugarten. Bernice Neugarten, "A Developmental View of Adult Personality," *Relations of Development and Aging*, James E. Birren (ed.) (Springfield, Ill.: Charles C Thomas, 1964), p. 189. Sociologists have also been stumped by the same problems, says Dr. Orville G. Brim, Jr., the former president of the Russell Sage Foundation. Scolding his colleagues for ignoring the years beyond youth, Brim insists: "The most important, most difficult question about adult socialization is how much change can take place in adult personality." Social research has failed to answer this crucial question, failed to even try answering it, he observes. Orville G. Brim, "Adult Socialization," *Socialization and Society*, John Clausen (ed.) (Boston: Little, Brown, 1968), p. 195.

4. Researchers at Duke University's School of Medicine have disproved many of our negative stereotypes about the elderly. They have found, for example, that large numbers of people over sixty-five do not live in institutions, homes, or hospitals. Only 4 per cent do. Also, health and physical ability do not inevitably decline steadily. The patterns vary enormously, and many of the aged remain so physically fit that they climb mountains, run marathons, and swim great distances. Citing one study of men in their seventies who improved their health so much after a one-year exercise program that their body reactions were like those of men thirty years younger, these researchers claim that physical decline is due more to lack of exercise than to the aging process. Similarly, sexual activity and desire do and can continue. And, contrary to popular belief, mental facilities and intelligence do not necessarily diminish with aging, although the speed of response may slow somewhat. Many aged people continue to be very creative in later life. Moreover, despite widespread employment prejudice, the productivity of older workers does not decrease. In fact, older workers are not less productive, less reliable, or more prone to accidents or absenteeism than younger ones. Finally,

say these experts, the most crucial factor for successful aging is continuing high levels of physical, mental, and social activity. Ewald W. Busse and Eric Pfeiffer, *Behavior and Adaptation in Late Life* (Boston: Little, Brown, 1969). See also Alex Comfort, *A Good Age* (New York: Crown, 1976).

5. C. G. Jung, *The Development of Personality* (Princeton, N.J.: Princeton University Press, 1970), Vol. 17 of the Collected Works, p. 171

6. Henri F. Ellenberger, *The Discovery of the Unconscious* (New York: Basic Books, 1970), p. 672

7. Jung, *The Development of Personality*, p. 193.

8. C. G. Jung, *The Structure and Dynamics of the Psyche* (Princeton, N.J.: Princeton University Press, 1969), Vol. 8 of the Collected Works, p. 389.

9. Jung, *The Structure and Dynamics of the Psyche*, p. 396.

10. For a comparative analysis of Freud and Jung, see Ira Progoff, *The Death and Rebirth of Psychology* (New York: McGraw-Hill, 1956). See also Progoff, *Jung's Psychology and Its Social Meaning* (New York: The Julian Press, 1953).

11. Adelaide Bry (ed.), *Inside Psychotherapy* (New York: Basic Books, 1972), pp. 24-25.

12. On Erikson's stages of development, see: Erik H. Erikson, *Childhood and Society* (New York: W. W. Norton, 1963), pp. 247-74; Erikson, *Insight and Responsibility*, pp. 111-57; and Richard I. Evans, *Dialogue with Erik Erikson* (New York: Harper & Row, 1967).

13. See Robert Coles, *Erik H. Erikson: The Growth of His Work* (Boston: Little, Brown, 1970).

14. Erikson, *Young Man Luther*, p. 254.

15. Erikson, *Insight and Responsibility*, p. 130.

16. Erikson, *Childhood and Society*, p. 268.

17. Erikson, *Insight and Responsibility*, p. 134.

18. On the Yale study of the male mid-life period, see: Daniel J. Levinson, Charlotte M. Darrow, Edward B. Klein, Maria H. Levinson, and Braxton McKee, "The Psychosocial Development of Men in Early Adulthood and the Mid-life Transition," *Life History Research in Psychopathology* (Minneapolis: University of Minnesota Press, 1974), Vol. 3.

19. McKee quote: from Maggie Scarf, "Husbands in Crisis," *McCall's* (June 1972).

20. Levinson quote: from Maggie Scarf, "Time of Transition: The Male in the Mid-life Decade," (Mar. 1972) (unpublished version of *McCall's* article).

21. Levinson quote: from Peter T. Chew, "Good Old Charlie and Faithful Jane," *The National Observer* (Apr. 5, 1971).

Chapter 7: Penis Angst *and the Balm of Nubile Girls.*

1. Alex Comfort (ed.), *The Joy of Sex* (New York: Crown, 1972), p. 243.
2. On the male climacteric, see: Edward Weiss and O. Spurgeon English, *Psychosomatic Medicine* (Philadelphia: W. B. Saunders, 1957), pp. 375-414; H. S. Kupperman, "Hypogonadism in the Adult Male," *Human Endocrinology* (1963), Vol. II; John F. Oliven, *Sexual Hygiene and Pathology* (Philadelphia: J. B. Lippincott, 1965), pp. 335-51; Silvano Arieti (ed.), *American Handbook of Psychiatry* (New York: Basic Books, 1966), Vol. III, pp. 69-87; and Robert H. Williams (ed.), *Textbook of Endocrinology* (Philadelphia: W. B. Saunders, 1968), pp. 1,010-11.
3. "The most pernicious of all sexual fictions is the nearly universally accepted belief that sexual effectiveness inevitably disappears as the human being ages," say Masters and Johnson. "It simply isn't true." William H. Masters and Virginia E. Johnson, "Ten Sex Myths Exploded," *Playboy* (Dec. 1970). See also Masters and Johnson, *Human Sexual Inadequacy* (Boston: Little, Brown, 1970).
4. "An Interview with Masters and Johnson on 'Human Sexual Inadequacy,'" *Medical Aspects of Human Sexuality* (July 1970).
5. On the multiple causes of impotence, see Masters and Johnson, *Human Sexual Response* (Boston: Little, Brown, 1966), pp. 263-69.
6. Dr. Robert Rose and his colleagues at the Boston University School of Medicine have found that the testosterone level of men under stress is dramatically lower than for those who are not. This was the result when they compared two groups of men under stress—soldiers awaiting attack, and infantrymen undergoing difficult basic training—with another group doing routine jobs. The same result held when they studied a group of men, first, as they went through the initial weeks of rigorous training for officers' candidate school, and then again, when they had "made it." The hormone levels dropped when the men were under stress, and rose again when they were more relaxed. "Stress seems to have an inhibiting effect on hormone secretion," Rose concludes. "It almost looks like a see-saw relationship; as the stress goes up, the testosterone goes down." Maggie Scarf, "He and She: The Sex Hormones and Behavior," the New York *Times* magazine (May 7, 1972).
7. Helen Singer Kaplan, *The New Sex Therapy* (New York: Brunner/Mazel, 1974), p. 146.
8. This reasoning was confirmed in an unusual sociological study

of a West Coast cocktail lounge that was patronized primarily because it facilitated casual affairs between "high status" older men, all married, and young single women. The rules of this mating game were clearly understood by everyone, including the bartenders and waitresses. Most revealing, however: The men in this study flatly stated that "they deserved romantic interludes with attractive, decent women because earlier in life they did not have the time for such interludes, and such women were not available to them." Julian Roebuck and S. Lee Spray, "The Cocktail Lounge: A Study of Heterosexual Relations in a Public Organization," *Medical Aspects of Human Sexuality* (June 1971).

9. Alison Lurie, *The War Between the Tates* (New York: Random House, 1974).

10. Martha L. Stein, *Lovers, Friends, Slaves . . . The Nine Male Sexual Types: Their Psycho-sexual Transactions with Call Girls* (New York: Berkley/Putnam's, 1974).

11. "Tragically, yet understandably, tens of thousands of men have moved from effective sexual functioning to varying levels of secondary impotence as they age, because they did not understand the natural variants that physiological aging imposes in previously established patterns of sexual functioning," say Masters and Johnson. Masters and Johnson, *Human Sexual Inadequacy*, p. 316. See also: Kaplan, *The New Sex Therapy;* Isadore Rubin, *Sexual Life in the Later Years* (SIECUS Study Guide No. 12, 1970); Harold I. Lief, "Sex in Older People," *Sexual Behavior* (Oct. 1971); Carol Tavris, "Good News About Sex," *New York* (Dec. 6, 1976); and Warren Mintz, "The Male Sexual Cycle," *The Humanist* (Nov./Dec. 1976).

12. Virginia E. Johnson and William H. Masters, "Why 'Working at' Sex Doesn't Work," *Redbook* (Apr. 1973).

13. Kaplan, *The New Sex Therapy*, p. 519.

Chapter 8: The Quaking Marriage

1. Social scientists are now discovering that men and women tend to develop in different directions during the middle years: Men are moving toward more expressive, interpersonal values and goals (love affairs, painting, writing, more meaningful relationships), while women are heading toward more instrumental ones (a job, more money, or more influence). This same conclusion has been reached with entirely different methods by both Bernice Neugarten, professor of human development at the University of Chicago, and Marjorie Fiske, a social psychologist who heads the Langley Porter Neuropsychiatric Institute in San Francisco. Neugarten's findings are based on psychological testing, or projective data; Fiske's on

in-depth interviewing about values and goals. Both researchers have applied their methods to large samples: Neugarten's is upper-middle-class; Fiske's is middle- and lower-middle-class. Bernice Neugarten (ed.), *Personality in Middle and Late Life* (New York: Atherton, 1964), pp. 44-89; and M. Fiske Lowenthal and David Chiriboga, "Transition to the Empty Nest," *Arch. Gen. Psychiatry* (Jan. 1972), Vol. 26, pp. 8-14.

2. C. G. Jung, *The Strucutre and Dynamics of the Psyche* (Princeton, N.J.: Princeton University Press, 1969), Vol. 8 of the Collected Works, p. 398.

3. Morton Hunt, *The Affair* (New York: World, 1969), p. 177.

4. Ibid., p. 183.

5. Ibid., pp. 269-70.

6. Melvin B. Goodman, M.D., and Shirley B. Goodman, C.S.W., "The Victims of Psychotherapy" (1971) (unpublished).

Chapter 9: Double Bind: Generation in the Middle ↝

1. Butler quote from a book review in *Psychiatry* (Feb. 1971), Vol. 34, p. 107.

2. On the generation that has always been "in the middle": Eda LeShan, an educator and family therapist, writes: "We are not only middle-aged, but we feel caught in the middle of our past and our present. What is perhaps most special about us is that we have always been in the middle! We were raised to have respect for our elders, and to see it as a central focus of our lives to please our parents; we are still trying to do this. But we also came to resent this role, and to feel cheated. Sometimes we sacrificed far too much in this homage; sometimes we even sold our souls for parental approval and satisfaction. We were the first parents in the era of the child-centered family; when we became parents, our children tended to come first; *we* worked hard at pleasing *them!* We were the first crop of parents to take our children's failures and limitations as an indication of *our* inadequacy, not theirs; the first to believe, even briefly, that one could aspire to being a perfect parent. We found ourselves in the middle, trying to please both an older and a younger generation." Eda J. LeShan, *The Wonderful Crisis of Middle Age* (New York: David McKay, 1973), pp. 15-16.

3. William Gibson, *A Mass for the Dead* (New York: Atheneum, 1968), p. 266.

4. On Freud: See Henry F. Ellenberger, *The Discovery of the Unconscious* (New York: Basic Books, 1970), pp. 418-570. The quote is from p. 447.

5. Klein quote: from Maggie Scarf, "Husbands in Crisis," *McCall's* (June 1972).

6. King quotes from Enid Nemy, "How Did Alan King's Son

Become an Addict? Both Try to Explain," the New York *Times* (Aug. 1, 1972).

7. Ibid.
8. Ibid.
9. "Alan King Tells Why He Turned His Son In," New York *Post* (April 16, 1973).
10. The Fiske study of the supposed generation gap between high school students and their parents focused on fifty-two high school seniors and fifty-four parents whose youngest child was a senior, all middle- and lower-middle-class families. See Majda Thurnher, Donald Spence, and M. Fiske Lowenthal, "Value Confluence and Behavioral Conflict in Intergenerational Relations," *J. of Marriage and the Family* (May 1974), Vol. 36, No. 2, pp. 308-19.
11. Quotes on "interlocking crises" and the "loving fight" from L. David Levi, Helm Stierlin, and Robert J. Savard, "Father and Sons: The Interlocking Crises of Integrity and Identity," *Psychiatry* (Feb. 1972), Vol. 35. Psychiatrist Helm Stierlin and his associates based their conclusions on a five-year study of twenty-six troubled adolescents and their families. The children, all fifteen and sixteen and mostly boys, were referred by schools in the Washington, D.C., area because of various difficulties and underachievement. The fathers, who ranged in age from forty-two to fifty-nine, were mostly between forty-five and fifty.
12. John Leonard, "Father Never Knows Best—and the TV Tells Us So," New York *Times* (Nov. 6, 1975).
13. Nichols quote from "The New Fathers," *Life* (July 14, 1972).
14. Levi, Stierlin, and Savard, op. cit.

Chapter 10: Making It: The Urge for Independence

1. Larry L. King, "Most likely to Succeed," *New Times* (Nov. 16, 1973).
2. Ibid.
3. On the paradox of success, see: Richard M. Huber, *The American Idea of Success* (New York: McGraw-Hill), 1971.
4. See Ely Chinoy, *Automobile Workers and the American Dream* (Boston: Beacon Press, 1955).
5. *But What if the Dream Comes True?* a "CBS Reports" documentary produced by Robert Markowitz and written by him with Charles Kuralt (Nov. 25, 1971).
6. Ibid.
7. Ibid.

Chapter 11: A New Frontier: The Inner Self

1. Robert N. Butler, "Looking Forward to What?" *American Behavioral Scientist* (Sept./Oct. 1970).

2. Wayne Anderson, *Gauguin's Paradise Lost* (New York: The Viking Press, 1971), p. 222.

3. Ibid., p. 237.

4. Ibid., p. 4.

5. John B. Koffend, *A Letter to My Wife* (New York: Saturday Review Press, 1972), p. 6.

6. Ibid., p. 181.

7. Ibid., p. 98.

8. Ibid., p. 63.

9. Ibid., p. 216.

10. Judy Klemesrud, "An Author Who Felt Lost in Paradise," the New York *Times* (Oct. 27, 1972).

11. Koffend, op. cit., p. 117.

12. Ibid., p. 101.

13. On keeping men young, see: Thomas Meehand, "The Booming Business in Men's Toiletries," *Cosmopolitan* (Apr. 1972); "Plastic Surgery," the New York *Times* (Sept. 27, 1971); "Face-lifts for Men," *Look* (Dec. 1, 1970); "Face-lifting Erases Age in Men, Too," the New York *Times* (June 28, 1971); "A Happy Speciality," *Newsweek* (May 31, 1971); and "A Lift for Men," *Time* (Oct. 11, 1971).

14. On the youth revolution, see: John W. Aldridge, *In the Country of the Young* (New York: Harper & Row, 1970); Nancy Mayer, "The Party Is Over on Madison Avenue," *Lithopinion* (Winter 1971); and Nancy Mayer, "How the Middle Class Turns On," *New York* (Oct. 20, 1969).

15. See James L. Grold, "The Middle-aged, Middle-class Dropout," *Modern Medicine* (Nov. 29, 1971), pp. 51-54.

16. "The Great Escape," *The Wall Street Journal* (Feb. 22, 1971).

17. Ibid.

18. Ibid.

19. Ibid.

20. John Coleman resigned the presidency of Haverford last year to become chairman of the Edna McConnell Clark Foundation. On Coleman's sabbatical, see: Israel Shenker, "College Head's Sabbatical: Two Months at Menial Jobs," the New York *Times* (June 10, 1973); and "Learning with a Shovel," *Time* (June 25, 1973).

21. John R. Coleman, *Blue-collar Journal: A College President's Sabbatical* (Philadelphia: J. B. Lippincott, 1974), p. 8.

22. Ibid., pp. 166-67.

23. Ibid., p. 252.
24. On the *Odyssey* as a journey of self-exploration, see Sidney M. Jourard, "On Being Persuaded Who You Are," *Association for Humanistic Psychology Newsletter* (Jan. 1975).
25. F. Scott Fitzgerald, *The Last Tycoon,* (New York: Charles Scribner, 1941).
26. Theodore Roszak, *Unfinished Animal* (New York: Harper & Row, 1975), p. 19.

Chapter 12: New Directions: Work

1. On men who have changed careers: for examples, case histories, and a discussion of problems, see: Damon Stetson, *Starting Over* (New York: Macmillan, 1971); and the Spring 1973 issue of *Industrial Gerontology,* which is devoted to second careers and contains an extensive bibliography.
2. Peter F. Drucker, *The Age of Discontinuity* (New York: Harper & Row, 1969), p. 292.
3. Ibid., p. 296.
4. Ibid., p. 292.
5. Nancy K. Schlossberg, "Men in Transition: A Study of Adult Male Undergraduates at Wayne State University, 1967" (unpublished).
6. Ann Bayer, "Beginning Again in the Middle," *Life* (June 12, 1970).
7. On excessively rigid requirements of schools: The reality of this prejudice against the older student has been cited in many studies of career change. Columbia University Professor Dale L. Hiestand flatly states: "The majority of universities and schools seem to have policies which directly restrict opportunities for older applicants even though they do not make a formal statement to that effect." Dale L. Hiestand, *Changing Careers After Thirty-five* (New York: Columbia University Press, 1971), p. 61.
8. Harding Lemay, *Inside, Looking Out* (New York: Harper & Row, 1971), p. 279.
9. Industrial gerontologist Harold L. Sheppard insists that the mid-life need for new work options, far from being an elitist concept, extends also to the working-class man. In a study of malaise among male union members over forty, he found that 35 per cent—based on their own aspirations and goals—were good second-career candidates. See H. L. Sheppard and N. Q. Herrick, *Where Have All the Robots Gone?* (New York: Free Press/Macmillan, 1972).
10. Rita Reif, "They Fled Urban Pressures for a Sanctuary in the Wilderness," the New York *Times* (Aug. 20, 1972).
11. Lisa Hobbs, *Running Towards Life* (New York: McGraw-Hill, 1971), pp. 59-60.

12. Ibid., p. 61.
13. Ibid., p. 4.
14. Ibid., p. 85.
15. Ibid., p. 122.
16. Ibid., p. 38

Chapter 13: New Directions: Marriage

1. Maggie Scarf, "Husbands in Crisis," *McCall's* (June 1972).
2. Ibid.
3. Morton Hunt, "The Future of Marriage," *Playboy* (Aug. 1971).
4. For books on marriage, see: Nena and George O'Neill, *Open Marriage* (New York: M. Evans, 1972); Dr. George R. Bach and Peter Wyden, *The Intimate Enemy* (New York: William Morrow, 1969); and Carl R. Rogers, *Becoming Partners: Marriage and Its Alternatives* (New York: Delacorte, 1972).

Chapter 14: The Metamorphosis from Boy/Man to Man

1. Sam Keen, *Beginnings Without End* (New York: Harper & Row, 1975), pp. ix-x.
2. Harry Levinson, *Executive Stress* (New York: Harper & Row, 1964), p. 278.
3. Margaret Clark and Barbara G. Anderson, *Culture and Aging* (Springfield, Ill.: Charles C Thomas, 1967).
4. This material is reprinted from Nancy Mayer, "Leisure—or a Coronary?" *Travel and Leisure* (Jan. 1972).
5. A. H. Ismail and L. E. Trachtman, "Jogging the Imagination," *Psychology Today* (Mar. 1973).
6. Keen, op. cit., pp. 74-75.

Chapter 15: Coming of Age in America

1. On making our institutions more responsive to human needs, see: "The Sacred and the Political in American Life" (an interview with Robert Bellah), *Psychology Today* (Jan. 1976); Harry Levinson, "Easing the Pain of Personal Loss," *Harvard Business Review* (Sept.-Oct. 1972); Ira Progoff, *The Symbolic and the Real* (New York: McGraw-Hill, 1963); E. F. Schumacher, *Small Is Beautiful: Economics as if People Mattered* (New York: Harper & Row, 1973).
2. On reordering the life cycle, see Robert N. Butler, M.D., *Why Survive? Being Old in America* (New York: Harper & Row, 1975), esp. Chap. 13.
3. H. L. Sheppard and N. Q. Herrick, *Where Have All the Robots Gone?* (New York: Free Press/Macmillan, 1972).

4. Alvin Toffler, *Future Shock* (New York: Random House, 1970), pp. 340-343.
5. Sidney M. Jourard, *The Transparent Self* (New York: D. Van Nostrand, 1971), esp. Chap. 5.
6. The acronym SAGE stands for Senior Actualization and Growth Explorations. In addition to Gay Luce, the current co-directors of SAGE are Kenneth Dychtwald, Eugenia Gerrard, and Elizabeth Bexton.
7. Laughingbird, "SAGE," *New Age Journal* (1975), Vol. 1, No. 9.
8. Ibid.
9. Butler, op. cit., p. 388.

BIBLIOGRAPHY.

Aldridge, John W. *In the Country of the Young*. New York: Harper & Row, 1970.

Anderson, Wayne. *Gauguin's Paradise Lost*. New York: The Viking Press, 1971.

Angyal, András. *Neurosis and Treatment: A Holistic Theory*. New York: John Wiley & Sons, 1965.

Arieti, Silvano (ed.). *American Handbook of Psychiatry*, Vol. III. New York: Basic Books, 1966.

Axelson, L. J. "Personal Adjustment in the Postparental Period," *Marriage and Family Living*, 22 (1960).

Bach, Dr. George R.; and Wyden, Peter. *The Intimate Enemy*. New York: Wm. Morrow, 1969.

Baker, Elliott. *Pocock & Pitt*. New York: G. P. Putnam's Sons, 1971.

Balswick, Jack O.; and Peek, Charles W. "The Inexpressive Male: A Tragedy of American Society," *The Family Coordinator*, October 1971.

Barfield, Richard; and Morgan, James. *Early Retirement: The Decision and the Experience*. Ann Arbor: Institute of Social Research, U. of Michigan, 1970.

Barker-Benfield, G. J. *Male Attitudes Toward Women and Sexuality in Nineteenth-century America*. New York: Harper & Row, 1976.

Barron, F. *Creativity and Psychological Health*. Princeton, N.J.: D. Van Nostrand, 1963.

Bartlett, L. E. *New Work/New Life*. New York: Harper & Row, 1976.

Bayer, Ann. "Beginning Again in the Middle," *Life*, June 12, 1970.

Bednarik, Karl. *The Male in Crisis*. New York: Alfred A. Knopf, 1970.

Bell, Daniel. *Work and Its Discontents*. Boston: Beacon Press, 1956.

Biggs, D., *Breaking Out*. New York: David McKay, 1973.

Birren, James E. (ed.). *Relations of Development and Aging*. Springfield, Ill.: Charles C. Thomas, 1964.

Block, Jack. *Lives Through Time*. Berkeley, Calif.: Bancroft Books, 1971.

Brim, Orville G. "Adult Socialization." In Clausen, John (ed.). *Socialization and Society*. Boston: Little, Brown, 1968.

Bry, Adelaide (ed.). *Inside Psychotherapy*. New York: Basic Books, 1972.

Buhler, Charlotte; and Massarik, Fred (eds.). *The Course of Human Life*. New York: Springer, 1968.

Busse, Ewald W.; and Pfeiffer, Eric. *Behavior and Adaptation in Late Life*. Boston: Little, Brown, 1969.

Butler, Robert N. "Looking Forward to What?" *American Behavioral Scientist*, September/October 1970.

Butler, Robert N., M.D. *Why Survive? Being Old in America*. New York: Harper & Row, 1975.

Cannon, Walter B. *The Wisdom of the Body*. New York: W. W. Norton, 1932.

Chew, Peter T. "Good Old Charlie and Faithful Jane," *The National Observer*, April 5, 1971.

Chilman, Catherine S. "Families in Development at Mid-state of the Family Life Cycle," *The Family Coordinator*, October 1968.

Chinoy, Ely. *Automobile Workers and the American Dream*. Boston: Beacon Press, 1955.

Clark, Margaret; and Anderson, Barbara G. *Culture and Aging*. Springfield, Ill.: Charles C Thomas, 1967.

Clausen, John (ed.). *Socialization and Society*. Boston: Little, Brown, 1968.

Coleman, John R. *Blue-collar Journal: A College President's Sabbatical*. Philadelphia: J. B. Lippincott, 1974.

Coles, Robert. *Erik H. Erikson: The Growth of His Work*. Boston: Little, Brown, 1970.

Comfort, Alex. *A Good Age*. New York: Crown, 1976.

————(ed.). *The Joy of Sex*. New York: Crown, 1972.

Committee on Work and Personality in the Middle Years. *Bibliography*. New York: Social Science Research Council, July 1977.

Cuber, J. F.; 4nd Haroff, P. B. *The Significant Americans*. New York: Appleton-Century-Crofts, 1965.

Cumming, Elaine; and Henry, William E. *Growing Old: The Process of Disengagement*. New York: Basic Books, 1961.

Dahlberg, Charles Clay. "Sexual Contact Between Patient and Therapist," *Contemporary Psychoanalysis*. Vol. 6, Spring 1970.

Davitz, Joel; and Davitz, Lois. *Making It from 40 to 50*. New York: Random House, 1976.

de Beauvoir, Simone. *The Coming of Age*. New York: G. P. Putnam's Sons, 1972.

de Grazia, Sebastian. *Of Time, Work and Leisure*. New York: The Twentieth Century Fund, 1962.

Deutscher, I. *Married Life in the Middle Years.* Kansas City Community Studies, 1959.

Deutscher, M. "Adult Work and Developmental Models," *American Journal of Orthopsychiatry,* Vol. 38, No. 5 (October 1968).

Drucker, Peter F. *The Age of Discontinuity.* New York: Harper & Row, 1969.

Dunbar, Flanders. *Mind and Body: Psychosomatic Medicine.* New York: Random House, 1947.

Dunne, John Gregory. *Vegas: A Memoir of a Dark Season.* New York: Random House, 1974.

Ellenberger, Henri F. *The Discovery of the Unconscious.* New York: Basic Books, 1970.

Engel, George L. *Psychological Development in Health and Disease.* Philadelphia: W. B. Saunders, 1962.

Epstein, Joseph. *Divorced in America.* New York: E. P. Dutton, 1974.

Epstein, Seymour, *The Dream Museum.* New York: Doubleday, 1971.

Erikson, Erik H. *Young Man Luther.* New York: W. W. Norton, 1962.

————. *Childhood and Society.* New York: W. W. Norton, 1963.

————. *Insight and Responsibility,* New York: W. W. Norton, 1964.

Evans, Richard I. *Dialogue with Erik Erikson.* New York: Harper & Row, 1967.

Farrell, Warren. *The Liberated Man.* New York: Random House, 1975.

Fasteau, Marc Feigen. *The Male Machine.* New York: McGraw-Hill, 1974.

Feifel, Herman (ed.). *The Meaning of Death.* New York: McGraw-Hill, 1959.

Filene, Peter Gabriel. *Him/Her/Self: Sex Roles in Modern America.* New York: Harcourt Brace Jovanovich, 1974.

Finkle, A. L., et al. "Sexual Potency in Aging Males," *JAMA.,* 170, 1959.

Fishwick, Marshall. *The Hero, American Style.* New York: David McKay, 1969.

Fitzgerald, F. Scott. *The Last Tycoon.* New York: Charles Scribner's Sons, 1941.

Frenkel-Brunswik, Else. "Adjustments and Reorientation in the Course of the Life Span." In Bernice Neugarten (ed.). *Middle Age and Aging.* Chicago: University of Chicago Press, 1968.

Freud, Sigmund. *Civilization and Its Discontents.* London: Hogarth Press, 1961.

Fried, Barbara. *The Middle-age Crisis.* New York: Harper & Row, 1967.

Friedan, Betty. *The Feminine Mystique.* New York: W. W. Norton, 1963.

Friedman, Meyer, M.D.; Brown, Alvin E.; and Rosenman, Ray H., M.D. "Voice Analysis Test for Detection of Behavior Pattern," *JAMA.*, May 5, 1969.

Friedman, Meyer, M.D.; and Rosenman, Ray H., M.D. "Etiology and Pathogenesis of Coronary Arteriosclerosis," *Cardiovascular Disorders.* Philadelphia: F. A. Davis, 1968.

——. *Type A Behavior and Your Heart.* New York: Alfred A. Knopf, 1974.

Friedman, Meyer; and Uhley, Herman. "Management of Coronary Artery Disease," *Postgraduate Medicine,* 42:3 (September 1967).

Gardner, John W. *Self-Renewal.* New York, N.Y.: Harper & Row, 1963.

——. *No Easy Victories.* New York: Harper & Row, 1968.

Garvin, Richard M.; and Burger, Robert E. *Where They Go to Die.* New York: Delacorte, 1968.

Gibson, William. *A Mass for the Dead.* New York: Atheneum, 1968.

Goldner, Fred H. "Demotion in Industrial Management," *American Sociological Review,* 30, 5 (October 1965).

Goode, William J. *Readings on the Family and Society.* Englewood Cliffs, N.J.: Prentice-Hall, 1964.

—— (ed.). *The Family.* Englewood Cliffs, N.J.: Prentice-Hall, 1964.

Goodman, Melvin B., M.D.; and Goodman, Shirley B., C.S.W. "The Victims of Psychotherapy," 1971 (unpublished).

Grold, L. James. "The Middle-aged, Middle-class Dropout," *Modern Medicine,* November 29, 1971.

Gould, Roger. "The Phases of Adult Life: A Study in Developmental Psychology," *American Journal of Psychiatry,* November 1972.

Gurin, Gerald; Veroff, Joseph; and Feld, Sheila. *Americans View Their Mental Health.* New York: Basic Books, 1960.

Gutmann, D. "Ego Psychological and Developmental Approaches to the 'Retirement Crisis' in Men," (paper presented at National Institute of Child Health and Human Development Conference, Washington, D.C., April 3–5, 1967).

Haan, Norma. "Personality Development from Adolescence to Adulthood in the Oakland Growth and Guidance Studies," *Seminars in Psychiatry,* 4 (4) (November 1972).

Harlow, Harry F.; and Zimmerman, Robert R. "Affectional Responses in the Infant Monkey," *Science,* 130 (1959).

Heller, Joseph. *Something Happened.* New York: Alfred A. Knopf, 1974.

Hiestand, Dale L. *Chainging Careers After Thirty-five.* New York: Columbia University Press, 1971.

Hobbs, Lisa. *Running Towards Life.* New York: McGraw-Hill, 1971.

Havighurst, R. J. "Successful Aging," *Gerontologist,* 1:8-13 (1961).

Holmes, Thomas H.; and Masuda Minoru. "Psychosomatic Syndrome," *Psychology Today,* April 1972.

Huber, Richard M. *The American Idea of Success.* New York: McGraw-Hill, 1971.

Hughes, E. C. *Men and Their Work.* Chicago, Ill.: The Free Press of Glencoe, 1958.

Hunt, Morton M. *The Natural History of Love.* New York: Alfred A. Knopf, 1959.

———. *The World of the Formerly Married.* New York: McGraw-Hill, 1966.

———. *The Affair.* New York: World Publishing Company, 1969.

———. "The Future of Marriage," *Playboy,* August 1971.

Ismail, A. H.; and Trachtman, L. E. "Jogging the Imagination," *Psychology Today,* March 1973.

Jaffe, A. J. "The Middle Years," special issue of *Industrial Gerontology,* September 1971.

Janeway, Elizabeth. *Man's World, Woman's Place.* New York: Wm. Morrow, 1971.

Jacques, Elliott. "Death and the Mid-life Crisis," *The International Journal of Psycho-Analysis,* October 1965.

Jennings, Eugene E. *The Executive in Crisis.* East Lansing, Mich.: MSU Business Studies, 1965.

Johnson, Virginia E.; and Masters, William H. "Why 'Working at' Sex Doesn't Work," *Redbook,* April 1973.

Jourard, Sidney M. *The Transparent Self.* New York: D. Van Nostrand, 1971.

———. "On Being Persuaded Who You Are," *Association for Humanistic Psychology Newsletter,* January 1975.

Jung, C. G. *The Structure and Dynamics of the Psyche* (Vol. 8 of the Collected Works). Princeton, N.J.: Princeton University Press, 1969.

———. *The Development of Personality.* (Vol. 17 of the Collected Works). Princeton, N.J.: Princeton University Press, 1970.

Kaplan, Helen Singer. *The New Sex Therapy.* New York: Brunner/Mazel, 1974.

Kardiner, Abram. *The Individual and His Society.* New York: Columbia University Press, 1939.

Kaye, Harvey E., M.D. *Male Survival.* New York: Grosset & Dunlap, 1974.

Keen, Sam. *Beginnings Without End.* New York: Harper & Row, 1975.

King, Larry L. "Most Likely to Succeed," *New Times,* November 16, 1973.

Kinsey, A. C.; Pomeroy, W. B.; and Martin, E. E. *Sexual Behavior in the Human Male*. Philadelphia: W. B. Saunders, 1948.

Klemesrud, Judy. "An Author Who Felt Lost in Paradise," *New York Times*, October 27, 1972.

Koffend, John B. *A Letter to My Wife*. New York: Saturday Review Press, 1972.

Komarovsky, Mirra. *Blue-collar Marriage*. New York: Random House, 1964.

Kupperman, H. S. "Hypogonadism in the Adult Male," *Human Endocrinology*, Vol. II (1963).

Langer, T. S.; and Michael, S. T. *Life Stress and Mental Health: The Mid-town Manhattan Study*. London: Collier-Macmillan, 1963.

Laughingbird. "SAGE," *New Age Journal*, Vol. 1, No. 9 (1975).

Lemay, Harding. *Inside, Looking Out*. New York: Harper & Row, 1971.

Leonard, George B. *The Transformation: A Guide to the Inevitable Changes in Humankind*. New York: Delacorte, 1972.

Leonard, John. "Father Never Knows Best—and the TV Tells Us So," *New York Times*, November 6, 1975.

LeShan, Eda J. *The Wonderful Crisis of Middle Age*. New York: David McKay, 1973.

Levi, L. David; Stierlin, Helm; and Savard, Robert J. "Father and Sons: The Interlocking Crises of Integrity and Identity," *Psychiatry*, Vol. 35 (February 1972).

Levinson, Daniel J.; Darrow, Charlotte M.; Klein, Edward B.; Levinson, Maria H.; and McKee, Braxton. "The Psychosocial Development of Men in Early Adulthood and the Mid-life Transition," in *Life History Research in Psychopathology*, Vol. 3, Univ. of Minnesota Press, 1974.

Levinson, Harry, *Emotional Health: The World of Work*, New York: Harper & Row, 1964.

———. *Executive Stress*. New York: Harper & Row, 1964.

———. "On Being a Middle-aged Manager," *Harvard Business Review*, July-August 1969.

———. "Easing the Pain of Personal Loss," *Harvard Business Review*, September-October 1972.

Lewis, Sinclair. *Babbitt*. New York: Random House Modern Library, 1922.

Lidz, Theodore. *The Person: His Development Throughout the Life Cycle*. New York: Basic Books, 1968.

Lief, Harold I. "Sex in Older People," *Sexual Behavior*, October 1971.

Lindbergh, Anne Morrow. *Gift from the Sea*. New York: Pantheon Books, 1955.

Linder, Staffan B. *The Harried Leisure Class*. New York: Columbia University Press, 1970.

Lowenthal, M. Fiske; and Chiriboga, David. "Transition to the Empty Nest," *Arch. Gen. Psychiatry*, Vol. 26 (January 1972).

Lurie, Alison. *The War Between the Tates*. New York: Random House, 1974.

McMorrow, Fred. *Midolescence: The Dangerous Years*. New York: Quadrangle/The New York Times Book Co.; 1974.

McQuade, Walter. "What Stress Can Do to You," *Fortune*, January 1972.

———; and Aikman, Ann. *Stress*. New York: E. P. Dutton, 1974.

MacIver, R. M. *The Challenge of the Passing Years*. New York: Pocket Books, 1962.

Maslow, Abraham, *Motivation and Personality*. New York: Harper & Row, 1954.

———. *Toward a Psychology of Being*. New York: D. Van Nostrand, 1962.

———. *The Farther Reaches of Human Nature*. New York: Viking Press, 1971.

Masters, William H. "Sex Steroid Influence on the Aging Process," *Amer. J. Obstet. Gynec.*, 74 (1957).

———; and Johnson, Virginia E. *Human Sexual Response*. Boston: Little, Brown, 1966.

———. *Human Sexual Inadequacy*. Boston: Little, Brown, 1970.

Mayer, Nancy. "How the Middle Class Turns On," *New York*, October 20, 1969.

———. "The Party Is Over on Madison Avenue," *Lithopinion*, Winter 1971.

———. "Leisure—or a Coronary?" *Travel and Leisure*, January 1972.

Mead, Margaret. *New Lives for Old*. New York: New American Library, 1956.

Meehand, Thomas. "The Booming Business in Men's Toiletries," *Cosmopolitan*, April 1972.

Miller, Jason. *That Championship Season*. New York: Atheneum, 1972.

Mintz, Warren. "The Male Sexual Cycle," *The Humanist*, November/December 1976.

Morris, Desmond. *Intimate Behavior*. New York: Random House, 1971.

Nemy, Enid. "How Did Alan King's Son Become an Addict? Both Try to Explain," New York *Times*, August 1, 1972.

Neugarten, Bernice, "A Developmental View of Adult Personality." In Birren, James E. (ed.). *Relations of Development and Aging*. Springfield, Ill.: Charles C Thomas, 1964.

———. "The Awareness of Middle Age." In Neugarten, Bernice L. (ed.). *Middle Age and Aging*. Chicago: University of Chicago Press, 1968.

————. (ed.). *Personality in Middle and Late Life.* New York: Atherton, 1964.

Neugarten, B. L.; and Garron, D. "The Attitude of Middle-aged Persons Toward Growing Older," *Geriatrics,* 14:21-24 (January 1959).

Oates, Wayne E. *Confessions of a Workaholic.* Nashville, Tenn.: Abingdon Press, 1972.

Oliven, John F. *Sexual Hygiene and Pathology.* Philadelphia: J. B. Lippincott, 1965.

O'Neill, Nena; and O'Neill, George. *Open Marriage.* New York: M. Evans, 1972.

Orwell, George. *Coming Up for Air.* New York: Harcourt, Brace & World, 1939.

Peterson, James A. *Married Love in the Middle Years.* New York: Association Press, 1968.

Podhoretz, Norman. *Making It.* New York: Random House, 1967.

Pressey, Sidney L.; and Kuhler, Raymond G. *Psychological Development Through the Life Span.* New York: Harper & Row, 1957.

Previn, Dory, *On My Way to Where.* New York: Saturday Review Press, 1971.

Progoff, Ira. *Jung's Psychology and Its Social Meaning.* New York: The Julian Press, 1953.

————. *The Death and Rebirth of Psychology.* New York: McGraw-Hill, 1956.

————. *The Symbolic and the Real.* New York: McGraw-Hill, 1963.

Ramey, Estelle, M.D. "Weaker Male Sex Needs Women's Help," *Modern Medicine,* January 10, 1972.

Reichard, S; Livson, F.; and Peterson, P.G. *Aging and Personality: A Study of Eighty-seven Older Men.* New York: John Wiley & Sons, 1962.

Reif, Rita. "They Fled Urban Pressures for a Sanctuary in the Wilderness," New York *Times,* August 20, 1972.

Rhinehart, Luke *The Dice Man.* New York: Wm. Morrow, 1971.

Roebuck, Julian; and Spray, S. Lee. "The Cocktail Lounge: A Study of Heterosexual Relations in a Public Organization," *Medical Aspects of Human Sexuality,* June 1971.

Rogers, Carl R. *Becoming Partners: Marriage and Its Alternatives.* New York: Delacorte, 1972.

————. *On Personal Power.* New York: Delacorte, 1977.

Rogin, Gilbert. *What Happens Next?* New York: Random House, 1971.

Rosenberg, George. *The Worker Grows Old.* San Francisco: Jossey-Bass, 1970.

Rosenman, Ray H., M.D. "Emotional Patterns in the Development of Cardiovascular Disease," *J. Am. College Health Assoc.,* Vol. 15, No. 3 (February 1967).

————. "Emotional Factors in Coronary Heart Disease," *Postgraduate Medicine*, 42:3 (September 1967).

————. "Prospective Epidemiological Recognition of the Candidate for Ischemic Heart Disease," *Psychotherapy and Psychosomatics*, Vol. 16, Nos. 4-5 (1968).

Roszak, Theodore. *Unfinished Animal.* New York: Harper & Row, 1975.

Rubin, Isadore. *Sexual Life in the Later Years.* New York: SIECUS Study Guide No. 12, 1970.

Scarf, Maggie. "Time of Transition: The Male in the Mid-life Decade," March 1972 (unpublished version of *McCall's* article).

————. "He and She: The Sex Hormones and Behavior," New York *Times Magazine*, May 7, 1972.

————. "Husbands in Crisis," *McCall's*, June 1972.

Schlossberg, Nancy K. "Men in Transition: A Study of Adult Male Undergraduates at Wayne State University," 1967 (unpublished).

Schumacher, E. F. *Small Is Beautiful: Economics as if People Mattered* New York: Harper & Row, 1973.

Seely, John R.; Sim, R. Alexander; and Loosley, Elizabeth W., *Crestwood Heights.* New York: John Wiley & Sons, 1963.

Selye, Hans. *The Stress of Life,* New York: McGraw-Hill, 1956.

Sheehy, Gail. *Passages.* New York: E. P. Dutton, 1976.

Sheppard, Harold L. "Who Are the Workers with the 'Blues'?" Washington, D.C., W. E. Upjohn Institute for Employment Research, September 1970.

————; and Herrick, N. Q. *Where Have All the Robots Gone?* New York: Free Press/Macmillan, 1972.

Shenker, Israel. "College Head's Sabbatical: Two Months at Menial Jobs," New York *Times*, June 10, 1973.

Shumaker, Benjamin. *Characteristics of Adult Males Who Voluntarily Seek Career Counseling Services.* Doctoral study, University of Michigan, 1970.

Simenon, Georges. *When I Was Old.* New York: Harcourt Brace Jovanovich, 1971.

Simon, Anne W. *The New Years: A New Middle Age.* New York: Alfred A. Knopf, 1968.

Soddy, Kenneth; with Kidson, Mary C. *Men in Middle Life.* Philadelphia: J. B. Lippincott, 1967.

Sofer, Cyril. *Men in Mid-career.* London: Cambridge University Press, 1970.

Stein, Martha L. *Lovers, Friends, Slaves . . . The Nine Male Sexual Types; Their Psycho-sexual Transactions with Call Girls.* New York: Berkley/Putnam's, 1974.

Stern, Richard. *Other Men's Daughters.* New York: E. P. Dutton, 1973.

Stetson, Damon. *Starting Over.* New York: MacMillan, 1971.

Stokes, W. R. "Sexual Functioning in the Aging Male," *Geriatrics*, 6 (1951).

Super, Donald. *The Psychology of Careers.* New York: Harper & Row, 1957.

Tarnowieski, Dale. *The Changing Success Ethic: An AMA Survey Report.* New York, 1973.

Tavris, Carol. "Good News About Sex," *New York,* December 6, 1976.

Terkel, Studs. *Working: People Talk About What They Do All Day and How They Feel About What They Do.* New York: Pantheon Books, 1972.

Thurnher, Majda; Spence, Donald; and Lowenthal, M. Fiske. "Value Confluence and Behavioral Conflict in Intergenerational Relations," *J. of Marriage and the Family,* Vol. 36, No. 2 (May 1974).

Toffler, Alvin, *Future Shock.* New York: Random House, 1970.

Trice, Harrison; and Belasco, James A. "The Aging Collegian." In Maddox, George (ed.). *The Domesticated Drug: Drinking Among Collegians.* New Haven: College and University Press, 1970.

Trice, Harrison M.; and Roman, Paul Michael. "Occupational Risk Factors in Mental Health and the Impact of Role Change Experience." In Leedy, Jack (ed.). *Compensation in Psychiatric Disability and Rehabilitation.* Springfield, Ill.: Charles C Thomas, 1971.

Updike, John, *Rabbit Redux.* New York: Alfred A. Knopf, 1971.

Vaillant, George E.; and McArthur, Charles C. "Natural History of Male Psychologic Health. I. The Adult Life Cycle from 18-50," *Seminars in Psychiatry* 4 (4) (November 1972).

Van Gennep, Arnold. *The Rites of Passage.* Chicago: University of Chicago Press, 1960.

Vedder, C. (ed.). *Problems of the Middle-aged.* Springfield, Ill.: Charles C Thomas, 1965.

Weiss, Edward; and English, O. Spurgeon. *Psychosomatic Medicine.* Philadelphia: W. B. Saunders, 1943.

Whyte, William H. *The Organization Man.* New York: Simon & Schuster, 1956.

Williams, R. H.; and Wirths, C. G. *Lives Through the Years.* New York: Atherton Press, 1965.

Williams, Robert H. (ed.). *Textbook of Endocrinology.* Philadelphia: W. B. Saunders, 1968.

Wilson, M. *Good Company: A Study of Nyakyusa Age-villages.* Boston: Beacon Press, 1963.

About the Author

Nancy Mayer has been a writer/editor in the mental health field for ten years. As a free-lance journalist, she has published numerous articles in *New York, Cosmopolitan, Travel & Leisure,* and other national magazines. A graduate of Radcliffe, she has also worked at the Mount Sinai Medical Center and at the *New York Review of Books.* She is now completing her educational and training requirements to become a psychotherapist. She lives in Manhattan.

Index

Buy them at your local
bookstore or use coupon
on next page for ordering.

SIGNET

FOR LOVERS ONLY

By the year 2000, 2 out of 3 Americans could be illiterate.

It's true.

Today, 75 million adults...about one American in three, can't read adequately. And by the year 2000, U.S. News & World Report envisions an America with a literacy rate of only 30%.

Before that America comes to be, you can stop it...by joining the fight against illiteracy today.

Call the Coalition for Literacy at toll-free **1-800-228-8813** and volunteer.

Volunteer Against Illiteracy. The only degree you need is a degree of caring.